Teacher's Book

A RESOURCE FOR PLANNING AND TEACHING

Level 3.2 Celebrate

Introductory Selection: **Miss Nelson Is Missing!**

Theme 1 **Oink, Oink, Oink**

Theme 2 **Community Ties**

Theme 3 **Disaster!**

Theme 4 **What's Cooking?**

Theme 5 **Weather Watch**

Theme 6 **What a Day!**

Senior Authors

J. David Cooper
John J. Pikulski

Authors

Kathryn H. Au
Margarita Calderon
Jacqueline C. Comas
Marjorie Y. Lipson
J. Sabrina Mims
Susan E. Page
Sheila W. Valencia
MaryEllen Vogt

Consultants

Dolores Malcolm
Tina Saldivar
Shane Templeton

INVITATIONS TO LITERACY

D1473319

Houghton Mifflin Company • Boston

Atlanta • Dallas • Geneva, Illinois • Palo Alto • Princeton

Literature Reviewers

Librarians: **Consuelo Harris,** Public Library of Cincinnati, Cincinnati, Ohio; **Sarah Jones,** Elko County Library, Elko, Nevada; **Maeve Visser Knoth,** Cambridge Public Library, Cambridge, Massachusetts; **Valerie Lennox,** Highlands Branch Library, Jacksonville, Florida; **Margaret Miles,** Central Library, Sacramento, California; **Danilta Nichols,** Fordham Library, New York, New York; **Patricia O'Malley,** Hartford Public Library, Hartford, Connecticut; **Rob Reid,** L.E. Phillips Memorial Public Library, Eau Claire, Wisconsin; **Mary Calletto Rife,** Kalamazoo Public Library, Kalamazoo, Michigan

Teachers: **Debora Adam,** South Dover Elementary School, Dover, Delaware; **Linda Chick,** Paloma School, San Marcos, California; **Bea Garcia,** Kolfax Elementary School, Denver, Colorado; **Flavia Gordon-Gunther,** Morningside Elementary School, Atlanta, Georgia; **Linda Macy,** Washington Elementary School, Wichita, Kansas; **Paul Warnke,** Onate Elementary School, Albuquerque, New Mexico; **Margaret White,** Hilton Head Elementary School, Hilton Head, South Carolina

Program Reviewers

Debora Adam, South Dover Elementary School, Dover, Delaware; **Sue Bradley,** Ardmore Elementary School, Bellevue, Washington; **Marsha Kiefer,** Truman Elementary School, Rolla, Missouri; **Paul Warnke,** Onate Elementary School, Albuquerque, New Mexico

Be a Writer Feature

Special thanks to the following teachers whose students' compositions are included in the Be a Writer features in this level:

Leticia Albright, E. A. Jones Elementary School, Missouri City, Texas; **Alice Holstein,** Newton, Massachusetts; **Ron Gunter,** Taylors Elementary School, Taylors, South Carolina; **Theresa Callicott,** North Jackson Elementary School, Jackson, Mississippi; **Betsy Turner,** Clays Mill Elementary School, Lexington, Kentucky; **Jane Merritt,** Mountainside Elementary, Fort Carson, Colorado

Credits

Cover photography by Tony Scarpetta

Photography: Tony Scarpetta, pp. 16D, 37O, 58L, 58M, 58N, 84N, 84O; Tracy Wheeler Studio, pp. 16G, 37M, 58O, 121O, 121P, 123A

Banta Digital Group, pp. 16C, 16D, 37N, 37P, 58E, 84M, 84N, 84O, 121N, 121P, 123A

Sook Nyul Choi, p.41A; Kindra Clineff, p.84M; Suki Coughlin, p.17A; Lawrence Migdale, p.91G; Margaret Miller, p.61A

Illustration: Charles M. Schulz, p.84M; Jim Gordon, p.121H

Acknowledgments

Special thanks to David E. Freeman and Yvonne S. Freeman for their contribution to the development of the instructional support for students acquiring English.

Printed in U.S.A.

ISBN 0-395-91448-5

.23456789-WC-04 03 02 01 00 99 98

WHAT'S COOKING?

Performance Standards

During this theme, all students will

- recognize how food is a way of sharing and bringing people together
- write a research report
- compare selections by completing a chart
- make predictions based upon inferences made about various story elements
- edit writing, with an emphasis on organizing information

Table of Contents

THEME: What's Cooking?

LITERATURE FOR SMALL-GROUP INSTRUCTION

 PAPERBACK **PLUS**

 PAPERBACK **PLUS**

 SOAR TO **SUCCESS!**

EASY

Who Put the Pepper in the Pot?

by Joanna Cole

In the same book . . .
• food riddles
• kitchen safety rules
• recipes from around the world

AVERAGE/CHALLENGING

Everybody Cooks Rice

by Norah Dooley

In the same book . . .
• recipes for international rice dishes
• a world map
• facts about seven different countries

THE INTERMEDIATE INTERVENTION PROGRAM

Level 3 Books

A collection of books with teacher support for small-group intervention

Bibliography
Books for Independent Reading

 Multicultural

 Science/Health

 Math

 Social Studies

 Music

Art

VERY EASY

Two for Stew
by Laura Numeroff and Barney Saltzberg
Simon 1996 (32p)
A young woman and her poodle have to change their plans when their favorite restaurant is out of its famous stew.

Tasting Things
by Alan Fowler
Childrens 1992 (32p)
A simple science book explains one of the most important senses.
Available in Spanish as *El gusto de las cosas.*

Green Corn Tamales/Tamales de elote
 by Gina Rodríguez
Hispanic Books 1994 (36p)
The members of a Hispanic American family gather
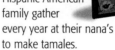
every year at their nana's to make tamales.

Eating the Alphabet: Fruits and Vegetables from A to Z
by Lois Ehlert
Harcourt 1989 (32p); also paper
Different fruits or vegetables, many unusual, are pictured for each letter of the alphabet.

The First Strawberries: A Cherokee Story
by Joseph Bruchac
Dial 1993 (32p)
Delicious strawberries prompt the first man and woman to make peace after a quarrel.

This Is the Way We Eat Our Lunch
by Edith Baer
Scholastic 1995 (40p)
The reader goes on a tour of the world to see what other kids eat for lunch.

EASY

Mr. Putter and Tabby Bake the Cake
by Cynthia Rylant
Harcourt 1994 (44p) paper
Mr. Putter and his cat bake a Christmas fruitcake for their neighbor.

Stone Soup
by Marcia Brown
Scribner's 1947 (48p); Aladdin 1986 paper
A favorite classic. **Available in Spanish as *Sopa de piedras.***

The Popcorn Book
by Tomie dePaola
Holiday 1993 (28p)
Tony and Tim give a brief history of popcorn. **Available in Spanish as *El libro de las palomitas de maíz.***

Chop, Simmer, Season
by Alexa Brandenberg
Harcourt 1997 (32p)
Two young chefs bake bread, toss a salad, and grill fish as they prepare a feast for their guests.

Seven Loaves of Bread
by Ferida Wolff
Tambourine 1993 (32p)
When Milly gets sick and Rose does the baking, the entire farm starts to go hungry.

How to Make an Apple Pie and See the World
 by Marjorie Priceman
Knopf 1994 (32p)
A closed market doesn't daunt a girl determined to find the ingredients for apple pie.

May'naise Sandwiches & Sunshine Tea
 by Sandra Belton
Four Winds 1994 (32p)
Big Mama shares with her granddaughter memories of a special lunch she shared with a friend when she was a girl.

Goody O'Grumpity
by Carol Ryrie Brink
North-South 1994 (32p)
When Goody O'Grumpity bakes her spice cake, all the children come running to have a taste.

Mel's Diner
by Marissa Moss
Bridgewater 1994; also paper
Mabel, who loves helping out in her parents' diner, wants to have her own diner when she grows up.

AVERAGE

Aunt Flossie's Hats (And Crab Cakes Later)
by Elizabeth Fitzgerald Howard
Clarion 1991 (32p); also paper
Sara and Susan's visits to Aunt Flossie end with delicious crab cakes.

Cam Jansen and the Mystery of the Stolen Corn Popper
by David A. Adler
Puffin 1992 (64p)
Cam is sure she knows who stole the corn popper from the department store.

The Edible Pyramid: Good Eating Every Day
by Loreen Leedy
Holiday 1994; also paper
Learn the right things to eat at a restaurant called The Edible Pyramid.

Sunday Potatoes, Monday Potatoes
by Vicky Schiefman
Simon 1994 (40p)
Plain old potatoes every day and then on Sunday—potato pudding! Recipe included.

Peas and Honey: Recipes for Kids (with a Pinch of Poetry)
by Kimberly Colen
Boyds Mills 1995
Simple recipes, plus poems by Jack Prelutsky, Aileen Fisher, and others.

The Rajah's Rice: A Mathematical Folktale from India
 by David Barry
Freeman 1994 (32p)
Chandra outwits the Rajah by using her math knowledge.

The Rattlebang Picnic
by Margaret Mahy
Dial 1994 (32p)
When the McTavish family runs into trouble, Granny's rock-hard pizza gets them out of a jam.

Everybody Bakes Bread
by Norah Dooley
Carolrhoda 1995 (40p);
also paper
Carrie searches the neighborhood for a three-handled rolling pin and finds neighbors baking breads from many countries.

Latkes and Applesauce
by Fran Manushkin
Scholastic 1990 (32p);
also paper
A blizzard ruins a poor family's apples and potatoes, but not their celebration of Hanukkah.

How Pizza Came to Queens
by Dayal Kaur Khalsa
Crown 1989 (32p)
When Mrs. Pellegrino visits from Italy, she brings along a delicious new recipe.

Dumpling Soup
by Jama Kim Rattigan
Little 1993 (32p)
Every New Year's Eve, Marisa's family gathers at Grandma's for dumpling soup.

Oh, How Waffle! Riddles You Can Eat
by Judith Matthews and Ray Robinson
Holiday 1992 (32p)
Delicious puns and wordplay abound in the book of food riddles.

Carlos and the Squash Plant/Carlos y la planta calabaza
by Jan Romero Stevens
Northland 1993 (32p)
After ignoring his mother's warnings about washing, Carlos finds a squash plant growing from his ear. **In English and Spanish.**

Jalapeño Bagels
by Natasha Wing
Atheneum 1996 (32p)
For International Day at school, Pablo takes bagels that represent his Mexican and Jewish heritage.

Siggy's Spaghetti Works
by Peggy Thomson
Tambourine 1993 (32p)
Children tour a spaghetti factory and learn the history of spaghetti and how it's made.

Roses Sing on New Snow
by Paul Yee
Macmillan 1992 (32p)
Maylin finally receives recognition for cooking in her father's restaurant.

CHALLENGING

Chocolate by Hershey
by Betty Furford
Carolrhoda 1994 (64p)
A biography about the man who invented the famous Hershey bar.

Cody Coyote Cooks! A Southwest Cookbook for Kids
by Denise Skrepcinski, et al
Tricycle 1996 (84p)
A collection of Southwestern recipes, Coyote trickster tales, craft suggestions, and facts about the Southwestern states.

Cranberries: Fruit of the Bog
by Diane L. Burns
Carolrhoda 1994 (48p)
Children learn where and how cranberries are grown in an account of cranberry farming in Wisconsin.

Corn Belt Harvest
by Raymond Bial
Houghton 1991 (48p)
The planting, cultivation, and harvesting of corn is traced through the seasons.

The Sacred Harvest: Ojibway Wild Rice Gathering
by Gordon Regguinti
Lerner 1992 (48p); also paper
A young Ojibway boy goes to his first wild rice harvest with his father.

Books for Teacher Read Aloud

Clambake: A Wampanoag Tradition
by Russell M. Peters
Lerner 1992 (48p); also paper
Steven, a Mashpee Wampanoag, hosts a clambake for his friends and relatives.

The Pizza Mystery
by Gertrude Chandler Warner
Whitman 1993 (128p); also paper
In this Boxcar Children mystery, someone is trying to put Piccolo's Pizzeria out of business.

Food Fight! Poets Join the Fight Against Hunger
edited by Michael Rosen
Harcourt 1996 (56p)
Thirty-three well-known poets write about food, from the common to the exotic.

Technology Resources

Software

Great Start™ Macintosh or Windows CD-ROM software. Includes story summaries, background building, and vocabulary support for each selection in the theme. Houghton Mifflin Company.

Spelling Spree™ Macintosh or Windows CD-ROM software. Includes spelling, vocabulary, and proofreading practice. Houghton Mifflin Company.

Channel R.E.A.D. Videodiscs "Suspended in Space" Houghton Mifflin Company.

Internet: Education Place (www.eduplace.com) Visit the Reading/Language Arts Center in the Teachers' Center to find projects, games, and theme-related links and activities.

Teacher's Resource Disk Macintosh or Windows software. Houghton Mifflin Company.

Writing Software The Learning Company's Ultimate Writing & Creativity Center. Macintosh or Windows software. The Learning Company®.

Video Cassettes

Chicken Sunday *by Patricia Polacco.* Weston Woods

Eating Right with Harv and Marv. Alfred Higgins Prod.

How to Eat Fried Worms *by Thomas Rockwell.* Listening Library

Mouse Soup *by Arnold Lobel.* Am. Sch. Pub.

Audio Cassettes

"The Doughnuts" from **Homer Price** *by Robert McCloskey.* Weston Woods

Food for Growing Bodies. Nat'l. Geo

Audio Tapes for "What's Cooking?" Houghton Mifflin Company.

Filmstrips

Stone Soup *by Marcia Brown.* Weston Woods Available in Spanish and bilingual.

Our Foods and Where They Come From. Nat'l Geo.

AV addresses are on pages H9–H10.

Theme at a Glance

	Reading		Writing and Language Arts	
Selections	**Comprehension Skills and Strategies**	**Word Skills and Strategies**	**Responding**	**Writing**
Tony's Bread	Folktales, 21 Making Judgments, 27 ✓ Following Directions, 31, 37C–37D Sequence of Events, 33 Reading Strategies, 18, 20, 26, 28	✓ Multiple-Meaning Words, 37G–37H; Dictionary, 37H; Words from Italian, Words That Exclaim, Notebook, 37I	Personal Response, 37 Anthology Activities, 37 Home Connection, 37 Literature Discussion, 37A Selection Connections, 37A	Folktale Characteristics, 35 Play, 37E
Sandwiches from Around the World			Discussion, 40 Home Connection, 40	Sandwich Recipes, 41
Halmoni and the Picnic	Compare and Contrast, 47 Problem Solving/Decision Making, 49 ✓ Predicting Outcomes, 53, 58B–58C Reading Strategies, 44, 48, 50, 54	✓ Using Context, 58F–58G; r-Controlled Vowels, 58G; Words from Places, Regional Words, Prefix uni-, 58H	Personal Response, 58 Anthology Activities, 58 Home Connection, 58 Literature Discussion, 58A Selection Connections, 58A	Conveying Characters' Feelings, 55 Invitation, 58D
Spaghetti! Spaghetti!/ I'd Never Eat a Beet			Discussion, 60	Poem, 61 Menu, 61
Henry and Beezus	Predicting Outcomes, 67 Following Directions, 69 Realistic Fiction, 71 Reading Strategies, 62, 64, 70 ✓ Sequence of Events, 77, 84B–84C	✓ Prefixes un- and re-, 84F–84G; Analogies, Exact Words for said, Prefixes bi- and tri-, 84H	Personal Response, 84 Anthology Activities, 84 Home Connection, 84 Literature Discussion, 84A Selection Connections, 84A	Character Development, 65 ✓ Avoiding Stringy Sentences, 84D–84E
Get the Facts on Fast Foods			Discussion, 86, 88 Home Connection, 89	
Reading-Writing Workshop **Be a Writer: Oranges**				Research Report, 90–91F Topic Sentences, 91A; Supporting Details, 91B; Introductions and Conclusions, 91C
Chicken Sunday	✓ Author's Viewpoint, 97 Problem Solving/Decision Making, 99, 121C–121D Sequence of Events, 117 Reading Strategies, 94, 102, 104, 112, 114	✓ Homophones, 121G–121H; Phonograms, 121H; "Wonderful" Words, Word Family for decorate, Words for Hats, 121I	Personal Response, 121 Anthology Activities, 121 Home Connection, 121 Selection Connections, 121A Literature Discussion, 121B	Poetic Language, 95 Poem, 121E
Fun Food Facts			Discussion, 123	Stories, 123

✓ *Indicates Tested Skills.* See page 16F for assessment options.

Theme Concept

Food is an important aspect of a culture's identity.

Pacing

This theme is designed to take 4 to 6 weeks, depending on your students' needs.

Multi-age Classroom

Grade 2 – Good Friends
Grade 4 – Meet the Challenge

Cross-Curricular

Spelling*	Grammar, Usage and Mechanics	Listening and Speaking	Viewing	Study Skills	Content Area
✓ Spelling the First Sound in *city* and *just,* 37J	✓ Helping Verbs, 37K–37L	Performing Reader's Theater, Listening to *Tony's Bread*, Speaking Italian, 37M	Looking at Tomie dePaola's Artwork, Watching Bread Bake, Observing Shapes of Bread, 37N		**Health:** Making *Panettone,* 37O; Listing Rules for Kitchen Safety, 37P; **Science:** Making a Table of Enriched Breads, 37P **Social Studies:** Shipping *Panettone* from Milan, 37P
			Breads from Around the World, 41	✓ Globes, 39, H2	**Social Studies:** Ethnic Breads, 41
✓ Words Ending with *-er* or *-le,* 58I	✓ Irregular Verbs, 58J–58K	Chanting Jump Rope Rhymes, Greetings in Korean, Visiting with Grandparents, 58L	Chopsticks Demonstration, A Video About Korean Americans, Signs and Symbols, 58M		**Health:** Making Kimbap, 58N **Math:** Measuring Distances, 58O **Social Studies:** Charting Korean Exports, Learning About Customs, 58O
					Health: Food Bulletin Board, 61
✓ The VCCV Pattern, 84I	✓ Punctuating Dialogue, 84J–84K	Making Apologies, Listening to Dogs Howl, Selecting Music for Chase Scenes, 84L	A Video About Dogs, Animal Comic Strips, Observing Dogs in the Community, 84M	Library: Fiction Books, 79, H3	**Health:** Riding It Right: Bicycle Safety; Making Barbecue Sauce, 84N **Science:** Parts of a Bicycle, 84O **Math:** Compiling Dog Statistics, 84O
			Food Commercials, 85	Reading a Chart, 87, H4	**Math:** Comparing Calories, 88 **Science:** Circulatory System, 88; Fatty Foods, 89; **Health:** Diet, 89
Words Often Misspelled, 91E					
✓ Homophones, 121J	✓ Commas in a Series, 121K–121L	Listening to Gospel Music, Speaking Russian, Listening to Klezmer Music, 121M	Comparing Patricia Polacco's Artwork, Watching a Video, Looking at Hats, 121N		**Art:** Making Pysanky Eggs, 121O **Science:** Experimenting with Eggs, 121P **Math:** Hat Prices, Shaping Up Eggs, 121P
Theme Assessment Wrap-Up: Spelling Review, 123B					**Math:** Comparing Measurements, 123 **Health:** Nutrition Information, 123

*Additional spelling lists with practice, LAB, pp. 149–158 (optional)

Meeting Individual Needs

 Students Acquiring English
Activities and notes offer strategies to help students' comprehension.

 Challenge
Challenge activities and notes stimulate critical and creative thinking.

 Extra Support
Activities and notes offer strategies to help students experience success.

Through Literature...

Instructional Reading

Anthology
Level 3.2, pp. 12–123

Teacher's Book
What's Cooking?

Supported/Independent Reading

Watch Me Read Books
Corn
Soup of the Day
Help from Harry
Mother's Day Special

Average/Challenging Paperback Plus
Everybody Cooks Rice
by Norah Dooley

Easy Paperback Plus
Who Put the Pepper in the Pot?
by Joanna Cole

Bibliography
Teacher's Book,
pp. 16A–16B

Extra Support/Students Acquiring English

 Great Start™ CD-ROM software
What's Cooking?

 Audio Tapes
for What's Cooking?

 SOAR TO **SUCCESS!**
The Intermediate
Intervention Program

Extra Support Handbook
Levels 3.1–3.2,
pp. 50–66, 112–115

Students Acquiring English Handbook
Levels 3.1–3.2,
pp. 134–167, 240–243

Language Resources:
Chinese, Hmong,
Cambodian, Vietnamese

Extension/Challenge

Teacher's Book
• Theme Projects
• Communication Activities
• Cross-Curricular Activities

Home/Community Connections
Levels 3.1–3.2

Internet:
Education Place
www.eduplace.com

Through Instruction...

Teaching Choices Reading, Writing, Language Arts, Cross-Curricular

Teacher's Book
Choose among skill Minilessons,
Interactive Learning Lessons, and
Reteaching Lessons and activities
to meet students' needs.

Literacy Activity Book
Level 3.2, pp. 1–52

Extra Support/Students Acquiring English

Extra Support Handbook
Levels 3.1–3.2,
pp. 50–66, 112–115

Students Acquiring English Handbook
Levels 3.1–3.2,
pp. 134–167, 240–243

 Channel R.E.A.D. Videodiscs
• "Suspended in Space"

Extension/Challenge

Teacher's Book
• Spelling Challenge Words
• Performance Assessment

Internet:
Education Place
www.eduplace.com

 Spelling Spree
CD-ROM

 The Learning Company's Ultimate Writing & Creativity Center software

Planning for Assessment

Performance Standards During this theme, all students will learn to

- *Recognize how food is a way of sharing and bringing people together*
- *Write a research report*
- *Compare selections by completing a chart*

- *Make predictions based upon inferences made about various story elements*
- *Edit writing, with an emphasis on organizing information*

Informal Assessment

Informal Assessment Checklist, pp. H7–H8

- Reading and Responding
- Following Directions, Predicting Outcomes, Sequence, Problem Solving/Decision Making
- Avoiding Stringy Sentences
- Word Skills and Strategies
- Grammar
- Listening and Speaking
- Attitudes and Habits

Literacy Activity Book

- Selection Connections, p. 2
- Comprehension Check, pp. 4, 17, 27, 43
- Comprehension Skills, pp. 5, 18, 29, 44
- Writing Skills, pp. 7, 19, 31, 45
- Word Skills, pp. 8, 20, 32, 46

Reading-Writing Workshop

- Writing a Report, pp. 90–91F
- Scoring Rubric, p. 91F

Performance Assessment

- Planning a Picnic, p. 123A
- Scoring Rubric, p. 123A

Retellings—Oral/Written

- *Teacher's Assessment Handbook*

Formal Assessment

Integrated Theme Test

Test applies the following theme skills to a new reading selection:
- Reading Strategies
- Following Directions, Predicting Outcomes, Sequence, Problem Solving/Decision Making
- Word Skills and Strategies
- Writing Fluency
- Grammar and Spelling (optional)
- Self-Assessment

Theme Skills Test

- Following Directions, Predicting Outcomes, Sequence, Problem Solving/Decision Making
- Multiple-Meaning Words, Using Context, Prefixes *un-* and *re-*, Homophones
- Writing Skills
- Study Skills
- Spelling
- Grammar

Benchmark Progress Test

- Give a Benchmark Progress Test two or three times a year to measure student growth in reading and writing.

Managing Assessment

Monitoring Independent Work

Question: How can I monitor students' independent reading and writing?

Answer: Try these tips:

- For monitoring reading, use a book log that includes a place for students to write the date, what they are reading, and a few comments. Have students use their logs to share favorite books and to do a class chart of types of books they are reading.

- To add interest and variety, use book logs for a two-week period several times during the year rather than all year long. Also, have students design new book logs for each two-week period.

- Use students' writing folders, portfolios, or journals to monitor independent writing. Students may want to keep lists of their writing projects. Have them share their lists with classmates and bring them to their writing conferences with you.

- Focus on a few students each time you have independent reading and writing. Notice students who are able to stick with their reading and writing and those who need extra support. Record your observations on the Informal Assessment Checklist.

For more information on this and other topics, see the *Teacher's Assessment Handbook*.

Portfolio Assessment

The portfolio icon signals portfolio opportunities throughout the theme.

Additional Portfolio Tips:
- Helping Students Make Selections for the Portfolio, p. 123B
- Evaluating Oral Language, 123B

Launching the Theme

Literacy Activity Book, p. 2

Name

What's Cooking?

Fill in the chart as you read the stories.

	What is the important food?	Why is the food important?
Tony's Bread		
Halmoni and the Picnic		

Literacy Activity Book, p. 1

What's Cooking?

What does your family like to eat when you are having a celebration? Describe the meal.

_____
_____
_____
_____

Complete the word web with words and phrases that describe a special meal you have had.

A Special Meal

What's Cooking? **1**

Selection Connections

Ask students to complete *Literacy Activity Book* page 1 using what they know about cooking. Then discuss the Selection Connections chart on *Literacy Activity Book* page 2. Note that students will return to this chart after reading each selection and after completing the theme.

See the Houghton Mifflin **Internet** resources for additional activities.

See the **Teacher's Resource Disk** for theme-related support material.

Theme Concept Food is an important aspect of a culture's identity.

Setting the Scene

Introduce the title: "What's Cooking?"

Discussion prompts:

* What foods do you eat or know of that originated with a particular cultural group? (Italian: pasta, pizza, etc.; Chinese: wonton soup, egg roll, fried rice, etc.; Mexican: tacos, burritos, etc.)

* Where might people go, or what might they do, if they wanted to try a food that's popular with a different cultural group? (visit a restaurant; get a recipe and cook it themselves; go to a cultural festival; visit a friend from that cultural group)

* If you could choose one food to try from another cultural group, which would you choose? Why? (Answers will vary.)

Have a Tasting Party

Invite parents and grandparents to make foods that are favorites with their cultural groups for an international food festival with your class. Encourage students to try new taste treats and compare them with foods they have eaten. Caution: Be sensitive to any student who does not wish to try other dishes. He or she may have allergies or be unable to eat certain kinds of food.

Interactive Bulletin Board

Assemble a bulletin board displaying pictures of students' favorite foods. Students can add drawings and pictures from magazines during the theme. Suggest that students arrange the foods by food group headings such as *meat, vegetable/fruit, bread,* and *dairy.*

Choices for Projects

Create a Class Cookbook
Cooperative Learning

Encourage students to bring in favorite recipes. Have students work in groups to compile and sort all recipes into sections such as *meat and poultry, fish, eggs, vegetables, soups,* and *salads.* Copy the recipes. Then have students create colorful covers for the take-home cookbooks. Suggest that the class vote on the best title for the cookbook.

- Compile and sort recipes. Paste the recipes on different colored paper.

- Use tabs for section dividers.

- Print the title on the cookbook cover.

Materials
- construction paper, different colors
- safety scissors
- glue

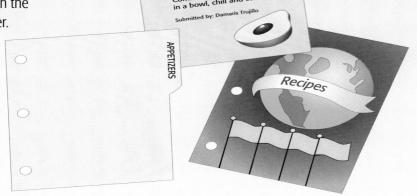

Write a Memory

Ask students to think about foods they associate with certain people or places. Give an example from your childhood, such as the smell of cookies in a parent's kitchen, the smell and taste of food eaten at a sporting event, or a special stew cooked by a neighbor. Have students write descriptions or poems about memories of people and places associated with food. Display the descriptions or poems in booklets.

Independent Reading and Writing

Plan time each day for independent reading and writing. For independent reading, provide books from the Bibliography on pages 16A–16B, have students bring in books of their own choosing, or encourage students to read the Paperback Plus books for this theme:

Easy reading: *Who Put the Pepper in the Pot?* by Joanna Cole

Average/challenging reading: *Everybody Cooks Rice* by Norah Dooley

For independent writing, encourage students to choose their own writing activities. For those who need help getting started, suggest one or more activities on pages 37F, 58E, 84E, and 121F.

See the *Home/Community Connections Booklet* for theme-related materials.

Portfolio Opportunity

- Save the *Literacy Activity Book* p. 2 to show students' ability to compare selections.
- The Portfolio Opportunity icon highlights other portfolio opportunities throughout the theme.

SELECTION:
Tony's Bread

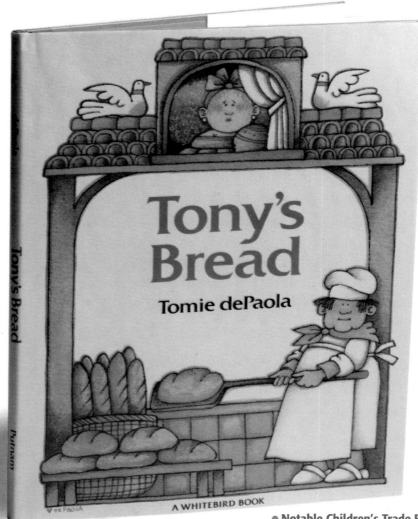

A WHITEBIRD BOOK

● Notable Children's Trade Book
  in the Field of Social Studies
● Child Study Children's Books of
  the Year

AWARD WINNER

by Tomie dePaola

Other Books by the Author
The Legend of the Bluebonnet
The Quicksand Book
Strega Nona Meets Her Match

Selection Summary

This folktale explains how the Italian bread that is shaped like a flowerpot came to be called *panettone,* or Tony's bread. The tale begins in a village outside Milano, where Tony and his daughter Serafina live. Tony and Serafina each have a dream: He longs to become a famous baker; she longs to be married. When Angelo, a nobleman, comes to the village and falls in love with Serafina, he plots to make the dreams of both Tony and Serafina come true. By the end of the story, Angelo and Serafina are married, and Tony has won fame for the delicious bread he has invented—*panettone.*

Lesson Planning Guide

FIVE-DAY PLANS
See pages 28–29 of the
Five-Day Lesson Plans booklet.

	Skill/Strategy Instruction	Meeting Individual Needs	Lesson Resources
1 **Introduce** *the* **Literature** *Pacing: 1 day*	**Preparing to Read and Write** Prior Knowledge/Building Background, 17C **Selection Vocabulary, 17D** • spoiled • court • nobleman • proposal • adoration • assured **Spelling Pretest, 37J** • once • just • city • large • slice • age • jam • circle	**Support in Advance,** 17C **Students Acquiring English,** 17C **Other Choices for Building Background,** 17C **Spelling Challenge Words,** 37J • princess • village • except • jewelry	*Literacy Activity Book,* Selection Vocabulary, p. 3 **Transparency:** Vocabulary, 4–1 **Great Start** CD-ROM software, "What's Cooking?" CD
2 **Interact** *with* **Literature** *Pacing: 1–3 days*	**Reading Strategies** Think About Words, 18, 20, 28 Monitor, 18, 26 **Minilessons** Genre: Folktales, 21 Making Judgments, 27 ✓ Following Directions, 31 Sequence of Events, 33 Writer's Craft: Folktale Characteristics, 35	**Choices for Reading,** 18 **Guided Reading,** 18 Comprehension/Critical Thinking, 22, 28, 34 **Students Acquiring English,** 19, 22, 26, 27, 31, 32, 33, 37 **Extra Support,** 20 **Challenge,** 19	**Reading-Writing Workshop,** Research Report, 90–91F *Literacy Activity Book,* Selection Connections, p. 2; Comprehension Check, p. 4 **Audio Tape** for What's Cooking?: *Tony's Bread* The Learning Company's Ultimate Writing & Creativity Center software
3 **Instruct** *and* **Integrate** *Pacing: 1–3 days*	✓ **Comprehension:** Following Directions, 37C **Writing:** Play, 37E **Word Skills and Strategies:** ✓ Multiple-Meaning Words, 37G Dictionary: Multiple-Meaning Words, 37H **Building Vocabulary:** Vocabulary Activities, 37I ✓ **Spelling:** Spelling the First Sound in *city* and *just,* 37J ✓ **Grammar:** Helping Verbs, 37K–37L **Communication Activities:** Listening and Speaking, 37M; Viewing, 37N **Cross-Curricular Activities:** Health, 37O–37P; Science, 37P; Social Studies, 37P	**Reteaching:** Following Directions, 37D **Activity Choices:** Shared Writing: A Play; Creative Writing: A Folktale; Friendly Letter; Jingle, 37F **Reteaching:** Multiple-Meaning Words, 37H **Activity Choices:** Words from Italian, Words That Exclaim, Vocabulary Notebook, 37I **Challenge Words Practice,** 37J **Reteaching:** Helping Verbs, 37L **Activity Choices:** Listening and Speaking, 37M; Viewing, 37N **Activity Choices:** Health, 37O–37P; Science, 37P; Social Studies, 37P	**Watch Me Read** *Corn* **Reading-Writing Workshop,** Research Report, 90–91F **Transparencies:** Comprehension, 4–2; Writing, 4–3; Word Skills, 4–4; Grammar, 4–5 *Literacy Activity Book,* Comprehension Skill, p. 5; Writing Skills, p. 7; Word Skills, p. 8; Building Vocabulary, p. 9; Spelling, pp. 10–11; Grammar, pp. 12–13 **Spelling Spree** CD-ROM The Learning Company's Ultimate Writing & Creativity Center software **Audio Tape** for What's Cooking?: *Tony's Bread*

✓ *Indicates Tested Skills.* See page 16F for assessment options.

Introduce *the* Literature

Preparing to Read and Write

Support in Advance

Use this activity with students who need extra support before participating in the whole-class activity.

Discussing a Baker's Job Begin a discussion about baking by having students look at the illustration on page 26. Ask the following:

- What is the man doing? (kneading dough; making bread)

- Where is he doing this? (in a bakery)

- What is this man's profession? (He's a baker.)

Invite students to share information about different types and shapes of bread.

Management Tip You may wish to have the rest of the class work on a theme project while you do the Support in Advance activity.

Students Acquiring English

Have students begin a wall chart with words they know that are related to baking. As they read the story, they can add words such as the following: *dough, flour, ingredients, loaf, mix, pastry, rise,* and *slice.* Encourage them to also add words they hear on television or see in advertisements.

Great Start
For students needing extra support with key concepts and vocabulary, use the "What's Cooking?" CD.

Prior Knowledge/Building Background

Key Concept
Bread and
Panettone

Encourage students who have made bread before to describe and pantomime the process. Elicit suggestions for how a basic bread recipe could be varied to make the bread into something for a special occasion.

Then tell students that they are going to read a folktale about the origin of a bread called *panettone* (pah-nah-TOE-nay). Graph what students know about this bread, providing additional information as necessary. You may want to have students look at the photograph of *panettone* on page 37.

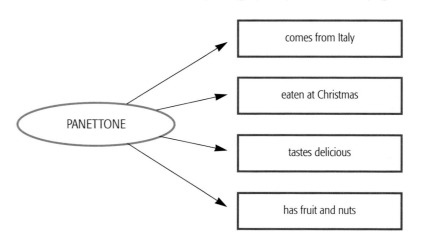

Other Choices for Building Background

Identifying Setting

Extra Support As students preview the illustrations on pages 18–22, help them identify the setting of the story as a village in Italy long ago. Encourage discussion about the architecture, the clothing, and the language that is spoken there. (Italian)

Quick Writing

Challenge The storyline of many folktales revolves around a young man attempting to win the love of a young woman. Have students discuss such tales. Then have them develop a list of steps involved in the typical courtship process in folktales.

Selection Vocabulary

Key Words

spoiled

court

nobleman

proposal

adoration

assured

Display Transparency 4–1. Draw attention to the connected words, noting that these words have similar meanings. Ask students how they can use the synonyms to figure out the meanings of the words they don't know. Then have volunteers read aloud the connected words. Work as a class to answer each question that follows.

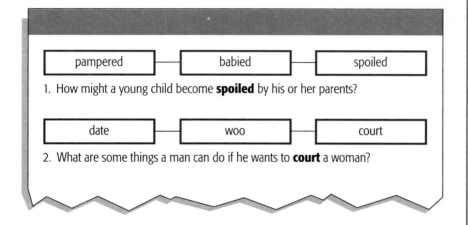

| pampered | — | babied | — | spoiled |

1. How might a young child become **spoiled** by his or her parents?

| date | — | woo | — | court |

2. What are some things a man can do if he wants to **court** a woman?

Vocabulary Practice Have students work independently or in pairs to complete *Literacy Activity Book* page 3.

Transparency 4–1

Caring Words

| pampered | — | babied | — | spoiled |

1. How might a young child become **spoiled** by his or her parents?

| date | — | woo | — | court |

2. What are some things a man can do if he wants to **court** a woman?

| plan | — | offer | — | proposal |

3. Describe a **proposal** for earning extra money.

| promised | — | convinced | — | assured |

4. What can you do to be **assured** that you will do well on a test?

| love | — | worship | — | adoration |

5. What can you do to show your **adoration** for someone?

| prince | — | lord | — | nobleman |

6. Would you expect a **nobleman** to be rich or poor?

WHAT'S COOKING?
Tony's Bread
SELECTION VOCABULARY

TRANSPARENCY 4–1
TEACHER'S BOOK PAGE 17D

Social Studies

Teacher FactFile

Bread: The Staff of Life

- Bread is the most widely eaten food on earth.

- Because bread provides energy and protein, it is often called the *staff of life*.

- Prehistoric people made flat bread by mixing grain meal and water.

- Ancient Egyptians learned to make yeast bread around 2600 B.C. and passed the knowledge on to the Romans, who spread it through Europe.

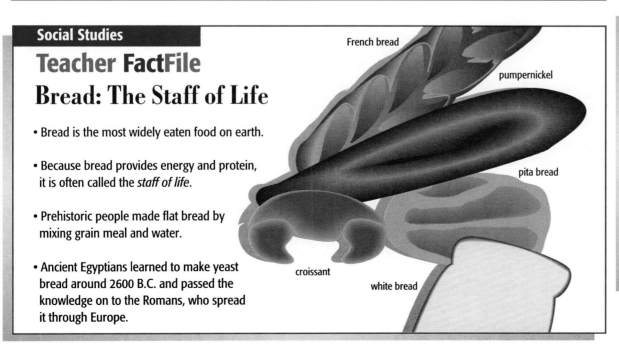

French bread

pumpernickel

pita bread

white bread

croissant

Literacy Activity Book, p. 3

TV Time

Read the summary from the TV weekly and answer the questions.

Clarabella: The Miniseries A **nobleman** falls in love with the **spoiled** daughter of a village blacksmith. His **adoration** for her is as big as the Adriatic Sea, and he sets out to **court** her. His marriage **proposal** is accepted only after the daughter is **assured** that he will continue to spoil her.

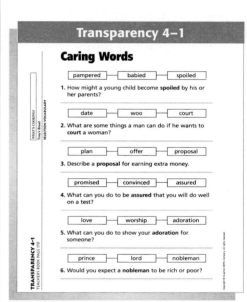

❶ Why might the daughter be **spoiled**?

❷ What could the **nobleman** do to **court** the daughter?

❸ What is something for which you have an **adoration**?

❹ What does it mean that the daughter accepted the marriage **proposal**?

❺ How might you be **assured** that people will do what they say they will do?

What's Cooking? 3

Interact *with* **Literature**

Reading Strategies

▶ **Think About Words Monitor**

Teacher Modeling Discuss how good readers get involved in the stories they read by using clues to figure out what is happening.

Think Aloud

This story has an unfamiliar setting and some words in a language that I don't know. If I'm having trouble understanding anything, I can look at the illustrations and go back over what I've read. If I come to any words I don't know, I can stop and think about them and look for clues to their meaning.

Predicting/Purpose Setting

After students have looked at the first couple of pages, have them predict why the young woman is so sad.

Choices for Reading

Independent Reading	Cooperative Reading
Guided Reading	Teacher Read Aloud

Guided Reading

Have students who are using the Guided Reading option read to the end of page 23.

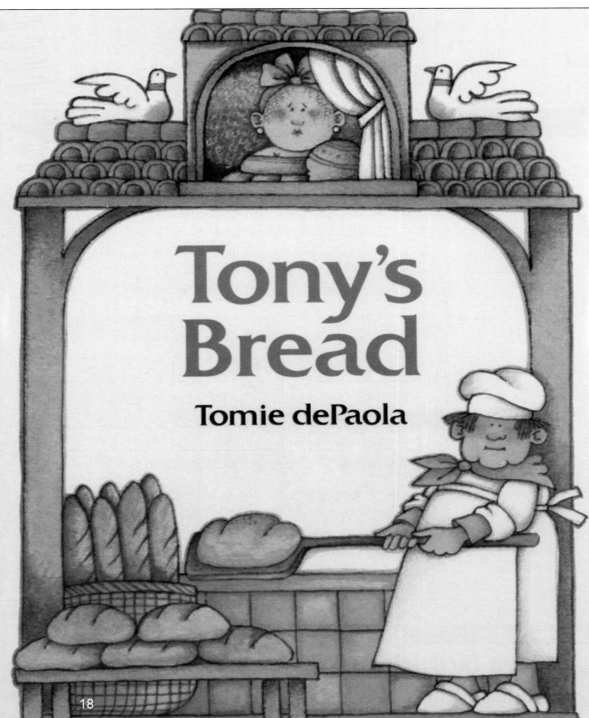

Tony's Bread
Tomie dePaola

18

Quick REFERENCE

Visual Literacy

Symbols *Tony's Bread* is part of Tomie dePaola's "Whitebird Book" series. Students may enjoy looking for the white bird symbol on page 18 and elsewhere in the story, as well as in other books by dePaola, such as *Strega Nona Meets Her Match*.

Once, a long time ago, in a small village outside the grand city of Milano, there lived a baker named Antonio. But everyone called him Tony.

Tony made bread and only bread in his bakery. It was good and simple and the villagers loved it. But Tony had a dream. One day he would have a bakery of his own in Milano and become the most famous baker in all of northern Italy.

 Students Acquiring English

Nicknames If necessary, point out that *Tony* is a nickname, or shortened form, for *Antonio*. Ask students to give examples of nicknames used in their primary language.

Visual Literacy

Signs Students may notice the picture sign above the door of Tony's bakery. Discuss when and why such wordless signs might be useful. (if one couldn't read; if one was traveling in a country where he or she didn't know the language)

 Challenge

Using a map or globe, have students speculate which of the smaller towns around Milan, Italy, might have been Tony's village. Students can also trace a route from that town to Milan and calculate how far apart the two places are.

Interact
with
Literature

Reading Strategies

▶ **Think About Words**

Discuss with students how they might use context clues to figure out a general meaning for the word *widower*.

Think Aloud

The paragraph says Tony lived with his daughter. It also says he had raised Serafina since she was little. Since there's no mention of Serafina's mother, I can guess that a *widower* is a man who doesn't have a wife anymore.

Now, Tony lived with his only daughter, Serafina. He was a widower and he had raised Serafina from the time she was *una piccola bambina* — a little girl. And how he had spoiled her!

"Antonio treats Serafina like *una principessa*" — a princess — said Zia Clotilda.

"The finest clothes, the finest jewelry, anything her heart desires," said Zia Caterina.

"She never has to lift a finger. All she does is sit, looking out the window eating *dolci*" — sweets — said Zia Clorinda.

"Now that she is old enough to marry, Tony thinks that no man is good enough for his Serafina," the three sisters whispered to each other.

20

QuickREFERENCE

Vocabulary

Pronunciations

- *una piccola bambina:* OO-nuh PEE-koh-luh bam-BEE-nuh
- *una principessa:* OO-nuh preen-chee-PAY-suh

Extra Support

Translations The author has provided translations for the Italian words and phrases. Point out that *una piccola bambina* is followed by a dash (—) and its English translation: *a little girl.* Have students find other such examples.

Vocabulary

Pronunciations

- *zia:* ZEE-uh (aunt)
- *dolci:* DOHL-chee

That *was* true. Tony did think that no man was worthy of his darling daughter. He would not even talk to the young men in the village who wanted to court Serafina.

So, poor Serafina would sit at the window behind the curtains, eating her *dolci* and crying.

21

MINILESSON

Genre

Folktales

Teach/Model

Encourage students to talk about their favorite folktales—stories that have been handed down and retold through the years. Work together to compile a list of characteristics common to most folktales:

- They're always set in the past, and the time and place are usually established quickly.

- They contain details that reflect a particular culture.

- Repetition is a basic element, with three often an important number.

- Characters are generally portrayed as one-dimensional (for example, good, evil, brave, foolish, or lazy).

- They usually end on a happy note, with good being rewarded and evil being punished.

Practice/Apply

Students may enjoy hosting a folktale story hour for a younger class. Suggest that students practice reading their folktale aloud several times.

Interact *with* Literature

Guided Reading

Comprehension/Critical Thinking

1. How does Tony treat his daughter, Serafina? (He treats her like a princess, giving her anything she wants—except the one thing she wants most, a husband.)

2. Why do you think Tony believes there are no young men in the village suitable to become Serafina's husband? (He's probably overly protective of her because she's his only daughter.)

3. Do you feel sorry for Serafina? Why or why not? (Answers will vary, but should be supported by reasons from the story.)

Predicting/Purpose Setting

Ask students to predict what Angelo's plan will be and whether it will be successful. Then have them read pages 24–29 to find out if their predictions are correct. Questions for checking comprehension can be found on page 28.

One day, Angelo, a wealthy nobleman from Milano, was passing through the village. As he went by Tony's house, the wind blew the curtains away from the window, and there sat Serafina. Angelo and Serafina looked into each other's eyes and it was love at first sight for both of them.

The three sisters were standing nearby. "Dear ladies," Angelo asked them, "who is that lovely creature sitting at that window? *Che bella donna!* — What a beautiful woman! Is she married or spoken for?"

22

Informal Assessment

If students' responses to the Guided Reading questions indicate that they understand what the dreams of the three main characters are, you may wish to have them finish reading the story independently or with a partner.

QuickREFERENCE

Vocabulary
Pronunciations
- *che bella donna:* kay BEL-luh DOE-nuh

Students Acquiring English

Expressions Be sure students comprehend the meanings of the expressions *love at first sight* ("they loved each other immediately") and *spoken for* ("already engaged or committed to marry someone").

Vocabulary

Word Origins Students may be interested to know that the name *Serafina* is a form of the word *seraphim*, a special type of angel, while the name *Angelo* literally means "angel."

"Ah, young *signore*," said Zia Clotilda. "That is Serafina, the daughter of Tony the baker. No, she is not married."

"And not likely to be for a long time," said Zia Caterina.

"No one is good enough for Tony's little Serafina," Zia Clorinda explained.

"Well, we'll see about that," said Angelo. "Now, aunties, tell me all you can about her."

The young nobleman and the three sisters sat and talked and talked and talked. And before long, Angelo knew all about Serafina and Tony the baker. And he knew all about Tony's dream of becoming the most famous baker in all of northern Italy.

"*Grazie*, aunties" — thank you — said Angelo. "I think I have a plan that will give Tony his dream and give me the wife of my dreams. But I will need your help. This is what I want you to do . . ."

23

 Journal

Aspirations Tony dreams of becoming the most famous baker in all of northern Italy. Invite students to complete the following sentence in their journals: *I dream of becoming the most famous _____ in all of _____.*

The next day, a letter arrived at the bakery for Tony

Dear Signore Baker,

I am Angelo, a nobleman from Milano. I was passing through your village and was lucky enough to taste your fine bread!

Would you be so kind as to meet me in front of the church after Mass on Sunday so we may talk. I have a <u>proposal</u> to make to you.

Angelo, di Milano.

24

QuickREFERENCE

★★★ Multicultural Link

Heritage Tomie dePaola's family is from Italy. He shows obvious pride in his Italian heritage by sprinkling *Tony's Bread* with Italian words and by setting the story in a town in Italy.

Invite students to discuss their cultural heritage. Give students whose first language is not English a chance to say words in their primary language and to tell the class about the city or town they came from originally.

and a secret letter arrived at Tony's house for Serafina.

Dear Bella Serafina, ♡ ♡ ♡

I saw you at your window and I love you!

Here's a ring to keep as a symbol
of my _adoration_.

It will not be long before we are
HUSBAND and WIFE!

♡ Angelo, your true love.

25

Visual Literacy

Letters Have students compare the letters, noting that Angelo used the same stationery for both but that his letter to Tony was more formal. (He used _Signore_ in the greeting and signed his full name, while he greeted Serafina by her first name.)

Social Studies Link

Rings Rings are often used to symbolize an engagement or marriage. The ancient Romans were the first to use wedding rings. Early wedding rings were simple iron bands. The practice of adorning rings with gems began around A.D.1200.

Interact *with* Literature

Reading Strategies

 Monitor

The abrupt change of scene from page 26 to page 27 may confuse some students. If necessary, model how students can monitor their reading.

___

Think Aloud

This scene is confusing to me because on the previous page Tony was in his bakery talking with the three sisters. It seems like I missed something. But when I go back a few pages, I remember that Angelo asked Tony to meet him on Sunday after Mass. And, in the picture on page 27, Tony and Serafina seem dressed up, like they've just come from church. So, I conclude that this scene takes place on a different day than the one on page 26.

And Zia Clotilda, Zia Caterina and Zia Clorinda did their part.

"Oh, Tony, did you see that rich young man from Milano?" Zia Clotilda asked.

"He wanted to know all about you. It seems he just loved your bread!" said Zia Caterina.

"Nothing like it in all Milano, he said," Zia Clorinda told Tony. "Why, I wouldn't be surprised if he wanted to meet you, the way he went on."

"Well, dear ladies, funny you should say that, because he does want to meet me — after Mass on Sunday," said Tony. "His name is Angelo di Milano."

"Imagine that!" the three women exclaimed. *"Che bella fortuna"* — What good luck for you. "And for Serafina!" they whispered to each other.

26

QuickREFERENCE

Vocabulary

Pronunciations

- *che bella fortuna:* kay BEL-luh for-TOO-nuh

Students Acquiring English

MEETING INDIVIDUAL NEEDS

Word Meaning Point out that when Tony says *"funny you should say that,"* he doesn't mean that the sisters have told him a joke or said something comical. In this sense, *funny* means "unusual" or "odd."

Self-Assessment

Have students evaluate how their reading strategies have helped them enjoy and comprehend the story thus far.

"And so, Signor Antonio, I would be most pleased if you and your lovely daughter would come to Milano as my guests," Angelo said.

"And if you like our city, I would be proud to set you up in a fine bakery of your own near the Piazza del Duomo — the cathedral square. Your fame would be assured, Signor Antonio. I will see to that."

Tony couldn't believe his ears. His dream was about to come true. "Why, thank you, Signor Angelo. But please, call me Tony. All my friends do."

"Also Signor Tony," Angelo continued. "The advantages for your beautiful daughter would be great. I admit I would not find it unpleasant for Serafina to sit beside me at my great table as my wife — the daughter of Tony, the most famous baker of Milano."

27

Students Acquiring English

Expressions Note the meanings of *set you up* ("provide everything you need"), *couldn't believe his ears* ("couldn't believe what he was hearing") and *come true* ("to really happen, to change from a dream to reality").

Vocabulary

Pronunciations
- *signor:* seen-YOR ("mister")
- *piazza del Duomo:* pee-AHT-suh del doo-OH-moh

MINILESSON

Making Judgments   REVIEW & MAINTAIN

Teach/Model

Ask students whether they think Tony should trust Angelo. Point out that as readers they have a distinct advantage over Tony: they can see things about Angelo that he can't see. By carefully weighing the evidence on both sides, they can make a judgment about whether to trust Angelo.

Work with students to add up reasons why Angelo should or should not be trusted.

Reasons to Trust Angelo	Reasons Not to Trust Angelo
• He has good manners. • He seems to love Serafina.	• He's a stranger. • He secretly asks the sisters to help him. • He sends Serafina a secret letter. • He flatters Tony.
2 reasons to trust him	4 reasons not to trust him

Encourage students to discuss whatever judgments they make about Angelo.

Practice/Apply

Encourage teams of students to choose sides and to debate these questions:

- Should Tony leave his small village for the big city?

- Does Serafina really love Angelo?

SKILL FINDER

Full lesson/Reteaching, Theme 6, pp. 255C–255D

Minilessons, Theme 1, p. 47; Theme 6, pp. 239, 285

Interact
with
Literature

Reading Strategies

► **Think About Words**

Discuss what clues students can use to figure out what a *laughingstock* is ("someone who is the object of laughter"):

- What two words do you see in *laughingstock*? (*laughing* and *stock*)

- From the context, does it sound like a *laughingstock* is something Tony wants to be? (No, he's sad when he says it; he'd rather leave Milano than become one.)

 **Guided Reading**

Comprehension/Critical Thinking

1. What convinced Tony to accept Angelo's proposal? (Angelo appealed to his dream of becoming the most famous baker in northern Italy.)

2. Why did Tony become depressed when he toured Milano? (He felt he could never compete with the fine bakeries there.)

3. How would you describe Angelo? Do you think Tony should trust him? (He's clever; he goes after what he wants; he's a little deceitful.)

Predicting/Purpose Setting

Ask students to predict what might happen to change Tony's mind. Then have them finish reading the story.

That did it! Tony agreed, and off he and Serafina went with Angelo. Together they walked all the small streets around the cathedral square and visited all the bakeries and pastry shops.

They tasted *torta* — cake — and *biscotti* — cookies — and *pane* — bread. And Tony was depressed. The bread alone was like nothing Tony had ever tasted: bread made out of the finest, whitest flour; bread shaped like pinwheels; bread with seeds of all sorts scattered over the top.

28

QuickREFERENCE

Vocabulary
Pronunciations
- *torta:* TOR-tuh
- *biscotti:* bi-SKOT-tee
- *pane:* PAHN-eh

"It is no use, Signor Angelo," said a very sad Tony. "I can never compete with all these fine bakeries and pastry shops. All I can make is bread, and very simple bread at that. I would be the laughingstock of Milano. It is better if Serafina and I just go home."

"No, never!" Angelo shouted.

"Oh, Papa, no," Serafina cried. Not only was she in love with Angelo, but she was looking forward to living in that grand house with all those good things to eat.

29

Visual Literacy

Signs Have students find the Italian words for cookies (*biscotti*), cake (*torta*), and bread (*pane*) in the illustration. Students may be interested to know that *Motta* is the name of a café and company in Milan famed for its *panettone*, which today is exported to the United States. Perhaps Tomie dePaola included the name *Motta* in this illustration as a humorous nod to present-day Milan since, at this point in the story, *panettone* hasn't been invented yet!

Social Studies Link

Milan Milan is Italy's second-largest city. It became a trading center in the A.D. 100s. After the Roman Empire fell, trading ceased and Milan became a small town. The city later regained importance, becoming a leader in the Renaissance.

Interact
with
Literature

"If only you could make bread that tasted as good and sweet as this candied fruit and these raisins," Serafina said.

"Or," Angelo said, getting another idea, "as rich and sweet as this cup of punch made from milk and eggs and honey!"

"Milk, eggs, honey," Tony said, thinking out loud.

"Candied fruit," Serafina said. "Raisins," Angelo chimed in.

"That's it!" all three shouted.

"I shall make the richest, lightest, most wonderful bread anyone has ever tasted — out of the whitest flour, the biggest eggs, the creamiest milk, the sweetest candied fruit and the plumpest raisins," Tony shouted.

30

Informal Assessment

Oral Reading To check oral reading fluency, ask individual students to read aloud pages 30–31. Students should first be allowed to reread the pages silently. The Oral Reading Checklist in the *Teacher's Assessment Handbook* provides criteria for assessment.

QuickREFERENCE

Health Link

Raisins Raisins are a good source of vitamins A and B, thiamine, and riboflavin. Minerals such as calcium, potassium, and iron are also in these dried grapes. Raisins give quick energy boosts because the body quickly absorbs their sugars.

Math Link

Pounds It takes about $4\frac{1}{2}$ pounds of grapes to make one pound of raisins. How many pounds of grapes would it take to make two pounds of raisins? (9) Three pounds? ($13\frac{1}{2}$) Five pounds? ($22\frac{1}{2}$)

"Oh, Papa," Serafina cried, kissing her father.

"Servants," Angelo called, and he sent them off to buy all the fine ingredients Tony would need.

The next morning, Tony, Serafina and all the supplies headed back to the little village.

And Tony began to work. Day after day he experimented until he had mixed the lightest, richest dough with as many raisins and as much candied fruit as he could put into it.

Now he was ready to bake. He sent word to Angelo in Milano that he should come to the bakery the next afternoon.

Then he set out the dough in large bowls and went to bed. As Tony slept, the dough began to rise and rise and rise.

The next morning he filled every pan in his shop. One piece of dough was left over so he threw it in a flower pot and baked it too.

31

Science Link

Bakers add yeast to bread, which breaks down sugar in bread into carbon dioxide gas. The gas bubbles make dough rise. If students examine a slice of bread they will observe holes in the bread left by bubbles trapped in the dough.

Students Acquiring English

When Tony *sent word to Angelo*, it means he sent a message to Angelo, either written or orally.

Math Link

Division Invite students to cite similarities between Tony's leftover dough and remainders in division. (A person can divide either dough or numbers into equal parts and end up with a remainder.)

Following Directions

Teach/Model

How did Tony know what steps to follow to make his new bread? Point out that although Tony was experimenting with a new recipe, he probably followed the same steps he had always used for making bread. Work with students to reconstruct the steps. The clue words will help you.

Clue Words	Step
First	He experimented until he had mixed just the right dough.
Next	He put the dough in large bowls to rise overnight.
Next morning	He put the dough into pans.
After that	He put the pans in the oven to bake.
Finally	He removed the baked bread from the oven and sliced it for eating.

Discuss the importance of following steps in the right order. What might have happened if Tony had omitted a step or done something out of order?

Practice/Apply

Have partners rewrite the steps into a numbered list of directions, such as *1. Mix the dough*. They can then takes turns pantomiming the directions.

SKILL FINDER

Full lesson/Reteaching, pp. 37C–37D

Minilessons, p. 69; Theme 2, p. 171

When Angelo arrived, the bread was just coming out of the oven. Everyone held his breath and waited while Tony cut a slice of his new bread. Angelo tasted it. Serafina tasted it. Tony tasted it. Zia Clotilda, Zia Caterina, Zia Clorinda all tasted it.

"That's it!" they shouted.
"I'll take these loaves back to Milano to see what my friends say," Angelo said, and off he went.

32

QuickREFERENCE

Visual Literacy

Shapes Have students look carefully at the loaves of bread on page 32 and identify the one that was baked in the flowerpot. Encourage students to verbalize how they could tell.

Students Acquiring English

Spelling You may wish to point out that *loaves* is the plural form of *loaf* and explain the following English spelling rule: to form the plural of some nouns ending in *f* or *fe*, change the *f* to *v* and add *es*. (examples: *leaf, leaves, knife, knives*)

In just a few days a letter and a large cart filled with ingredients arrived in the village.

Dear Tony,
  Here are more supplies,
  Make as much bread as you can,
and send it to me.
  Then, when I send for you,
I promise you will enter Milano
with flags flying and Serafina
will be mine.
  Your future son-in-law,
    Angelo

P.S.
  Please bake all the loaves in flowerpots.
My friends like the shape of that
loaf the best.

33

Interact
with
Literature

Guided Reading

Comprehension/Critical Thinking

1. How did Tony come up with the recipe for *panettone*? (He experimented with milk, eggs, honey, and other ingredients.)

2. How did Tony accidentally invent the unique shape of *panettone*? (He had dough left over but no more pans, so he baked the dough in a flowerpot.)

3. Do you think inventions are generally the result of skill or luck? (Probably a little of both: Tony worked hard to find just the right combination of ingredients for panettone, but he would never have discovered the shape if he hadn't run out of regular pans!)

4. Do you think Tony, Angelo, and Serafina will live happily ever after in Milano? Explain. (Accept reasonable responses supported by clues from the story.)

Self-Assessment

Encourage students to reflect on their own reading by asking themselves the following questions:

- Were any parts of the story confusing to me? What did I do to understand them?
- When I came across unfamiliar words, was I able to use strategies to figure out their meaning?

Just before Christmas, Angelo sent for Tony and Serafina. Sure enough, when their coach entered Milano, crowds were cheering and flags were flying.

"*Benvenuto, Tonio!*" — Welcome, Tony! — the crowds cheered. "*Benvenuto!*"

The bishop and the mayor were there to greet Tony and Serafina.

"And," said the mayor, "Milano is so happy to have you here, so we may always have enough of your wonderful bread!"

The next day when the bakery door was opened, the bishop's guards were called to keep order. All of Milano was there, except for Serafina and Angelo, who were being married quietly in a small chapel in the cathedral.

All during the wedding, they could hear the crowds cheering, calling for *pan di Tonio* — Tony's bread. And to this day, the *panettone* of Milano is eaten and enjoyed, especially at Christmas.

QuickREFERENCE

Social Studies Link

Cathedrals A *cathedral* is the church of a bishop in a Christian religion. Most cathedrals are shaped like a cross. A long center aisle and two side aisles extend from the entrance. The side aisles are the arms of the cross.

The Gothic-style Milan Cathedral is 520 feet long and 205 feet wide. Though its foundation was laid in 1385, it was not completed until 1813. Built of white Carrara marble, it has more than 3,000 statues decorating the inside and outside.

Vocabulary

Pronunciation
- *benvenuto:* ben-vay-NOO-toe

BRAVA SERAFINA, BRAVO ANGELO.
BRAVO TONY!

35

Writer's Craft
Folktale Characteristics

Teach/Model

Engage students in a discussion about how Tomie dePaola successfully incorporated the traditional elements of folktales in *Tony's Bread* while keeping his unique style of storytelling. If necessary, use the minilesson on page 21 to review characteristics of folktales.

Characteristic	Tony's Bread
set in the past	*Once, a long time ago . . .*
cultural details	Italian words, names, places
repeated elements/ the number 3	three sisters three letters
one-dimensional characters	Tony is simple. Angelo is clever.
a happy ending	Tony becomes famous. Angelo and Serafina get married.

Practice/Apply

Invite students to read and discuss some of dePaola's other folktales (*Jamie O'Rourke and the Big Potato, Strega Nona*). They may also want to compare the humor and illustrations in *Tony's Bread* with realistic fiction books by dePaola, such as *The Art Lesson*.

SKILL FINDER

Writing Activities: A Folktale, p. 37F

Reading-Writing Workshop, pp. 90–91F

Vocabulary

Pronunciation

• *bravo:* brah-VOE ("good job")

The Italian word *bravo* has come into common usage in English as an expression of approval. Ask students when they might have heard or used this term.

②

Interact *with* Literature

More About the Author-Illustrator

Tomie dePaola

Tomie dePaola is the award-winning author and illustrator of nearly 200 children's books, which have been published in more than fifteen countries. He has received the Regina Medal for lifetime contribution to children's literature and has had more of his books on the International Reading Association's *Children's Choice* list than any other author.

Becoming one of the best-known names in children's literature didn't happen without a large dose of rejection and frustration, though. For many years, while publishers were turning down his work, dePaola supported himself by teaching art classes, painting church murals, and designing greeting cards. (He once earned 15 dollars for designing a greeting card that eventually sold 80,000 copies.) When he was 31, he finally won his first assignment to illustrate a children's book. After that, the rest came easily, "like the other olives out of the bottle, after you pry out the first," he says.

One of dePaola's newest ventures is as the creative director of the Whitebird Books series, which seeks to discover new talent to bring folktales from around the world to a new generation of young readers.

MEET

Tomie dePaola

When he isn't writing and illustrating books such as *Strega Nona* and *The Legend of the Bluebonnet*, Tomie dePaola likes to spend time cooking and baking. His New Hampshire home has two full kitchens plus a grill room especially designed for baking bread and cooking meat. Tomie dePaola has been known to make a batch of *panettone* (pah-nah-TOE-nay) once in a while. There are a total of six ovens in his house. Sometimes, he cooks dinner for as many as thirty friends and uses all six ovens at the same time. *Buon appetito!*

Tomie dePaola in his grill room making an Italian bread called *pane pugliese* (PAH-nay pool-YAY-say)

Fresh Out of the Oven

RESPONDING

Create a Commercial
The Best Bread in Town

Tony needs to advertise his new bakery in Milano. Write and act out a commercial in which Tony convinces people to try his *panettone*.

Write a Folktale
Cook Up a Story

Tony's Bread explains how *panettone* was invented. Write a folktale about how another kind of bread was first made. You could choose pizza crust, pita bread, hot dog rolls, or another bread you like.

37

Responding Activities

Personal Response

- Encourage students to write their opinion of *Tony's Bread* in their journals. Which character did they like best? Least? What was their favorite part of the story?

- Allow students to respond to the selection any way they wish.

Anthology Activities

Invite students to select one of the activities on page 37, or choose one for them.

Home Connection

Italy in the News Suggest that students work with family members to clip out newspaper and magazine articles about Italy.

MEETING INDIVIDUAL NEEDS
Students Acquiring English

Make sure students understand that in the "Cook Up a Story" activity on page 37, the expression *cook up* means "to invent." You might suggest that this activity be done as a shared writing.

Informal Assessment

Students' responses should indicate a general understanding of the story.

Responding

More Choices for Responding

School Story Hour

Younger children love Tomie dePaola's stories. Your students might enjoy planning and conducting a storytelling hour for a younger class. Suggest that students first practice reading aloud *Tony's Bread* several times. Have them make invitations for the event.

1 Cut out an oven door from a piece of construction paper.

2 Glue the front of the oven to another piece of paper. Write your message inside.

3 Glue the oven door back on. Put your invitation in an envelope and deliver!

Guess what's cooking in Room 202? A storytelling hour just for you!

Materials
- construction paper
- scissors
- glue
- pens or marker
- manila envelopes

Literature Discussion

- How did adding the problem of a sad daughter enhance the telling of the story of how *panettone* came to be? What would the story have been like without that element?

- If you could rewrite the ending of the story, what would you change? Why?

- Do you think this is a believable story about how something was invented? Why or why not?

Selection Connections
LAB, p. 2

Have students complete the segment of the chart relating to *Tony's Bread.*

Talk Show

Cooperative Learning
Students can work with partners to present an interview about *Tony's Bread.* One student can be the talk-show host and the other can be Tony. The two can prepare questions and answers that take listeners through the process of how the bread was invented.

Informal Assessment

Check responses for a general understanding of the story.

Additional Support:
- Use Guided Reading questions to review and/or reread the selection.
- Have students work with partners to make a story map for the selection.
- Reread aloud any parts of the selection students found confusing.

More Choices for Responding

Ad Campaign

Have students work in small groups to create print ads for Tony's bread. They can also design a logo and make a sign for his new bakery in Milano.

Students Acquiring English Suggest that students look at a variety of print advertisements to see the kind of language used in advertising. Students can write catchy, one-word descriptions such as *Delicious!* or *Tasty!*

All Kinds of Shapes

Students Acquiring English If Tony hadn't had an empty flowerpot in his bakery, what else could he have baked his *panettone* in? Invite students to assemble and discuss a display of containers of various sizes that might make interesting shapes for *panettone.*

The Story Continues

Challenge Did everyone in *Tony's Bread* live happily ever after? Invite students to write a sequel that takes place several years after the invention of panettone. Let students discuss their ideas in small groups first. They might want to speculate on the following:

- How has fame changed Tony?
- Does Tony like living in the big city, or does he miss his small village?
- Are Angelo and Serafina happy? Is she still eating *dolci?*
- What became of Zia Clotilda, Zia Caterina, and Zia Clorinda?

Comprehension Check

Use the following questions and/or *Literacy Activity Book* page 4 to check understanding of the story.

1. How did Angelo help make the dreams of both Tony and Serafina come true? (He brought Tony to Milano and encouraged him to try a new bread recipe. He fell in love with Serafina.)

2. Do you think *panettone* would have been invented if Tony had stayed in his small village? (Probably not. Seeing the fine bakeries in Milano challenged him to come up with a new bread recipe.)

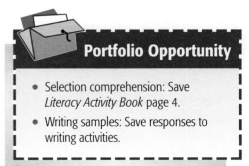

Literacy Activity Book, p. 4

Bread Today

Bread Today magazine wants to interview one of Tony's friends. Answer the questions for the magazine interview.

Bread Today INTERVIEW

Bread Today: Did Tony have any dreams while he was growing up?
Tony's Friend:

BT: Who first brought him to Milano, and why?
TF:

BT: But he returned to his home. Why?
TF:

BT: Where did Tony get the idea for *panettone?*
TF:

BT: What about Angelo and Serafina—how is that working out?
TF:

What's Cooking?

Portfolio Opportunity

- Selection comprehension: Save *Literacy Activity Book* page 4.
- Writing samples: Save responses to writing activities.

Instruct
and
Integrate

Comprehension

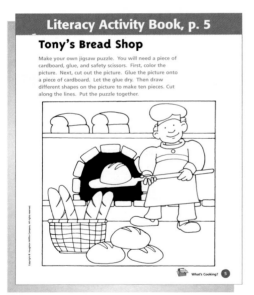

Literacy Activity Book, p. 5

Tony's Bread Shop

Make your own jigsaw puzzle. You will need a piece of cardboard, glue, and safety scissors. First, color the picture. Next, cut out the picture. Glue the picture onto a piece of cardboard. Let the glue dry. Then draw different shapes on the picture to make ten pieces. Cut along the lines. Put the puzzle together.

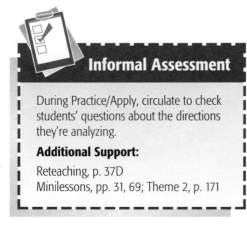

 What's Cooking? **5**

Informal Assessment

During Practice/Apply, circulate to check students' questions about the directions they're analyzing.

Additional Support:

Reteaching, p. 37D
Minilessons, pp. 31, 69; Theme 2, p. 171

INTERACTIVE LEARNING

TESTED SKILL

Following Directions

LAB, p. 5

Teach/Model

Invite a volunteer to write directions for going from the classroom to the cafeteria. Have the class fill in any missing steps. Then have other students attempt to follow the directions exactly.

Remind students that it is important to read directions carefully and to follow the steps in order. Explain that knowing how to follow directions will help students make things correctly and find their way to unfamiliar places.

Display Transparency 4–2, which has a partial recipe for Tony's bread, *panettone.* (A complete recipe appears on page 37O).

Panettone

1. Mix the dough in a big bowl and cover with a cloth.
2. Let the dough rise for about 2 hours, until it is double in size.
3. Meanwhile, grease two tube pans.
4. When the dough has risen, divide it in half.
5. Place each half in a greased tube pan.
6. Let the dough rise again for 1/2 hour.
7. Brush the tops with melted butter.
8. Bake in a 350° oven for about 1/2 hour.

Read the recipe with students and ask:

- What should you do first? (Read the recipe; gather ingredients.)

- What might happen if you didn't gather everything first? (You might discover too late that you're out of eggs!)

- According to this recipe, what should you gather? (bowl, cloth, pans)

- Can you grease the pans after you put the dough in them? (No.)

- What might happen if you baked the *panettone* longer than a half hour? (It might burn; it might be too dry.)

SKILL FINDER

Minilessons, pp. 31, 69;
Theme 2, p. 171

Practice/Apply
- Have students complete *Literacy Activity Book* page 5.

- Have students gather and analyze written directions (game instructions, a computer manual, recipes). Are the directions clear? Do any steps seem to be missing? What might happen if you do not follow the steps in order?

Reteaching

Following Directions

Read the following directions aloud and ask students to follow them. Remind students to do the steps in order and to finish each step before going on to the next one.

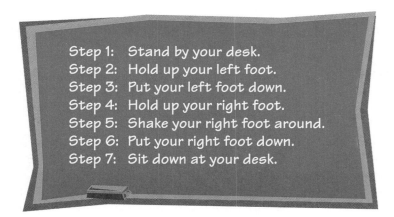

Step 1: Stand by your desk.
Step 2: Hold up your left foot.
Step 3: Put your left foot down.
Step 4: Hold up your right foot.
Step 5: Shake your right foot around.
Step 6: Put your right foot down.
Step 7: Sit down at your desk.

Ask students why it was important to finish doing Step 3 before going on to Step 4. (They could not hold up both feet at once!) Prompt them to discuss things they have done at home or in school that required them to follow directions. These activities might have included playing a board game or putting a toy together. Encourage volunteers to describe some of the steps they took.

With students, develop a list of directions for following directions. Students can make a poster to hang in the classroom.

Directions for Following Directions

▶ READ
all the directions carefully.

▶ GATHER
necessary ingredients, materials, or tools.

▶ FOLLOW
each step in order.

▶ FINISH
each step before going on to the next one.

Portfolio Opportunity

Save *Literacy Activity Book* page 5 as a record of students' understanding of following directions.

Instruct and Integrate

Writing Skills and Activities

Informal Assessment

INTERACTIVE LEARNING

Writing a Play

LAB, p. 7

Teach/Model

Discuss with students how a story is told when it is performed as a play. (by what the characters say and how they act) How does the audience know where the story takes place? (the stage sets and by what the characters say) Discuss with students how they often make up plays of their own and then act them out. They know what to say because they are both authors and actors. Explain that most adult plays are written by an author and performed by other people. The actors need a script to tell them what to say and how to act.

Explain that when writing a play script, an author thinks about the same things as when writing a story: the setting, the characters, and the action.

Display Transparency 4-3, which shows part of a scene from *Tony's Bread* rewritten as a play. Discuss these features:

Guidelines For Writing a Play

- A complete list of characters with brief labels is given first.

- A brief description of the setting and any special information about the characters follows.

- Spoken parts are preceded by the characters' names, written in all capital letters and followed by a colon. No quotation marks are used.

- Stage directions are in parentheses after the character's name. The directions, written as phrases, tell how the lines should be spoken or describe an action.

- Additional stage directions are given between sections of dialogue as necessary.

Help students see how the fifth paragraph on page 23 was turned into dialogue. Explain that a new scene begins whenever the setting changes. Point out that only critical stage directions are included. Many details are left up to the director and actors.

Practice/Apply

Work with students to complete the activity Shared Writing: A Play.

Writing Activities

Students can use The Learning Company's new elementary writing center for all their writing activities.

Shared Writing: A Play

Work with the class to rewrite *Tony's Bread* or another familiar story as a play or to create their own plot. If they choose to create their own plot, work with them to plan the characters, settings, and plot before they begin to write. Groups of students could role-play the dialogue for different parts of the play and then combine their efforts with your guidance. Provide an opportunity for students to perform their play for an audience.

Write a Friendly Letter

Have students note the design on Angelo's stationery. Invite students to design their own stationery and to use it to write friendly letters. Suggest that they write letters of appreciation to someone who has done something nice for them personally or perhaps to school personnel, such as the custodians, cafeteria workers, secretaries, or volunteers.

Write a Jingle
Cooperative Learning

Help students recall catchy jingles they have heard to advertise products. Suggest that students work in small groups to write a jingle for *panettone*. Students can brainstorm a list of descriptive words, names of ingredients, and words that rhyme with *panettone* that they can use in rhyming verses. Students can match their words with a familiar tune or make up a new tune.

Creative Writing: A Folktale

Invite students to write a folktale that includes the following elements:

- It is set in the past.

- It includes three of something, such as three tasks, three wishes, three tries, three bad characters, or a family with three people.

- It has a happy ending.

Invite students to illustrate their folktales and read them aloud or add them to the class library. *(See the Writer's Craft Minilesson on page 35.)*

Portfolio Opportunity

Save responses to activities on this page for writing samples.

Instruct *and* Integrate

Word Skills and Strategies

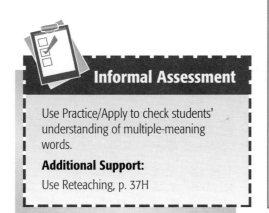

Informal Assessment

Use Practice/Apply to check students' understanding of multiple-meaning words.

Additional Support:
Use Reteaching, p. 37H

INTERACTIVE LEARNING

✓ TESTED SKILL Multiple-Meaning Words
LAB, p. 8

Teach/Model

Write these sentences on the board.

> Tony's *dream* was to become a famous baker.
>
> In the morning, Serafina woke from her *dream*.

Ask students if *dream* has the same meaning in both sentences. (no) Discuss with them the difference in meanings.

- In the first sentence, *dream* means "hope, wish."

- In the second sentence, it means "images seen during sleep."

Then ask students to tell you how they knew which meaning of *dream* you had in mind when you wrote each sentence. Elicit that the other words in the sentence make the meaning clear. Write this sentence on the board.

> Angelo gave Serafina a *ring*.

Ask students if they can make up a sentence or phrase using *ring* with a different meaning. (Samples: *ring a bell; circus ring; bathtub ring*) Elicit that

- many words have more than one meaning;

- readers can tell which meaning the writer had in mind from clues in the surrounding words.

Practice/Apply

Have students meet in small groups to search through the story for words that have more than one meaning. For each word they find, have them make up brief sentences or phrases using at least two different meanings of the word. Ask each group to share some of their words and meanings with the class.

The following multiple-meaning words are from the story:

long	punch	off	admit	keep	court	back
good	work	just	top	part	poor	left
simple	over	lived	headed	rich	crying	loaf
raised	set	can	bowls	funny	passing	lightest
spoiled	too	about	mine	please	coach	
so	treats	will	time	great	order	
kind	like	taste	old	crowds	shop	
sorts	looked	fine	called	even	sweet	

Multiple-Meaning Words

Copy the pictures onto the board; ask students what kind of top they see in each picture. (1. the top of a jar; 2. a mountaintop; 3. a spinning top) Elicit that *top* is one of many words that have more than one meaning. Remind students that when they come across multiple-meaning words in their reading, the other words in the sentence or paragraph serve the same purpose as the pictures on the board—they provide clues that let the reader know which meaning of the word is being used. Ask students which word clue makes the meaning of *top* clear in the following sentence:

Put the top back on the jelly jar. *(jar)*

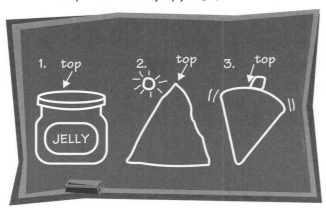

Word Skills Practice

Cumulative Skill Practice
Corn
by Janet Klausner

WATCH **ME** READ

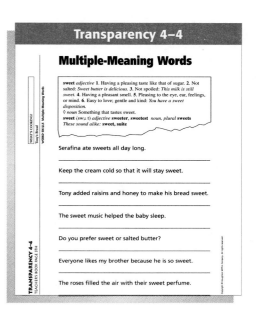

Transparency 4–4
Multiple-Meaning Words

MINILESSON

Dictionary Skills
Multiple-Meaning Words

Teach/Model Point to the entry for *sweet* on Transparency 4–4. Draw out from students that the numbers 1–6 indicate six different meanings of the adjective *sweet.* Elicit that sweet also has one noun definition, but it is not numbered because there is only one. Have volunteers read each definition aloud. Then have volunteers read aloud the first four sentences on the transparency, and work together to determine which meaning of *sweet* applies.

Practice/Apply Have students work independently to read the last three practice sentences, and select the appropriate meaning from the dictionary entry.

Advise students that each meaning is used only once. Then ask which meaning of *sweet* is used in each sentence. Have volunteers write the correct definition for each one.

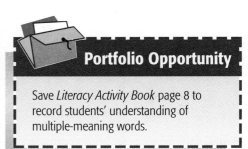

Portfolio Opportunity

Save *Literacy Activity Book* page 8 to record students' understanding of multiple-meaning words.

Instruct and Integrate

Building Vocabulary

High-Frequency Vocabulary Practice

Cumulative Skill Practice
Corn
by Janet Klausner

Words from Italian		
Food	**Music**	**Other**
pizza	opera	balcony
pepperoni	accordian	confetti
spaghetti	piano	umbrella
zucchini	violin	graffiti
macaroni	cello	portfolio
lasagna	oboe	tarantula
baloney	tuba	studio
pasta	piccolo	zany
pistachio	soprano	presto
broccoli	maestro	magenta

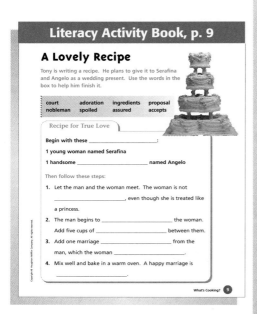

Literacy Activity Book, p. 9

A Lovely Recipe

Tony is writing a recipe. He plans to give it to Serafina and Angelo as a wedding present. Use the words in the box to help him finish it.

court	adoration	ingredients	proposal
nobleman	spoiled	assured	accepts

Recipe for True Love

Begin with these _____:

1 young woman named Serafina

1 handsome _____ named Angelo

Then follow these steps:

1. Let the man and the woman meet. The woman is not _____, even though she is treated like a princess.

2. The man begins to _____ the woman. Add five cups of _____ between them.

3. Add one marriage _____ from the man, which the woman _____.

4. Mix well and bake in a warm oven. A happy marriage is

What's Cooking? 9

Use this page to review Selection Vocabulary.

Vocabulary Activities

Words from Italian

While Tony was in Milano, he visited other bakeries and tasted the goods they made, such as their delicious biscotti. Ask students if they remember what *biscotti* means in Italian. (cookies) Point out that today many bakers in the United States also make special Italian cookies that they call biscotti, and that, as a result, the Italian word *biscotti* is becoming part of the English language. Tell students that many other words have also come to the English language from Italian.

Divide the class into small groups and assign each group several of the words from the list at left. Have students discuss the meanings of their words, sharing prior knowledge and using a dictionary when necessary. Then have the groups present their words and meanings to the class, writing each word on the board under the appropriate headings.

Words That Exclaim

Have students turn to page 35, and ask why people shout *"Bravo!"* (to show that they like something) Tell students that there are many other expressions that people use when they want to show a strong feeling. These expressions are called *exclamations.* Prompt students to think of exclamations. Ask "What might you say when . . . "

- you are cheering? (*yay, yippee, hurray, whoopee*)

- you have hurt yourself? (*ouch, ow*)

- you don't like something? (*boo, yuck, ugh, phooey*)

- you are surprised? (*wow, hey, huh, gee, golly*)

Write the exclamations on the board, and have volunteers say them with an appropriate tone of voice, facial expression, and gesture.

Vocabulary Notebook

Encourage students to keep their eyes and ears open for "food" words to add to their vocabulary notebooks. Prompt brainstorming by asking, "Where would you find food words . . . "

- in a supermarket? (signs and labels)

- in your kitchen? (food packages, cookbooks)

- in a restaurant? (menus)

- on television? (cooking shows, commercials)

Spelling

FIVE-DAY PLAN

DAY 1	DAY 2	DAY 3	DAY 4	DAY 5
Pretest; Minilesson; Challenge Words/ Additional Words (opt.); Take-Home Word Lists (LAB)	First LAB page; Challenge Words Practice (opt.)	Check first LAB page; Second LAB page (except writing application)	Check second LAB page; writing application (LAB)	Test

Teaching CHOICES

MINILESSON

Spelling Words
*once   *slice
*just   age
*city   jam
*large   circle

Challenge Words
*princess   *except
*village   *jewelry

Additional Spelling Words
jeans   circus
space   orange

*Starred words or forms of the words appear in *Tony's Bread*.

TESTED SKILL

The First Sound in *city* and *just*

LAB, p. 10–11

- Say the words *once* and *city.* Ask what consonant sound students hear in both words. (/s/) Write the words on the board. Ask students to name the consonant that spells the /s/ sound in each. (*c*)

- Ask which letter follows the *c* in *once.* (*e*) Then ask which letter follows the *c* in *city.* (*i*) Explain that *c* makes the /s/ sound when it is followed by *i* or *e.*

- Say the words *just* and *age.* Ask what consonant sound students hear in both words. (/j/) Write the words on the board. Ask students to name the consonant that spells the /j/ sound in each. (*j, g*)

- Ask what letter follows the *g* in *age.* (*e*) Explain that when *g* has the /j/ sound it is often followed by *e.*

- Write the Spelling Words on the board. Say the words and have students repeat them.

Spelling Assessment

Pretest

Say each underlined word, read the sentence, and then repeat the word. Have students write only the underlined words.

1. My father visits Italy <u>once</u> a year.
2. He <u>just</u> left this morning.
3. He was born in an Italian <u>city</u>.
4. His <u>large</u> family still lives there.
5. I'd like a big <u>slice</u> of that cake.
6. I said my first word at the <u>age</u> of one.
7. Toast with <u>jam</u> makes a good breakfast.
8. We sat in a <u>circle</u> and told stories.

Test

Spelling Words Use the Pretest sentences.

Challenge Words

9. The best bakery is in the <u>village</u> square.
10. Her <u>jewelry</u> is locked in a safe.
11. The <u>princess</u> is getting married.
12. Everybody went <u>except</u> for me.

SKILL FINDER	Daily Language Practice, p. 37L
	Reading-Writing Workshop, p. 91E

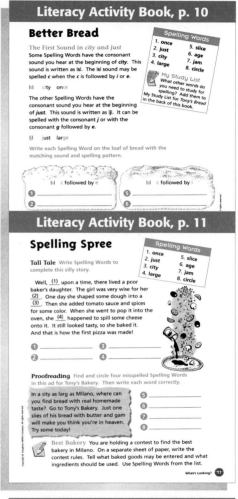

Literacy Activity Book, p. 10

Better Bread

The First Sound in *city* and *just*
Some Spelling Words have the consonant sound you hear at the beginning of *city.* This sound is written as /s/. The /s/ sound may be spelled *c* when the *c* is followed by *i* or *e.*

/s/ city once

The other Spelling Words have the consonant sound you hear at the beginning of *just.* This sound is written as /j/. It can be spelled with the consonant *j* or with the consonant *g* followed by *e.*

/j/ just large

Write each Spelling Word on the loaf of bread with the matching sound and spelling pattern.

Spelling Words
1. once   5. slice
2. just   6. age
3. city   7. jam
4. large 8. circle

My Study List
What other words do you need to study for spelling? Add them to My Study List for *Tony's Bread* in the back of this book.

/s/ c followed by ___
/j/ c followed by ___

Literacy Activity Book, p. 11

Spelling Spree

Tall Tale Write Spelling Words to complete this silly story.

Spelling Words
1. once   5. slice
2. just   6. age
3. city   7. jam
4. large 8. circle

Well, (1) upon a time, there lived a poor baker's daughter. The girl was very wise for her (2). One day she shaped some dough into a (3). Then she added tomato sauce and spices for some color. When she went to pop it into the oven, she (4) happened to spill some cheese onto it. It still looked tasty, so she baked it. And that is how the first pizza was made!

1. _____   3. _____
2. _____   4. _____

Proofreading Find and circle four misspelled Spelling Words in this ad for Tony's Bakery. Then write each word correctly.

In a sity as larg as Milano, where can you find bread with real homemade taste? Go to Tony's Bakery. Just one slies of his bread with butter and gam will make you think you're in heaven. Try some today!

5. _____
6. _____
7. _____
8. _____

Best Bakery You are holding a contest to find the best bakery in Milano. On a separate sheet of paper, write the contest rules. Tell what baked goods may be entered and what ingredients should be used. Use Spelling Words from the list.

What's Cooking? 11

Literacy Activity Book

Take-Home Word Lists: pp. 171–172

Students can use the **Spelling Spree CD-ROM** for extra practice with the spelling principles taught in this selection.

MEETING INDIVIDUAL NEEDS

Challenge

Challenge Words Practice Have students use the Challenge Words to write signs advertising a new bakery.

Instruct and Integrate

Grammar

FIVE-DAY PLAN

DAY 1	DAY 2	DAY 3	DAY 4	DAY 5
Daily Language Practice 1; Teach/Model; First LAB page	Daily Language Practice 2; Check first LAB page; Cooperative Learning	Daily Language Practice 3; Writing Application	Daily Language Practice 4; Reteaching (opt.); Second LAB page	Daily Language Practice 5; Check second LAB page; Students' Writing

---

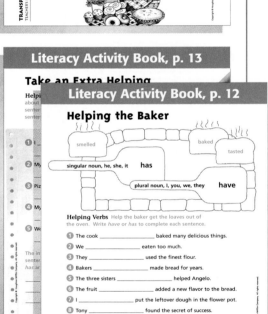

Transparency 4–5

Helping Verbs

Subject	Verb
A lonely woman	has looked out the window.
He	has spoiled his little girl.
The aunts	have listened to Angelo's plan.
We	have enjoyed the tale.

You _____ wanted a bakery of your own.

For years, I _____ dreamed about this.

The three sisters _____ talked to Angelo.

Their conversation _____ helped him with his plan.

A nobleman _____ fallen in love with Serafina

She _____ watched Angelo from her window.

We _____ noticed Antonio and his princess.

The bakeries _____ offered the finest pastry.

It _____ filled the air with a sweet smell.

A letter _____ arrived for the baker.

Tony _____ agreed to a marriage for Serafina.

They _____ raised a cheer for Tony.

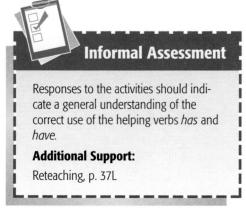

Literacy Activity Book, p. 13

Take an Extra Helping

Literacy Activity Book, p. 12

Helping the Baker

Helping Verbs Help the baker get the loaves out of the oven. Write *have* or *has* to complete each sentence.

1. The cook _____ baked many delicious things.
2. We _____ eaten too much.
3. They _____ used the finest flour.
4. Bakers _____ made bread for years.
5. The three sisters _____ helped Angelo.
6. The fruit _____ added a new flavor to the bread.
7. I _____ put the leftover dough in the flower pot.
8. Tony _____ found the secret of success.
9. Serafina _____ gained a wonderful new home.
10. You _____ learned the story of *panettone*.

12 What's Cooking?

Informal Assessment

Responses to the activities should indicate a general understanding of the correct use of the helping verbs *has* and *have*.

Additional Support:

Reteaching, p. 37L

INTERACTIVE LEARNING

TESTED SKILL

Helping Verbs

LAB, pp. 12–13

Sometimes the words *has* and *have* help other verbs to show past time. *Has* and *have* are called **helping verbs**.
- Use *has* with a singular noun in the subject and with *he, she,* or *it*.
- Use *have* with a plural noun in the subject and with *I, you, we,* or *they*.

Teach/Model

Write these first two sentences on the chalkboard, leaving extra space between words and omitting circles and underlines.

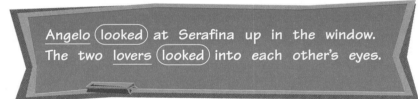

Angelo (looked) at Serafina up in the window.
The two lovers (looked) into each other's eyes.

Ask volunteers to read each sentence, to underline the noun in the subject, and to circle the verb. Elicit that

- a verb sometimes needs help to show past time
- a helping verb comes before the verb
- *have* and *has* can be helping verbs

Write the words *have* and *has* separately on tag board. Then write this next pair of sentences on a different chalkboard; omit *has* and *have*.

Discuss the examples. Hand the *has* card to a student who tapes it at the proper place back in the first pair of sentences you wrote. Repeat this with *have*. Have the new sentences read aloud.

Singular subject: The (city has) praised him.
Plural subject: The (aunts have) whispered to him.

SKILL FINDER
Reading-Writing Workshop, p. 91E

INTERACTIVE LEARNING *(continued)*

Display Transparency 4–5. Review the use of *have* and *has* in the examples. Ask volunteers to write *have* or *has* in each sentence.

Practice/Apply

Cooperative Learning: **Helping-Verb Clues** Have students form teams. Each team picks a character from *Tony's Bread* and writes a clue to the character's identity. Each clue is a sentence using *has* or *have* with a verb in past time, such as *I have admired Serafina from a distance.* (If teams omit *has* or *have*, or use *has* or *have* incorrectly, they are disqualified.) One teammate says the clue and calls on classmates to guess. (The team also may pantomime the character.) A correct guess is worth one point. After two incorrect tries from the class, the team earns ten points.

 Writing Application: A Friendly Letter Suggest that students write a letter to a friend telling about a dream they have. It might begin *I have dreamed for years of . . . .* Ask students to use *has* and *have* as helping verbs.

Students' Writing Have students check their writing in process for correct use of the helping verbs *has* and *have.*

More Practice

Houghton Mifflin English Level 3
Workbook Plus, pp. 55–56
Reteaching Workbook, p. 35

Write on Track
Write on Track SourceBook, p. 77

Reteaching **Helping Verbs**

 MEETING INDIVIDUAL NEEDS

Write these subjects on separate index cards.

Then place them face down, and write these predicates on the chalkboard.

I
You
We
They
The cooks
He
She
The cook

has measured the flour.
have measured the flour.

has counted the eggs.
have counted the eggs.

has stirred the dough.
have stirred the dough.

has baked the bread.
have baked the bread.

Pick a card. Work together to match it with four predicates. Have a volunteer say each new sentence. Then ask students to take turns matching cards. Collect the cards and display them in two categories: *have* cards and *has* cards. Use them to review how *has* is used with a singular noun, *she, he,* and *it,* while *have* is used with a plural noun, *I, you, we,* and *they.*

Daily Language Practice
Focus Skills

Grammar: Helping Verbs
Spelling: The first sound in *city* and *just*

Each day write one sentence on the chalkboard. Have each student write the sentence correctly on a sheet of paper. Tell students to correct any errors in the use of the helping verb *has* or *have* as well as any misspelled words. Have students correct their own paper as a volunteer corrects the sentence on the chalkboard.

1. Tony have dreamed of a bakery in a larje city.
Tony **has** dreamed of a bakery in a **large** city.

2. They has visited the sity just once.
They **have** visited the **city** just once.

3. You has handed a slise of bread to each aunt.
You **have** handed a **slice** of bread to each aunt.

4. Customers has asked for bread in the shape of a cercle.
Customers **have** asked for bread in the shape of a **circle**.

5. This woman have reached her dreams at an early aje.
This woman **has** reached her dreams at an early **age**.

Instruct *and* **Integrate**

Communication Activities

Guidelines for Reader's Theater

Write a script based on the story.

Assign parts for the main characters and the narrator who will read passages that do not contain dialogue.

Prepare sound effects.

Rehearse your parts.

Emphasize reading with expression.

Present the play to your classmates.

Audio Tape
for What's Cooking?: *Tony's Bread*

Listening and Speaking

Performing Reader's Theater

Cooperative Learning

Invite students to prepare a Reader's Theater presentation of *Tony's Bread.* To help them get started, review the Guidelines for Reader's Theater.

Listening to *Tony's Bread*

Invite students to listen to the audiotape for *Tony's Bread* several times. Then have them take turns retelling the story in their own words.

Speaking Italian

Multicultural Link Bring recordings in Italian to class. Review some of the words and ask students if they have heard any of them before. Write a few common Italian words and expressions on the board and have students practice saying them.

Resources
Living Language: Italian–Fast and Easy (Crown Publishers)

Good morning.	Buon giorno (bwohn JOR-no)
Good afternoon.	Buona sera (BWO-na SAY-ra)
How are you?	Come sta? (KO-may STA?)
I am well.	Sto bene (STO BAY-nay)
yes	si (SEE)
no	no (NO)
Good-bye.	Arrivederci (ar-ree-vay-DAYR-chee)

Challenge Have students compile an Italian phrase book. When the book is finished some students can role-play, using Italian.

Informal Assessment

Use the Guidelines for Reader's Theater to evaluate students' play presentation.

Additional Support:
- Review guidelines.
- Have students work in small groups to practice the story before sharing it with the class.

Viewing

Looking at Tomie dePaola's Artwork

Have students compare the illustrations from another Tomie dePaola book with those in *Tony's Bread*. Ask them to note similarities and differences in color treatments and details.

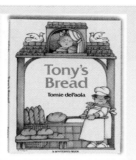

Watching Bread Bake

Tape a TV cooking demonstration of bread-making to play for students or take a trip to a bakery or the school cafeteria. After viewing, discuss the steps the baker took in preparing the bread and the utensils he or she used. Have students list and define baking terms such as *grease, blend,* and *dissolve.*

Observing Shapes of Bread

Let students look through magazines and newspapers for pictures of breads. Have them draw the different shapes in which bread is made. Then ask students to draw a slice from one of the breads. Discuss how the shape of the slice compares with the shape of the whole loaf of bread.

Portfolio Opportunity

Videotape students' Reader's Theater performances and save students' drawings of bread shapes in a portfolio of class projects.

3

Instruct *and* Integrate

Cross-Curricular Activities

Book List

Health

Bread by Dorothy Turner

How Bread Is Made by Neil Curtis and Peter Greenland

Social Studies

Count Your Way Through Italy by Jim Haskins

Italy by Jillian Powell

Ingredients

- 2 cakes compressed yeast
- 1 cup warm water
- $4\frac{1}{2}$ cups flour
- $\frac{1}{2}$ cup sugar
- $\frac{1}{2}$ cup softened butter
- 3 eggs
- 1 teaspoon salt
- 2 teaspoons grated lemon rind
- $\frac{1}{4}$ cup candied fruit
- $\frac{1}{4}$ cup raisins
- $\frac{1}{2}$ cup chopped nuts
- melted butter

Choices for Health

Making *Panettone*

Invite the class to work in groups to make Tony's special bread, *panettone*. Start this project in the morning to allow the dough to rise and for the time needed for baking.

Directions

1. Dissolve yeast in water for 10 minutes.

2. Stir in 1 cup of flour.

3. Cover and let rise in a warm place until double in size.

4. In a separate bowl, gradually add sugar to butter and beat until creamy.

5. Beat in eggs one at a time.

6. Add salt and lemon rind.

7. Beat the risen "sponge" of dough into this mixture.

8. Gradually add $3\frac{1}{2}$ cups flour and beat 5 minutes.

9. Add candied fruit, raisins, and nuts.

10. Cover bowl with a cloth and let dough rise for 2 hours, until double in size.

11. Divide dough in half and place each half in a greased tube pan.

12. Let dough rise again for $\frac{1}{2}$ hour.

13. Brush tops with melted butter.

14. Bake in a 350° oven for about $\frac{1}{2}$ hour.

Choices for Health *(continued)*

Listing Rules for Kitchen Safety

Make students aware of special precautions needed when cooking. Have them make a list of kitchen safety rules, and discuss each rule.

- Always have an adult with you while using a stove or oven.
- Use pot holders when removing anything hot from an oven or stove.
- Wipe up spills immediately.
- Have a fire extinguisher nearby.

Science

Making a Table of Enriched Breads

Have students look for ten USDA nutrition labels from breads that have been enriched. Ask students to find out which minerals or vitamins were added to each of the breads, then organize their findings into a table. Which breads were high in vitamins and minerals? Which were low?

Social Studies

Shipping *Panettone* from Milan

Challenge Have students pretend to send *panettone* to their hometown from Milan, Italy. What is the best way to do it without using air travel? What is the most direct route? Have them map the route, list the kinds of transportation they would use, and give directions to their house.

Portfolio Opportunity

Save the table of enriched breads in a portfolio to discuss nutrition in a science class.

Introduce the Literature

Activating Prior Knowledge

Work together with students to develop a word web for sandwiches. For example:

names for
taco
empanada

breads for
rye
pita

SANDWICHES

fillings for
peanut butter
cheese

times for
lunch
snack

Ask what students' favorite sandwiches are. You might even have them draw pictures or write directions for how to make them. Then explain that next they will read about sandwiches from all around the world.

Building Background

Preview the selection with students, noting the various ways information is presented. (Article uses a map and photographs, and gives pronunciations.)

Ask why the text at the top of pages 40–41 is shaded green. (It is a sidebar, a section that gives additional information.)

by Ann Hinga Klein

SANDWICHES from Around THE WORLD

Raise your hand if you like peanut butter and jelly sandwiches. Okay, now raise your hand if you like smoked eel sandwiches.

Just kidding! But did you know that in Holland, some kids really do like smoked eel sandwiches?

Kids around the world eat all kinds of sandwiches. We asked kids and parents from many different countries about the sandwiches they like to eat. Here is what they told us:

ETHIOPIA:

A popular bread called "injera" (in-JER-ah) looks like a big pancake. Ethiopian kids tear injera into pieces and use it to scoop up a reddish meat or vegetable sauce.

SWITZERLAND:

Some kids in Switzerland like strong cheese and salami on bread from a long loaf called a "baguette" (bag-ET).

38

Interact with Literature

 Students Acquiring English

Before reading the article, give students the opportunity to work with food-related vocabulary in context. Depending on their proficiency level, students might benefit from labeling and classifying pictures of foods they like and dislike or grouping (meat, fruit, vegetable) different sandwich fillings.

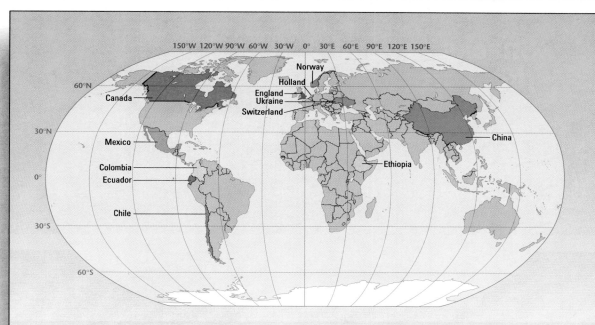

Map labels: Norway, Holland, England, Ukraine, Switzerland, Canada, Mexico, Colombia, Ecuador, Chile, China, Ethiopia. Degree markings: 150°W 120°W 90°W 60°W 30°W 0° 30°E 60°E 90°E 120°E 150°E; 60°N 30°N 0° 30°S 60°S

Avocado

ECUADOR:

Pork sandwiches are popular in Ecuador. Inside the bun, you will find a slice of roast pork, a bit of onion, a slice of tomato, lettuce, and some green avocado paste.

CHILE:

If you visit a friend in Chile, you might be served hot dogs with hot mayonnaise. Or your friend might offer you an avocado sandwich with onion. Did you say no thanks? Then how about an "empanada" (emp-in-AH-dah)? An empanada has cheese or meat in the middle, and a crust all around it.

39

Expanding Literacy
Social Studies Article

Instruct and Integrate **MINILESSON**

Study Skill
Globes

TESTED SKILL

Teach/Model

Ask students the following about the map on page 39:

- Why does the map have a round shape? (to imitate the earth's shape like a globe does)

- What makes different countries easy to find? (the callouts and various colors; the map also only shows countries discussed in the article.)

- Why is the country at the bottom in white? (It is the Arctic zone, which is cold and snowy.)

Also discuss these features.

Feature	Definition/Purpose
grid	These lines run vertically and horizontally around the globe. They divide the map into units that you can use to locate a country.
degrees	These measurements don't refer to temperature. Rather, they are a unit of measurement.

Practice/Apply

Ask students to place a ruler or their finger down the center of the map. Then have them identify which countries are in the eastern and western part of the globe. Also ask them to write quiz questions such as *Which country is the furthest north? south? east? west?*

 SKILL FINDER Full lesson, p. H2

 Interact with Literature

 MEETING INDIVIDUAL NEEDS **Extra Support**

Have students make a chart with information about each sandwich.

Name	Fillings	Your Opinion

Work with students acquiring English to identify different ways they can express their opinions. (Examples: *It sounds delicious. I'd like to try it. Sounds terrible.*)

Discussion

Discuss why it would be difficult to summarize this selection. (It contains a lot of specific information.) Use these questions to help students compare the sandwiches.

- Which sandwiches need to be broken open to be eaten? (the empanada and the piroshki)

- Which sandwiches contain lettuce? (pork sandwiches and taco sandwiches)

- Which sandwiches might often contain cheese? (the cheese and salami sandwich, the empanada, and a taco)

- Which sandwich would you like to try? Why?

Assign mixed groups of students to write factual questions about the sandwiches in the article. Then let groups quiz each other. Model with these questions.

- Which sandwich is served in an open shell? (the taco)

- Which sandwich contains eggs? (the smoked salmon sandwich)

 Home Connection

Encourage students to ask parents and/or grandparents to tell about sandwiches and snacks that they enjoyed as youngsters. Ask them to compare them with the sandwiches and snacks discussed in the article.

Snacks Around the World

Just like you, kids around the world want snacks when they get hungry between meals.

In Colombia, school kids munch potato chips, oranges, or pieces of pineapple.

In China, children nibble on popcorn, cookies, candy, or fruit for a treat. They can eat ice cream for a bedtime snack, but never right after a meal. That's because many parents believe that eating warm foods and cold foods at the same time will make their children's stomachs feel sick.

UKRAINE:
Ukrainians eat piroshki (per-OSH-kee). A piroshki has potatoes or meat inside and a crust all around the outside. Many Ukrainian people like their piroshki hot and spicy.

ENGLAND:
Jam sandwiches are after-school favorites in England. So are sandwiches with chocolate spread. Some English children like cheese-and-cucumber sandwiches. Others want just plain bread with butter.

40

In Mexico, children can buy snow cones in the market. The ice is in a huge block, and a person scrapes off small pieces and puts them in a cup. Kids can choose from 10 or 12 different syrup flavors. Children in Mexico also eat an orange fruit called a mango.

It is served on a stick and covered with hot chile pepper powder!

In **Canada**, children like clementines (CLEM-en-teens). These are sweet little oranges the size of golf balls.

Hot Peppers

MEXICO:

A taco is a sandwich in Mexico. You can buy a pork taco to eat for breakfast. Lunch is a big meal with soup, meat, and beans, but not sandwiches. People do eat sandwiches for supper in Mexico. Some people like roast chicken on thick slices of bread with sliced onions, tomatoes, and hot peppers. In some families, even the little children eat hot peppers.

NORWAY:

How about a sandwich of smoked salmon and scrambled eggs? That's what you might be served in Norway.

41

Social Studies Link

Cooperative Learning

Ask students to bring in recipes for ethnic breads. For example:

Irish soda bread

Gnocchi di patate (Italian dumplings)

Naan (Indian flat bread)

Challah (Jewish egg braid)

Kulich (Russian Easter bread)

If possible, bring in samples. Then divide students into small groups to compare the breads.

Viewing

Some form of bread is eaten in almost every country on earth. You may want to share with students *Bread, Bread, Bread* by Ann Morris (Lothrop, Lee & Shepard). The striking photographs show breads from around the world.

Writing

Ask students to write their own recipes for preparing favorite sandwiches. Suggest this format:

(Name) Sandwich
Ingredients (list all ingredients)
Steps (list in order)

SELECTION:

Halmoni and the Picnic

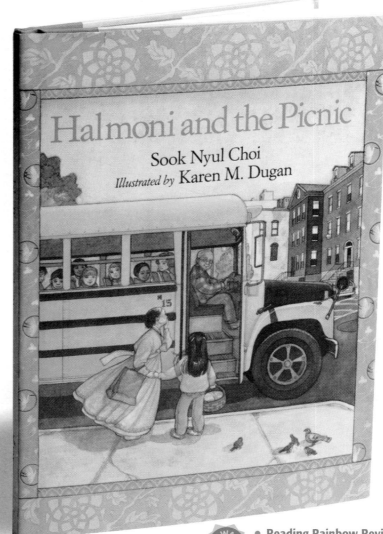

- Reading Rainbow Review Book
- American Bookseller "Pick of the Lists"

by Sook Nyul Choi

Selection Summary

Yunmi is worried about her grandmother, Halmoni, who has recently moved from Korea to live with Yunmi's family in the United States. Halmoni is uncomfortable in the strange new culture, and is too shy to speak English and make new friends.

Yunmi and her classmates Helen and Anna Marie decide to ask Halmoni to chaperon their class picnic. Halmoni agrees, and prepares a Korean dish called *kimbap* for the children. It is a big success, and the children even make up a jump-rope song about it. When the picnic is over, Halmoni says goodbye to the children in her new country's language, English.

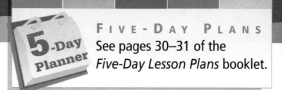
FIVE-DAY PLANS
See pages 30–31 of the
Five-Day Lesson Plans booklet.

Lesson Planning Guide

	Skill/Strategy Instruction	Meeting Individual Needs	Lesson Resources
1 **Introduce** *the* **Literature** *Pacing: 1 day*	**Preparing to Read and Write** Prior Knowledge/Building Background, 41C **Selection Vocabulary,** 41D • disturb • embarrassed • cautiously • relieved • dignified **Spelling Pretest,** 58I • grandmother • never • people • table • after • little • enter • apple	**Support in Advance,** 41C **Students Acquiring English,** 41C **Other Choices for Building Background,** 41C **Spelling Challenge Words,** 58I • together • wonder • wrinkle • another	*Literacy Activity Book,* Selection Vocabulary, p. 15 **Transparency:** Selection Vocabulary, 4–6 **Great Start** CD-ROM software, "What's Cooking?" CD
2 **Interact** *with* **Literature** *Pacing: 1–3 days*	**Reading Strategies** Predict/Infer, 44, 50 Self-Question, 44, 54 Think About Words, 48 **Minilessons** Compare and Contrast, 47 Problem Solving/Decision Making, 49 ✓ Predicting Outcomes, 53 Writer's Craft: Conveying Characters' Feelings, 55	**Choices for Reading,** 44 **Guided Reading,** 44 Comprehension/Critical Thinking, 46, 52, 56 **Students Acquiring English,** 48, 50, 56, 58 **Extra Support,** 47, 52 **Challenge,** 53	**Reading-Writing Workshop,** Research Report, 90–91F *Literacy Activity Book,* Selection Connections, p. 2; Comprehension Check, p. 17 **Audio Tape** for What's Cooking?: *Halmoni and the Picnic* The Learning Company's Ultimate Writing & Creativity Center software
3 **Instruct** *and* **Integrate** *Pacing: 1–3 days*	✓ **Comprehension:** Predicting Outcomes, 58B **Writing:** Invitation, 58D **Word Skills and Strategies:** ✓ Using Context, 58F Phonics: *r*-Controlled Vowels, 58G **Building Vocabulary:** Vocabulary Activities, 58H ✓ **Spelling:** Words Ending with *-er* or *-le,* 58I ✓ **Grammar:** Irregular Verbs, 58J–58K **Communication Activities:** Listening and Speaking, 58L; Viewing, 58M **Cross-Curricular Activities:** Health, 58N; Math, 58O; Social Studies, 58O	**Reteaching:** Predicting Outcomes, 58C **Activity Choices:** Invitation, Memorable Incident, Family Food, Showing Friendship, 58E **Reteaching:** Using Context, 58G **Activity Choices:** Words from Places, Regional Words, Prefix *uni-,* 58H **Challenge Words Practice,** 58I **Reteaching:** Irregular Verbs, 58K **Activity Choices:** Listening and Speaking, 58L; Viewing, 58M **Activity Choices:** Health, 58N; Math, 58O; Social Studies, 58O	Watch Me Read *Soup of the Day* **Reading-Writing Workshop,** Research Report, 90–91F **Transparencies:** Comprehension, 4–7; Writing, 4–8; Grammar, 4–9 *Literacy Activity Book,* Comprehension Skill, p. 18; Writing Skills, p. 19; Word Skills, p. 20; Building Vocabulary, p. 21; Spelling, pp. 22–23; Grammar, pp. 24–25 **Spelling Spree** CD-ROM **Audio Tape** for What's Cooking?: *Halmoni and the Picnic* The Learning Company's Ultimate Writing & Creativity Center software

✓ *Indicates Tested Skills. See page 16F for assessment options.*

1

Introduce *the* Literature

Preparing to Read and Write

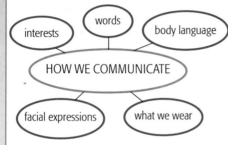

Support in Advance

Use this activity for students who need extra support before participating in the whole-class activity.

Web Invite students to think of the many ways people communicate with one another. Put responses in a word web.

- words
- interests
- body language
- HOW WE COMMUNICATE
- facial expressions
- what we wear

 Management Tip During the Support in Advance activity, have other students list some of their interests in their journals and list the people with whom they share these interests.

Students Acquiring English

Identify the main characters in the story: Yunmi, her grandmother, Halmoni, and her classmates, Anna Marie and Helen. Have students look through the story to find pictures of each character. Then work together to tell what the characters are doing in each picture and whether they look happy or sad.

Great Start
For students needing extra support with key concepts and vocabulary, use the "What's Cooking?" CD.

INTERACTIVE LEARNING

Prior Knowledge/Building Background

Key Concept
Feeling Accepted

Ask students what problems they might have living in a place where few people spoke their language or shared their customs. Encourage students who have visited other countries and students acquiring English to share their feelings.

Then discuss how this barrier can be overcome. Encourage students to share personal experiences. Brainstorm ways that the natives of one country can make a new citizen feel welcome. Write students' suggestions on the board. Have volunteers role-play some of the ideas.

> "talk" through gestures
> include in activities
> share languages
> ask questions about each other

Other Choices for Building Background

Role-Playing

 Challenge Prepare index cards with descriptions of different social situations. For example: *You are a shy person meeting someone for the first time*. Then have pairs of students draw the cards and role-play the situation.

Storyboards

Students Acquiring English Create three storyboards out of large sheets of paper. Have students use them to label and illustrate events in the beginning, middle, and end of the story.

INTERACTIVE LEARNING

Spelling
You may want to give the Spelling Pretest on page 58I before students read the selection.

Daily Language Practice
Use the activities on page 58K as a daily practice of the spelling and grammar skills taught with this selection.

Selection Vocabulary

Key Words

disturb

embarrassed

cautiously

relieved

dignified

Display Transparency 4–6. Work together with students to fill out the chart describing various emotional responses.

What Do You Do When You're . . .

Embarrassed?	Relieved?	Dignified?
blush	sigh	hold head high
head down	relax shoulders	show good manners

Extra Support You may wish to include these additional words from the story in this activity: *sighed, grinned, skipping,* and *hummed.*

Also, ask students to pantomime the following to show their understanding of the Key Words:

• how high winds *disturb* you when you walk against them

• how you would *cautiously* approach a cat you wanted to pet

Vocabulary Practice Have students work independently or together to complete the activity on page 15 of the *Literacy Activity Book.*

Transparency 4–6

Descriptive Words

What Do You Do When You're ...		
Embarrassed?	Relieved?	Dignified?

WHAT'S COOKING?
Hotmeat and the Picnic
SELECTION VOCABULARY

TRANSPARENCY 4–6
TEACHER'S BOOK PAGE 41D

Literacy Activity Book, p. 15

Act It Out

Write a definition for each word below. Then cut out the sentences at the bottom of the page and mix them up. Take turns with a partner picking a sentence and acting it out.

dignified: _____

embarrassed: _____

disturb: _____

cautiously: _____

relieved: _____

You drop a book on the floor, and you want to act **dignified** as you pick it up.

You just spilled your milk at lunch, and you feel **embarrassed**.

You are walking through a classroom and don't want to **disturb** the people who are hard at work.

You are at a busy street and must cross **cautiously**.

You feel **relieved** because you thought you were late for school but you really aren't.

What's Cooking? 15

Social Studies

Teacher FactFile

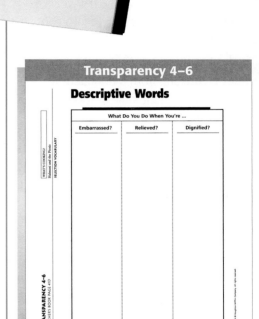

New York City, 1990

41% of the residents of New York City speak a language other than English at home.

POPULATION (MILLIONS)

White Black Hispanic Asian/Pacific Islander

Interact *with* Literature

More About the Author

Sook Nyul Choi

Born in Pyongyang, North Korea, Sook Nyul Choi spent two and a half years as a refugee in Pusan during the Korean War. She immigrated to the United States to pursue her college education. After graduating from Manhattanville College, she taught in New York City schools for almost twenty years while raising her two daughters.

In addition to having written *Halmoni and the Picnic*, Choi is the author of three autobiographical novels for young adults, *Year of Impossible Goodbyes*, *Echoes of the White Giraffe*, and *Gathering of Pearls*. She was the recipient of the 1992 Judy Lopez Book Award, presented by the Women's National Book Association.

Through her writing, Choi wants to bring to life the history and culture of Korea. "I hope that through my books, Americans can gain insight into this very different and interesting culture," she says.

A full-time writer and lecturer, Choi now lives in Cambridge, Massachusetts.

About the Author

Sook Nyul Choi grew up in North Korea. As a girl, she loved to read about faraway places, such as the United States. Years later, Sook Nyul Choi moved to the United States and became a teacher and then a writer. She likes to write about her homeland and about Korean people.

About the Illustrator

Karen M. Dugan had a lot of help illustrating *Halmoni and the Picnic*. To draw the setting accurately, she had a friend in New York City take pictures of the streets. She modeled the main character, Yunmi, after the author's own daughters. The author even made a Korean dish called *kimbap* and sent photos of it so Dugan could draw it.

42

Halmoni and the Picnic

Sook Nyul Choi

Illustrated by Karen M. Dugan

43

More About the Illustrator

Karen M. Dugan

Karen Dugan recalls making her first 'books' when she was in first grade by folding paper together and drawing out a story from start to finish.

Dugan graduated from art school but did not immediately embark on a career in art. She worked in an office, a hospital, and a museum. She also spent some time teaching. "Everything had its lessons," she says, "but the art kept pulling me back."

Returning to an early love, Dugan decided to focus on illustrating. She has since created the artwork for more than a dozen books for young people.

Interact
with
Literature

Reading Strategies

▶ **Predict/Infer**
Self-Question

Discussion Have students preview the illustrations. Discuss how a reader could infer different things from them and use them to make predictions. Ask what else a reader can use to make inferences. (important information in the text; prior knowledge) Then have students explain why asking yourself questions as you read is a useful strategy. (It gives you a purpose for reading and helps you check your understanding.)

Predicting/Purpose Setting

Suggest that students use the illustrations and the story title to predict what the story will be about.

Choices for Reading

Independent Reading	**Cooperative Reading**
Guided Reading	**Teacher Read Aloud**

Guided Reading

Students using this option should read pages 44–47. Comprehension questions are on page 46.

Hand in hand, Yunmi and her grandmother, Halmoni, walked toward St. Patrick's Elementary School. Taxi cabs darted between the big buses rumbling down busy Fourteenth Street. Yunmi squeezed Halmoni's hand and smiled. Halmoni nodded in acknowledgment, but kept her eyes on the street without smiling. Just like the day before, Halmoni looked sad as they drew closer to the school. She did not like going back to their empty apartment all alone.

Miss Stein, in her white uniform, was coming back from working the night shift at Beth Israel Hospital.

"Good morning, Miss Stein!" Yunmi called.

"Oh, hello, Yunmi," said Miss Stein, half smiling and half yawning.

"Yunmi," Halmoni said in Korean, "you must not call out to grown-ups. You should lower your eyes out of respect. It is rude for little ones to disturb their elders!"

Yunmi giggled. "Halmoni, people like it when I greet them. In America it isn't rude to call grown-ups by their names. Here it is rude *not* to say hello and *not* to look people in the eye when you speak to them."

Halmoni sighed. "I will never get used to living here."

44

Quick REFERENCE

Vocabulary

Pronunciation Ask students to try pronouncing the names *Halmoni* and *Yunmi*. Encourage them to compare the words to words they already know.

- *Halmoni* (HAHL mahnee)
- *Yunmi* (YOON mee)

Social Studies Link

Use a map or globe to point out Korea's location between China and Japan. At various points in history, Korea was controlled and greatly influenced by both countries. Koreans, though, are an ancient and homogeneous people.

✶✶ Multicultural Link

Traditional Korean values reflect the codes of Confucius. There ought to be "justice between ruler and subject, affection between father and son, prudence between husband and wife, order between old and young, and trust between friends."

45

Background: FYI

Koreans use several different forms of address, depending on the social relationship. They tailor the verbs or adjectives at the end of their sentences to reflect whomever they are addressing.

Visual Literacy

Encourage students to compare these aspects of city life in the illustration with their own neighborhoods.

- the walkup apartments above the store
- the variety shop
- the fire escape

Interact *with* Literature

 Guided Reading

Comprehension/Critical Thinking

1. **How does Halmoni feel? How do you know this?** (She is sad. She does not smile as she walks. Her expression turns sad as they get closer to the school. She says *"I will never get used to living here."*)

2. **Why is Halmoni so embarrassed?** (She is afraid her accent will make it hard for people to understand her.)

3. **How does Yunmi feel about Halmoni?** (She is concerned for her because she thinks Halmoni is lonely.)

4. **What else in America might someone new like Halmoni have difficulty adjusting to?** (Answers will vary. Encourage students to share personal experiences.)

Predicting/Purpose Setting

Have students discuss whether their predictions about what the story would be about were correct. Discuss what the problem in the story is, and then have students predict how it might be solved. Have students read pages 48–53.

46

Informal Assessment

If students' responses indicate that they understand the problem in the story, you may want to have them finish reading it independently or cooperatively.

Yunmi was sad for her grandmother, who found America too different from Korea.

"Halmoni," she said, "my friends like the bags of fruit you give them each morning."

"I am glad. It is always nice to share with friends," said Halmoni.

"Will you please say hello to my friends in English this morning? They will be so surprised to hear you talk to them. I know you can. Please, Halmoni?"

Halmoni replied, "No, I have only been here for two months. English words are still too difficult for my old tongue. I will sound funny. I will give them this fruit; that is my way of saying hello to them. Besides, you do enough talking for both of us!"

"Yunmi, Yunmi, wait for me!" they heard Anna Marie shout from behind them.

Then Helen came running up from a side street. "Hi, Anna Marie! Hi, Yunmi!"

They said hello to Halmoni. Halmoni nodded and gave one brown bag to each girl.

"Oh, thank you!" said Helen.

"Goody," said Anna Marie. "An apple, grapes, and cherries, too!" The girls said goodbye to Halmoni and headed toward the school yard.

Helen said, "Yunmi, your grandmother is so nice, but she never says anything. Why don't you teach her some English?"

Yunmi shook her head sadly. "My grandmother is <u>embarrassed</u> to speak with an accent. She could speak English if she wanted to. She is smart. She used to be a teacher in Korea."

47

Extra Support

If needed, explain that *accent* refers to the special way someone pronounces words, especially someone who is just learning a new language. An accent usually springs from a person's knowledge of letters and sounds in their primary language.

MINILESSON

Compare and Contrast

REVIEW & MAINTAIN

Teach/Model

Ask students how Halmoni and Yunmi are alike and different. Place responses in a diagram.

Yunmi		Halmoni
• speaks Korean and English	same family	• speaks Korean only
• many friends	speak Korean	• lonely

Explain to students that when you look for ways two people or things are alike, you are comparing; when you look for how they are different, you are contrasting.

Discuss how comparing and contrasting might help a reader. (It gives you a deeper understanding of the story. It helps you remember details.)

Practice/Apply

Have students compare and contrast the illustrations on pages 45 and 57. Ask:

- What is the same about each picture? (Halmoni and Yunmi; city street; holding hands)

- How are Halmoni and Yunmi's expressions different in the two pictures? (They look tense in one, and happy in the other.)

- In what other ways do the pictures differ? (On page 57 there are birds all around and many more people.)

SKILL FINDER

Full lesson/Reteaching, Theme 1, pp. 88B–88C

Minilessons, Theme 1, pp. 75 and 103

Interact *with* Literature

Reading Strategies

▶ **Think About Words**

Discuss these clues that a reader could use to figure out an approximate meaning of the word *determination*.

- *dialogue surrounding the word:* Helen says that they must do something, which implies a sense of immediacy. She expresses uncertainty (*"What can we do?"*) which prompts her friends to work together to find a solution.

- *other text clues:* The author says that the girls sat under the tree and did not play any games that morning.

- *picture clues:* The girls look like they are concentrating. The girl on the far right looks like she won't give up until they find a solution.

Helen thought for a while. "Maybe your grandmother is not happy here. When I'm not happy, I don't want to learn anything new. Maybe she's like me."

"That's true. I'm like that, too," Anna Marie agreed.

Yunmi sighed just like Halmoni and said, "I think she's lonely when I'm at school. My parents are so busy working that they have no time for her. I know she misses her old friends, but I don't want her to go back to Korea."

"She needs new friends!" Anna Marie exclaimed. "We can be her friends. We see her every day and we like her."

"We must do something to show her that we want to be her new friends," Helen said with determination. "What can we do?"

They entered the school yard and sat under the big oak tree thinking quietly. That morning they did not play tag or jump rope. When the bell rang, they went to their classroom and unpacked their bookbags in silence.

"Children, I have a special announcement to make this morning," Mrs. Nolan said. "Next Tuesday is our annual picnic in Central Park. We need a chaperon, so please ask your parents if one of them can come and help us."

Helen and Anna Marie raised their arms high, nearly falling off their chairs. Surprised, Mrs. Nolan said, "Yes, Helen, you first. What is it?"

Helen blushed, then asked, "Can Yunmi's grandmother be our chaperon, please?"

Mrs. Nolan said, "Of course. But Yunmi must ask her grandmother first. Will you, Yunmi?"

48

Self-Assessment

Reflecting Invite students to reflect on their reading with questions like the following:

- How are my predictions working out?
- How are the illustrations helping me to figure out what the characters are feeling?
- What parts of this story, if any, have been confusing?

QuickREFERENCE

Vocabulary

Word History The word *chaperon* literally means "hood or head covering." This was part of the costume of the Knights of the Garter, who were court attendants. The meaning of the word eventually changed to "escort."

Students Acquiring English

If students do not know what a *picnic* is, have them look at the illustration on page 53. Let students use the illustration to tell where picnics take place and what people do on a picnic. Ask volunteers to tell about a time they ate outdoors.

49

Problem Solving/ Decision Making

Teach/Model

REVIEW & MAINTAIN

Discuss why Mrs. Nolan's announcement seems the perfect solution to Halmoni's problem. Brainstorm what problems the picnic might address.

Problem	Solution
Halmoni is lonely.	She'll meet people at the picnic.
Halmoni is afraid to speak.	People at the picnic can ask her about Korean words.
Halmoni doesn't like New York.	The picnic will introduce her to Central Park.

Explain that finding a surprise solution like the girls did is just one way of solving a problem. Have students share other ways:

- thinking hard and researching

- asking for help

- brainstorming with others

Practice/Apply

Discuss Yunmi's decision not to discourage Halmoni from bringing kimbap to the picnic. Have students explain what she had to consider before making this decision.

- She had to consider Halmoni's feelings.

- She had to consider whether her classmates would make fun of Halmoni.

SKILL FINDER

Full lesson/Reteaching, pp. 121C–121D

Minilessons, p. 99; Theme 2, p. 141

Interact *with* Literature

Reading Strategies

▶ **Predict/Infer**

Discuss what readers know about the relationship between Halmoni and Yunmi so far. Then bring out these inferences that can be made:

- Yunmi is worried because she feels she has to ask Halmoni to the picnic, given her friends' enthusiastic response.

- She is hesitant to discuss bringing kimbap to the picnic because she is pleased that Halmoni is happy.

Have students predict whether Yunmi will persist in asking Halmoni not to take the kimbap to the picnic.

Helen and Anna Marie grinned and nodded at Yunmi with excitement. But Yunmi was suddenly confused and worried. What if Halmoni did not want to come? What if the children made fun of her pointed rubber shoes or her long Korean dress?

That afternoon Yunmi <u>cautiously</u> told Halmoni what had happened at school.

Halmoni blushed with pleasure. "Helen said that? Your teacher wants me?"

So <u>relieved</u> to see Halmoni looking happy, Yunmi nodded her head up and down.

Touching Yunmi's cheek, Halmoni asked, "And do you want me to go to the picnic with you?"

"Yes, yes, Halmoni, it will be fun. You will meet all my friends, and Mrs. Nolan, and we will be together all day long in Central Park."

"Then yes, I will come," Halmoni said.

Halmoni would not go to the picnic empty-handed. She prepared a huge fruit basket for the third graders. She also insisted on making large plates of kimbap and a big jug of barley tea. Kimbap is made of rice, carrots, eggs, and green vegetables wrapped in seaweed. Again, Yunmi was worried. Most of the children would bring bologna or peanut butter sandwiches, which they would wash down with soda pop. What if no one wanted to eat Halmoni's kimbap? What if they made faces?

"Halmoni, please do not take the kimbap to the picnic. It took you so long to make. Let's save it for us to eat later."

"Oh, it was no problem. It looks so pretty and it's perfect for picnics. I wonder if I made enough."

50

Informal Assessment

Oral Reading In order to check oral reading fluency, ask selected students to read aloud pages 50–52. Students should be allowed to first read these pages silently. Use the Oral Reading Checklist in the *Teacher's Assessment Handbook* as a guide for assessment.

Quick**REFERENCE**

Vocabulary

Pronunciation Encourage students to try pronouncing *kimbap*. Discuss how a reader might figure out its pronunciation.

- *kimbap* (KIHM bahp)

Students Acquiring English

MEETING INDIVIDUAL NEEDS

Discuss how a person might *blush* for a variety of reasons—either with pleasure (as here) or in embarrassment. Let students identify some situations that might make people blush.

Background: **F**y**I**

In Korean, *bap* means "rice." The seaweed used to make kimbap comes in sheets. The rice and vegetable mixture is spread on the sheet and rolled up. Then it is cut into small round pieces.

51

Interact *with* Literature

 Guided Reading

Comprehension/Critical Thinking

1. Were you surprised that Halmoni agreed so quickly to come to the picnic? Why or why not? (Responses will vary. Encourage students to use clues from the story to support their answers.)

2. Why does Halmoni prepare so much food for the picnic? (She is pleased that she has been asked to it, and wants to share in a way she is confident of—her cooking.)

3. How do you think Halmoni feels as she watches the children play in Central Park? (She is probably happy because she doesn't feel lonely, but she is still shy and wants to keep out of the way.)

Predicting/Purpose Setting

Ask students what they think of the idea of asking Halmoni to the picnic. Before reading the rest of the story, have them predict what else will happen at the picnic. Questions for discussing the conclusion of the story can be found on page 56.

On the morning of the picnic, Yunmi and her grandmother met the bus at school. Halmoni wore her pale blue skirt and top, called a ch'ima and chogori in Korean, with her white socks and white pointed rubber shoes.

When they arrived at Central Park, Halmoni sat under a big chestnut tree and watched the children play. The children took off their jackets and threw them in front of Halmoni. Smiling, she picked them up, shook off the grass and dirt, and folded each of them neatly. She liked the cool earth beneath her and the ringing laughter of the children.

At lunchtime, Halmoni placed the plates of kimbap on a large blue and white silk table cloth. Mrs. Nolan came over and gasped. "Oh, how beautiful they look! Children, come over and look at this. Yunmi's grandmother made my favorite lunch." Halmoni gave Mrs. Nolan a pair of chopsticks and poured a bit of soy sauce into a small dish. As the children munched on their sandwiches, they gathered around and watched Mrs. Nolan pop the little pieces of kimbap into her mouth.

Halmoni picked up one kimbap with her chopsticks and held it out to Helen. "Mogobwa," she said, which means "Try it." Helen understood and opened her mouth. Everyone watched her expression carefully as she chewed the strange-looking food. Her cautious chewing turned to delight. "Ummm, it's good!"

52

Vocabulary

Pronunciation Guide students to use their knowledge of phonics and their own knowledge of words to try to pronounce the words below.

- *ch'ima* (CHEE mah)
- *chogori* (joh GOH ree)
- *mogobwa* (MOH goh bwah)

 Extra Support

Invite students to demonstrate Helen's *cautious chewing* of the kimbap. Tell them to think about times they have tried a new food. Ask them also to show how Helen's expression gradually changes to one of delight.

Background: FYI

Chopsticks originated in China 2,400 years ago. The first part of the word comes from a word of Chinese origin meaning "fast or quick." Chopsticks come in many varieties such as wood, plastic, ivory, silver, and brass.

53

Challenge

Ask students to identify clues that reveal in what time of year the story is set. (in the spring; clues: the green grass and trees, the birds in the pictures on pages 46 and 57, *the cool earth* where Halmoni sits, the fact that school is still open)

Predicting Outcomes

TESTED
SKILL

Teach/Model

Ask a volunteer to read aloud the last two paragraphs on page 52. Discuss what they predict the outcome will be when the rest of Yunmi's class tries the kimbap. Explain to students that they can base their predictions on details from the story and what they already know. Work together to complete this chart.

What Happens in the Story:

• Mrs. Nolan tries the kimbap and likes it.

• Helen tries it and likes it too.

+

What I Know:

• People are more willing to try something if others recommend it.

Predicted Outcome:

The rest of the class will like Halmoni's kimbap.

Practice/Apply

Have students predict what the different outcomes for the story would be if the following had happened:

• Halmoni had declined to attend the picnic.

• Yielding to Yunmi's anxiety, Halmoni had not brought kimbap to the picnic.

SKILL FINDER

Full lesson/Reteaching, pp. 58B–58C

Minilessons, p. 67; Theme 1, p. 79

Interact
with
Literature

Reading Strategies

▶ **Self-Question**

Discuss the questions that might occur to a reader as he or she reads the scene in the park. Point out that questions like the following can help you see if you are understanding the story and what the characters are feeling.

- How does Halmoni feel about her kimbap?

- Why does Mrs. Nolan ask Yumni what to call her grandmother?

- Why does Halmoni start crying?

Then, Halmoni picked up another one and held it out for Anna Marie. "Nodo," she said, which means "You too." Anna Marie chewed slowly and then her face brightened, too. Helen and Anna Marie were ready for seconds, and soon everyone was eating the kimbap.

Halmoni smiled, displaying all her teeth. She forgot that in Korea it is not <u>dignified</u> for a woman to smile in public without covering her mouth with her hand.

After lunch, some children asked Halmoni to hold one end of their jump rope. Others asked if Halmoni would make kimbap again for next year's picnic. When Yunmi translated, Halmoni nodded and said, "Kurae, kurae," meaning "Yes, yes."

The children started to chant as they jumped rope:

> "One, two, pointed shoe.
> Three, four, kimbap more.
> Five, six, chopsticks.
> Seven, eight, kimbap plate.
> Kurae, kurae, Picnic Day!"

Halmoni smiled until tears clouded her vision. Her long blue ch'ima danced in the breeze as she turned the jump rope. She tapped her shoes to the rhythm of their song.

Mrs. Nolan asked Yunmi, "What should the class call your grandmother? Mrs. Lee?"

Yunmi said, "I just call her Halmoni, which means grandmother. In Korea, it is rude to call elders by their names."

54

Social Studies Link

Not for Girls! Students may be surprised to learn that jump rope started out as an activity for boys. It was considered unladylike for girls to jump rope.

Vocabulary

Pronunciation
- *nodo* (nah DOH)
- *kurae* (ghoo RAY)

★★★ Multicultural Link

Korean names traditionally appear with the family name first and the personal name last. This is often carried over when the names are written in English. Some Koreans, however, have adopted the Western style of placing the family name last.

55

Writer's Craft
Conveying Characters' Feelings

Teach/Model

Ask students how they know Halmoni is unhappy at the beginning of the story. Place responses in a chart like the following.

Halmoni's Words:
- "I will never get used to living here." (p. 44)
- "English words are still too difficult for my old tongue." (p. 47)

Halmoni's Actions:
- She kept her eyes on the street and didn't smile. (p. 44)
- She looked sad. (p. 44)

What the Author Says:
- She did not like going back to their empty apartment all alone. (p. 44)
- (Halmoni) found America too different from Korea. (p. 47)

Discuss how using all these different methods of showing how Halmoni is unhappy is much better than simply writing *Halmoni was unhappy.* Encourage students to use this technique in their own writing.

Practice/Apply

Ask students how the children in Yunmi's class felt about Halmoni. Have students tell how the author conveys the classmates' feelings. Then ask what Halmoni said and did to show she enjoyed being included.

SKILL FINDER Writing Activities: A Memorable Incident, p. 58E

Social Studies Link

Central Park Share these facts about Central Park with students.

- It is about 2.5 miles (4 km) long and 0.5 miles (0.8 km) wide.
- Clearing the sight in 1857 involved removing such things as bone-boiling works, farms, free-roaming livestock, and open sewers.
- The park's attractions include a zoo, an ice-skating rink, three small lakes, and an open-air theater.

 Home Connection

Public Parks Ask students to describe a park they like to play in and to recall experiences there. Discuss the value of public parks to the life of a community. You might want to bring in a schedule of events for a park in your area.

Interact *with* Literature

 Guided Reading

Comprehension/Critical Thinking

1. How did Halmoni feel at the picnic? How do you know? (She was pleased that everyone enjoyed the kimbap. She felt included in the fun because the children asked her to play jump rope with them.)

2. Why did Halmoni forget about covering her mouth when she smiled? (She was having such a good time that the thought escaped her.)

3. What do you think Halmoni was thinking about on the bus? (Answers will vary.)

4. Do you think Halmoni will continue trying to speak English from now on? Why or why not? (She probably will, because her confidence has been boosted by the picnic and she'll want to communicate and share with the children next time she sees them.)

Mrs. Nolan nodded and smiled. "Children, why don't we all thank Halmoni for her delicious kimbap?"

"Thank you for the kimbap, Halmoni!" the children shouted in unison. Halmoni's wrinkled face turned red and she looked down at her pointed shoes. She took a handkerchief from the large sleeve of her chogori and wiped her eyes.

Halmoni was deep in thought as the big bus wove through the New York City streets. When the bus arrived back at school, the children hurried off, shouting goodbye. Halmoni murmured in English, "Goodbye, goodbye."

Filled with pride, Yunmi grabbed Halmoni's hand and gave it a squeeze. Halmoni squeezed back. Yunmi grinned, thinking of Halmoni's big smile as the children sang about her in Central Park. Skipping along Fourteenth Street, Yunmi hummed the kimbap song.

She thought she heard Halmoni quietly humming along, too.

56

Self-Assessment

Ask students to assess their reading using these questions.

• How did asking myself questions help me to understand and appreciate the story more?

• Were the predictions I made close to how the story turned out? What surprised me in the story?

• Did I find this selection easy or hard to read? Why?

QuickREFERENCE

Vocabulary

Word Meaning Tell students that *in unison* means "all at once." Ask the group to read the thank-you to Halmoni in unison. Demonstrate saying something in a murmur. Have students read Halmoni's good-bye in a murmur.

Students Acquiring English

Have students work together to role-play the scene at Central Park. You or a student could read the story while students pantomime the actions and read the direct quotations.

57

Visual Literacy

Challenge students to find as many details in the picture on page 57 as they can. Some things they might miss or not recognize: entrance to the subway, newspaper vending machine, pizza store sign, taxicab.

Interact
with
Literature

Responding Activities

 Personal Response

- Have students write about how they felt when Halmoni murmured a word in English at the end of the story.

- Allow students to choose their own ways of responding to the selection.

Anthology Activities

Choose—or have students choose—an activity from page 58.

RESPONDING

Try One of These

Plan a Picnic

Let's Get Together

In a small group, plan a class picnic like the one Yunmi's class had. Where would it take place? What kinds of games would you play? Are there any special guests or foods you would like to bring?

Make a Card

Thank you, Halmoni!

Make a thank-you card that Helen or one of Yunmi's other classmates might send to Halmoni. Write a note thanking her for coming to the picnic and for bringing kimbap.

58

 Informal Assessment

Responses should show an understanding of different characters' feelings and the selection as a whole.

Additional Support:
- Use the Guided Reading questions to review and, if necessary, reread.
- Read aloud passages, as needed.

QuickREFERENCE

 Home Connection

Encourage students to share with their family what they learned about Korean culture. If you have any Korean students, you might have them invite a family member to speak to the class.

MEETING INDIVIDUAL NEEDS **Students Acquiring English**

Students may respond orally or by drawing, but encourage them to write as much as possible. For example, they could draw the location in the park for the "Let's Get Together" activity and label it, and later write a short description of it.

More Choices for Responding

Literature Discussion

- If Mrs. Nolan hadn't announced the picnic, what other idea do you think Yunmi and her friends might have thought of?

- If you wanted to do something nice for someone like Halmoni, where would you take him or her? What would you do together?

- Why are picnics a good way of bringing people together?

Class Game Day

Have students work together to plan a Class Game Day. On this day they will invite members of another class to their room to play various games. Students might volunteer for committees such as food, games, and invitations. Encourage them to be mindful of the interests and abilities of their guests in things they propose doing.

Play Ball !

Come to Our Class Game Day

When: February 25
Where: Room 5B
1:30-3:00

Write About Learning

Use this quote to recall for students Helen's insight about Halmoni: *"When I'm not happy, I don't want to learn anything new."* Then ask them to write about how they feel when they really want to learn something.

A Taste of Home

Students may like to share a favorite family dish by taking a picture of it and labeling the ingredients.

Create a Pictionary
Cooperative Learning

Invite pairs of students to make simple picture dictionaries that would be helpful to someone learning English.

Students Acquiring English
Encourage students to provide words in their primary language.

Selection Connections
LAB, p. 2

Have students complete the part of the chart relating to *Halmoni and the Picnic.*

Comprehension Check

Use these questions and/or *Literacy Activity Book* page 17 to discuss the selection:

1. Why does Halmoni give Yunmi's friends a bag of fruit each morning? (It is her way of saying hello and showing that she likes them.)

2. How does Mrs. Nolan help out at the picnic? (She encourages the class to try Halmoni's kimbap. She is polite, asking Yunmi the proper way to refer to her grandmother.)

3. Why is Yunmi filled with pride at the end of the story? (She is proud that Halmoni was accepted so completely.)

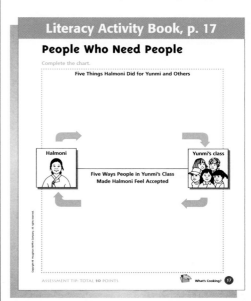

Literacy Activity Book, p. 17

People Who Need People

Complete the chart.

Five Things Halmoni Did for Yunmi and Others

Halmoni

Yunmi's class

Five Ways People in Yunmi's Class Made Halmoni Feel Accepted

ASSESSMENT TIP: TOTAL 10 POINTS   What's Cooking? 17

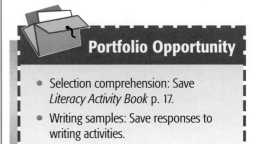

Portfolio Opportunity

- Selection comprehension: Save *Literacy Activity Book* p. 17.

- Writing samples: Save responses to writing activities.

Instruct
and
Integrate

Comprehension

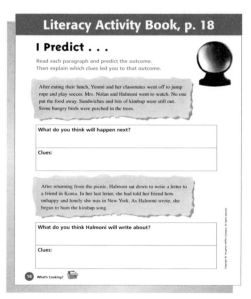

Literacy Activity Book, p. 18

I Predict . . .

Read each paragraph and predict the outcome.
Then explain which clues led you to that outcome.

After eating their lunch, Yunmi and her classmates went off to jump rope and play soccer. Mrs. Nolan and Halmoni went to watch. No one put the food away. Sandwiches and bits of kimbap were still out. Some hungry birds were perched in the trees.

What do you think will happen next?

Clues:

After returning from the picnic, Halmoni sat down to write a letter to a friend in Korea. In her last letter, she had told her friend how unhappy and lonely she was in New York. As Halmoni wrote, she began to hum the kimbap song.

What do you think Halmoni will write about?

Clues:

18 What's Cooking?

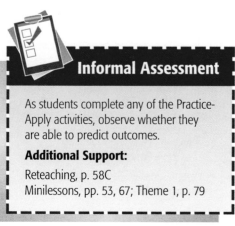

Informal Assessment

As students complete any of the Practice-Apply activities, observe whether they are able to predict outcomes.

Additional Support:

Reteaching, p. 58C
Minilessons, pp. 53, 67; Theme 1, p. 79

INTERACTIVE LEARNING

Predicting Outcomes
LAB, p. 18

TESTED SKILL

Teach/Model
Ask students if any of the outcomes in *Halmoni and the Picnic* surprised them. Explain that authors usually prepare their readers for certain outcomes by placing clues in the story. Readers can then use these clues—plus what they already know—to predict outcomes.

Display Transparency 4–7. Ask students to predict the outcome of each situation using what they know about Halmoni. Use this Think Aloud to model the first outcome.

Think Aloud

I think Halmoni will accept the class's invitation because she feels comfortable with the children now. From the story I know they like kimbap. In fact, Halmoni would probably take it as a compliment that they wanted to know how to make it. We're flattered when people take an interest in us. Also, I know that Halmoni enjoys giving food as a way of sharing herself. I remember she always gives Yunmi's friends bags of fruit each morning, and she brought a lot of food for the picnic.

Work together with students to continue filling out the chart. Encourage them to cite clues from the story and from their personal experience.

Situation	Predicted Outcome	Reasons
The class invites Halmoni to teach them how to cook kimbap.	Halmoni accepts.	• Halmoni knows they like kimbap. • She is flattered by the invitation. • She loves to share food.
Helen says hello to Halmoni one morning.	Halmoni says hello back.	• Halmoni trusts her enough to try English in front of her.

Practice/Apply
• Have students complete *Literacy Activity Book* page 18.

• Have students make up additional situations based on the story and then discuss possible outcomes.

SKILL FINDER
Minilessons, pp. 53, 67;
Theme 1, p. 79

Reteaching   Predicting Outcomes

Write each outcome below on the board. Then ask students to cite the events from the story that led up to each outcome. Encourage them to also mention things they already know that support each outcome. The page numbers are given in case you need or would like to reread the scenes with students.

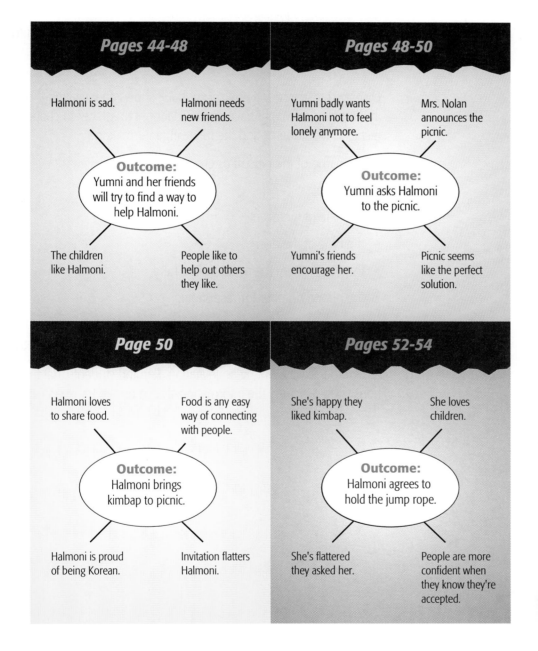

Pages 44-48

Halmoni is sad.

Halmoni needs new friends.

Outcome:
Yumni and her friends will try to find a way to help Halmoni.

The children like Halmoni.

People like to help out others they like.

Pages 48-50

Yumni badly wants Halmoni not to feel lonely anymore.

Mrs. Nolan announces the picnic.

Outcome:
Yumni asks Halmoni to the picnic.

Yumni's friends encourage her.

Picnic seems like the perfect solution.

Page 50

Halmoni loves to share food.

Food is any easy way of connecting with people.

Outcome:
Halmoni brings kimbap to picnic.

Halmoni is proud of being Korean.

Invitation flatters Halmoni.

Pages 52-54

She's happy they liked kimbap.

She loves children.

Outcome:
Halmoni agrees to hold the jump rope.

She's flattered they asked her.

People are more confident when they know they're accepted.

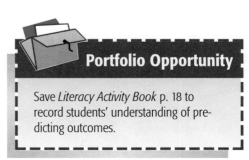

Portfolio Opportunity

Save *Literacy Activity Book* p. 18 to record students' understanding of predicting outcomes.

Instruct *and* Integrate

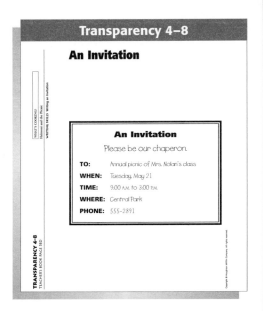

Transparency 4–8

An Invitation

An Invitation

Please be our chaperon.

TO: Annual picnic of Mrs. Nolan's class

WHEN: Tuesday, May 21

TIME: 9:00 A.M. to 3:00 P.M.

WHERE: Central Park

PHONE: 555-2891

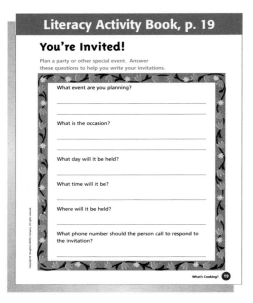

Literacy Activity Book, p. 19

You're Invited!

Plan a party or other special event. Answer these questions to help you write your invitations.

What event are you planning?

What is the occasion?

What day will it be held?

What time will it be?

Where will it be held?

What phone number should the person call to respond to the invitation?

What's Cooking? **19**

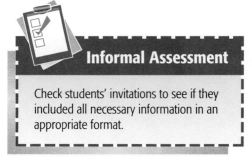

Informal Assessment

Check students' invitations to see if they included all necessary information in an appropriate format.

Writing Skills and Activities

INTERACTIVE LEARNING

Writing an Invitation

LAB, p. 19

Teach/Model

Discuss with students the purpose of an invitation. For what occasions do people send invitations? (Samples: birthdays, confirmations, bar mitzvahs, bat mitzvahs, weddings, other kinds of parties or celebrations) Discuss what information an invitation must include. (the occasion, date, time, place, name of party giver, how to respond)

Display Transparency 4–8. Explain that it shows an invitation the students in Yunmi's class might have sent to Halmoni to ask her to chaperon their picnic. Have students find the following information:

- the name of the person or group sending the invitation
- the event
- the date of the event
- the time of the event
- the place where the event will be held
- the phone number for responding

Discuss why it is important, as well as simply polite, to respond to an invitation to let the person know whether or not you will be attending.

Practice/Apply

Assign the activity Writing an Invitation. Remind students that their invitations should include the information shown on the transparency.

Writing Activities

A Memorable Incident

Remind students that Halmoni experienced different feelings: sad, embarrassed, happy. Write the word *Feelings* on the chalkboard. Ask students to name words that suggest different emotions, and use them to make a word web. Ask students to draw a picture of a situation that shows someone feeling one of these emotions. Then invite them to write a short account of the situation, showing how the person feels through their words, their actions, and their facial expressions. (*See the Writer's Craft Minilesson on page 55.*)

Writing an Invitation

Plan an occasion with students for writing an invitation. Would they like to invite someone from the community to visit their class? Would they like to invite parents or another class to share an activity? Have them write and send invitations. Have them use *Literacy Activity Book* page 19 to help them think of the information they need to include. Students may enjoy creating individual designs for their invitations.

A Family Food

Remind students that Halmoni brought kimbap, a special Korean food, to the picnic. Ask students to describe one of their family's favorite foods. Encourage them to describe one that is part of their family's culture. Students may enjoy having a food festival during which they share samples of the foods they describe.

Showing Friendship

Recall with students that Halmoni gave Yunmi's friends pieces of fruit to show friendship. Ask students in what other ways people can show friendship. Suggest that they write a paragraph telling about some of those ways.

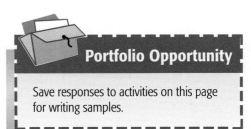

Portfolio Opportunity

Save responses to activities on this page for writing samples.

3

Instruct *and* Integrate

Word Skills and Strategies

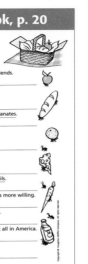

INTERACTIVE LEARNING

✓ TESTED SKILL Using Context
LAB, p. 20

Teach/Model

Write these sentences on the board. Ask a volunteer to read them.

> Yunmi squeezed Halmoni's hand and smiled.
> Halmoni nodded in acknowledgment but
> kept her eyes on the street without smiling.

Draw students' attention to the word *acknowledgment*. Elicit that a good reader can often figure out the meaning of a new word from

- discovering clues in the sentence or paragraph;
- thinking about a meaning that makes sense in those sentences.

Lead students to see that *response* could replace *acknowledgment*. Write the following on the board; discuss each different kind of context clue.

> Halmoni was shy, but Yunmi was gregarious. (*Gregarious* is contrasted with shy, so it must mean "outgoing and friendly.")

> In the park were gardens of white, yellow, and carmine roses. (*Carmine* is part of a series of colors, so it must be a color.)

> Halmoni wore her ch'ima and chogori, a pale blue skirt and top. (The words *ch'ima* and *chogori* are followed by a definition.)

Practice/Apply

Have students form small groups to find the following words in the story and discuss clues to their meaning. Sample answers are given.

embarrassed, p. 47	The phrase *with an accent* and the next sentence, *She could speak English if she wanted to,* hint that *embarrassed* means "ashamed."
chaperon, p. 48	The phrase *if one of them can come and help us* hints that *chaperon* means "an adult who helps at a gathering of young people."
kimbap, p. 50	The next sentence, *Kimbap is made of rice, carrots, eggs, and green vegetables wrapped in seaweed,* explains it.
rhythm, p. 54	The phrase *tapped her shoes* hints that it means "beat."

SKILL FINDER Word Skills and Strategies, Theme 1

Informal Assessment

Use Practice/Apply to check students' understanding of using context.

Reteaching

Using Context

Write each sentence from the chart at the right, including the underlining. Work together to circle and label each kind of clue. Use these prompts:

1. Is the word compared or contrasted with a more familiar word?

2. Is the word included in a series of more familiar words?

3. Is the word defined in the sentence or in another sentence?

4. What meaning would make sense?

Word Skills Practice

Cumulative Skill Practice
Soup of the Day
by Matt Cohen

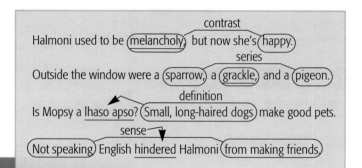

contrast
Halmoni used to be (melancholy,) but now she's (happy.)
series
Outside the window were a (sparrow,) a (grackle,) and a (pigeon.)
definition
Is Mopsy a lhaso apso? (Small, long-haired dogs) make good pets.
sense
(Not speaking) English hindered Halmoni (from making friends.)

M I N I L E S S O N

Phonics Review
r-Controlled Vowels

Teach/Model

Write this sentence and the five column heads on the chalkboard.

Halmoni had <u>tears</u> in <u>her</u> eyes when the children sang <u>their</u> song <u>for</u> her in the <u>park</u>.

Ask students which word in the sentence has the same vowel-plus-*r* sound they hear in *share*. (*their*) In *girl*? (*her*) In *your* (*for*) In *are*? (*park*) In *cheer*? (*tears*) Call on volunteers to write each word in the correct column. Elicit that

* the same vowel-plus-*r* sound can be spelled different ways;
* the same letters can spell different sounds, as in *share* and *are*.

share	girl	your	are	cheer
their	her	for	park	tears
bear	turn	more		here
where	heard	pour		weird

Practice/Apply

Write words from the story on separate slips of paper; distribute them. Ask students to group themselves by vowel-plus-*r* sound. Have groups list their words on the board. Review the spellings of each sound and the words in which the same letters spell different sounds, as in *earth* and *hear*.

her	darted	here	fourteenth	their
disturb	are	hear	your	share
heard	yard	nearly	for	embarrassed
girl	smart	tears	morning	parents
working	large		or	prepared
worried	barley		wore	carrots
hurried	park		New York	carefully

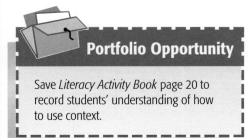

Portfolio Opportunity

Save *Literacy Activity Book* page 20 to record students' understanding of how to use context.

3

Instruct *and* Integrate

Building Vocabulary

Vocabulary Activities

Place	Word	Clue
Spain	spaniel	a kind of dog
Tangier, Morocco	tangerine	an orange-like fruit
Cantalupo, Italy	cantaloupe	a kind of melon
Lima, Peru	lima beans	a kind of vegetable
Taranto, Italy	tarantula	a kind of spider

Words from Places

Read this sentence aloud: *Some children brought bologna sandwiches to the picnic.* Ask students to guess which two words come from the names of places. (*bologna* and *sandwiches*) Explain that bologna, sometimes spelled *baloney,* was named after the Italian city of Bologna, which is famous for its sausages, and that sandwiches are named for Sandwich, England, where they were invented long ago by the Earl of Sandwich. Tell students that many words come from place names. Quiz students by giving them the place and, if necessary, the clue for the words on the chart above.

Prefix *uni-*

Challenge Write these sentences on the board: *Yunmi and her class-mates wore <u>uniforms</u> to school. As they jumped rope, they sang in <u>unison</u>.* What do the two underlined words have in common? (Both begin with *uni-*.) Explain that *uni-* is a prefix that means "one." Discuss how this meaning relates to *uniform* and *unison.* (People wear uniforms to show that they are all part of one group. When people sing in unison, they sound like a *single* voice.) Have small groups discuss how the meaning "one" relates to these words: *unicorn* (one horn); *unicycle* (one wheel); *universe* (the stars and planets form one world); *unique* (something unique is one of a kind); *unite* (joining together as one).

Regional Words

In the story, the children drink soda pop at their picnic. Ask if students know *soda pop* by another name, such as *tonic* or *cola.* Explain that many things are called by different names in different parts of the country. Then write each of the words at left on index cards and pass them out. Have a student read his or her word, asking, "Who has a word that means the same thing in another part of the country?" Students with synonyms should group their words on the board.

High-Frequency Vocabulary Practice

Cumulative Skill Practice
Soup of the Day
by Matt Cohen

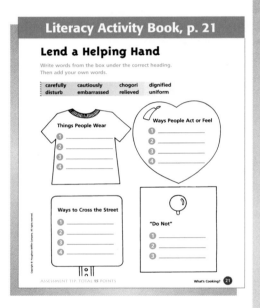

Literacy Activity Book, p. 21

Lend a Helping Hand

Write words from the box under the correct heading.
Then add your own words.

| carefully | cautiously | chogori | dignified |
| disturb | embarrassed | relieved | uniform |

Things People Wear

Ways People Act or Feel

Ways to Cross the Street

"Do Not"

Use this page to review Selection Vocabulary.

Regional Words

peanut, goober	baby carriage, baby buggy	brook, creek, stream
snap beans, string beans	flapjacks, griddle cakes, pancakes, hotcakes	sack, bag
earthworm, angleworm, fishworm		lightning bug, firefly
cellar, basement	thruway, freeway, expressway	pigsty, pigpen
skillet, frying pan		submarine sandwich, hoagie, hero

Spelling

FIVE-DAY PLAN

DAY 1	DAY 2	DAY 3	DAY 4	DAY 5
Pretest; Minilesson; Challenge Words/ Additional Words (opt.); Take-Home Word Lists (LAB)	First LAB page; Challenge Words Practice (opt.)	Check first LAB page; Second LAB page (except writing application)	Check second LAB page; writing application (LAB)	Test

Teaching CHOICES

MINILESSON

Words Ending with *er* or *le*

LAB, p. 22–23

TESTED SKILL

- Write the words *never* and *little* on the board. Say the words and have students repeat them. Ask students how many syllables are in each word. (two) Have students listen for the vowel sound in the second syllable as you repeat each word. Tell students that the weak vowel sound they hear in those syllables is called a *schwa* sound. Write the word *schwa* and the /ə/ symbol on the board.

- Write /ər/ on the board and repeat the word *never*. Explain that the /ər/ sounds are often spelled *er*. Underline *er* in *never*. Repeat this procedure with the /əl/ sound in *little*.

- Write the Spelling Words on the board. Tell students that each Spelling Word has the /ər/ sound spelled *er* or the /əl/ sound spelled *le*. Say the words and have students repeat them.

Spelling Words
*grandmother   *after
*never   *little
*people   *enter
*table   *apple

Challenge Words
*together   *wrinkle
*wonder   *another

Additional Spelling Words
butter   cracker
bubble   purple

*Starred words or forms of the words appear in *Halmoni and the Picnic*.

Spelling Assessment

Pretest

Say each underlined word, read the sentence, and then repeat the word. Have students write only the underlined words.

1. My grandmother is Japanese.
2. She never speaks to us in English.
3. She's shy around new people.
4. I'll set the table, if you clear it.
5. Let's go to the library after school.
6. My little sister always copies me.
7. Next year we'll enter the fourth grade.
8. I gave my teacher a big, red apple.

Test

Spelling Words Use the Pretest sentences.

Challenge Words
9. Try not to wrinkle your skirt.
10. I wonder why the sky is blue?
11. Help yourself to another cookie.
12. My friend and I sit together on the bus.

SKILL FINDER

Daily Language Practice, p. 58K
Reading-Writing Workshop, p. 91E

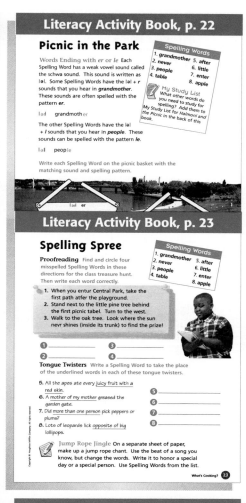

Literacy Activity Book, p. 22

Picnic in the Park

Words Ending with *er* or *le* Each Spelling Word has a weak vowel sound called the schwa sound. This sound is written as |əl. Some Spelling Words have the |ə| + r sounds that you hear in *grandmother*. These sounds are often spelled with the pattern *er*.

|əl   grandmoth*er*

The other Spelling Words have the |ə| + l sounds that you hear in *people*. These sounds can be spelled with the pattern *le*.

|əl   peop*le*

Write each Spelling Word on the picnic basket with the matching sound and spelling pattern.

Spelling Words
1. grandmother   5. after
2. never   6. little
3. people   7. enter
4. table   8. apple

My Study List What other words do you need to study for spelling? Add them to My Study List for *Halmoni and the Picnic* in the back of this book.

|əl   *er*

Literacy Activity Book, p. 23

Spelling Spree

Proofreading Find and circle four misspelled Spelling Words in these directions for the class treasure hunt. Then write each word correctly.

1. When you *entur* Central Park, take the first path *aftur* the playground.
2. Stand next to the little pine tree behind the first picnic *tabel*. Turn to the west.
3. Walk to the oak tree. Look where the sun *nevr* shines (inside its trunk) to find the prize!

Spelling Words
1. grandmother   5. after
2. never   6. little
3. people   7. enter
4. table   8. apple

1. _____   3. _____
2. _____   4. _____

Tongue Twisters Write a Spelling Word to take the place of the underlined words in each of these tongue twisters.

5. All the apes ate every juicy fruit with a red skin.
6. A mother of my mother greased the garden gate.
7. Did more than one person pick peppers or plums?
8. Lots of leopards lick opposite of big lollipops.

5. _____
6. _____
7. _____
8. _____

Jump Rope Jingle On a separate sheet of paper, make up a jump rope chant. Use the beat of a song you know, but change the words. Write it to honor a special day or a special person. Use Spelling Words from the list.

What's Cooking? 23

Literacy Activity Book

Take-Home Word Lists: pp. 171–172

Spelling Vocabulary Students can use the **Spelling Spree CD-ROM** for extra practice with the spelling principles taught in this selection.

MEETING INDIVIDUAL NEEDS   **Challenge**

Challenge Words Practice Have students use the Challenge Words to write sentences either about their grandparents or about other relatives.

Instruct *and* Integrate

Grammar

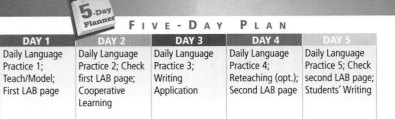

FIVE-DAY PLAN

DAY 1	DAY 2	DAY 3	DAY 4	DAY 5
Daily Language Practice 1; Teach/Model; First LAB page	Daily Language Practice 2; Check first LAB page; Cooperative Learning	Daily Language Practice 3; Writing Application	Daily Language Practice 4; Reteaching (opt.); Second LAB page	Daily Language Practice 5; Check second LAB page; Students' Writing

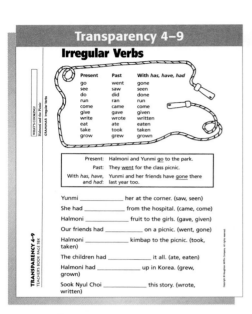

Transparency 4–9

Irregular Verbs

Present	Past	With *has, have, had*
go	went	gone
see	saw	seen
do	did	done
run	ran	run
come	came	come
give	gave	given
write	wrote	written
eat	ate	eaten
take	took	taken
grow	grew	grown

Present: Halmoni and Yunmi <u>go</u> to the park.
Past: They <u>went</u> for the class picnic.
With *has, have,* and *had:* Yunmi and her friends have <u>gone</u> there last year too.

Yunmi _____ her at the corner. (saw, seen)
She had _____ from the hospital. (came, come)
Halmoni _____ fruit to the girls. (gave, given)
Our friends had _____ on a picnic. (went, gone)
Halmoni _____ kimbap to the picnic. (took, taken)
The children had _____ it all. (ate, eaten)
Halmoni had _____ up in Korea. (grew, grown)
Sook Nyul Choi _____ this story. (wrote, written)

TRANSPARENCY 4–9
TEACHER'S BOOK PAGE 58K

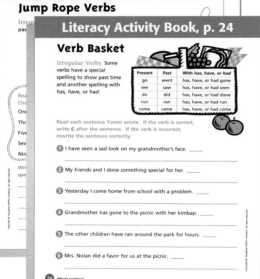

Literacy Activity Book, p. 25

Jump Rope Verbs

Literacy Activity Book, p. 24

Verb Basket

Irregular Verbs Some verbs have a special spelling to show past time and another spelling with *has, have,* or *had.*

Present	Past	With *has, have,* or *had*
go	went	has, have, or had gone
see	saw	has, have, or had seen
do	did	has, have, or had done
run	ran	has, have, or had run
come	came	has, have, or had come

Read each sentence Yunmi wrote. If the verb is correct, write **C** after the sentence. If the verb is incorrect, rewrite the sentence correctly.

1. I have seen a sad look on my grandmother's face. ___
2. My friends and I done something special for her. ___
3. Yesterday I come home from school with a problem. ___
4. Grandmother has gone to the picnic with her kimbap. ___
5. The other children have ran around the park for hours. ___
6. Mrs. Nolan did a favor for us at the picnic. ___

24 What's Cooking?

INTERACTIVE LEARNING

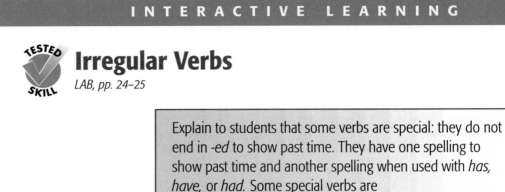

Irregular Verbs
LAB, pp. 24–25

> Explain to students that some verbs are special: they do not end in *-ed* to show past time. They have one spelling to show past time and another spelling when used with *has, have,* or *had.* Some special verbs are
> go see do run come give write eat take grow

Teach/Model Read these sentences.

They <u>entered</u> the yard and <u>sat</u> under the oak tree quietly.

They <u>went</u> to their classroom and <u>unpacked</u> their bags.

Have volunteers act out each sentence as you read it again. Tell students to listen for four verbs. Have volunteers list them on the chalkboard. Ask if the action is happening now or in the past. (past) Elicit that some verbs in past time do not end in *-ed*; they have special spellings. Model how these verbs change after *has, have,* or *had.* For example:

    go   went   has, have, or had gone

Invite students to find other verbs in *Halmoni and the Picnic* that express time past but do not end in *-ed.*

Display Transparency 4–9. Present the examples in the chart. Have a volunteer write the correct verb for each sentence.

Practice/Apply ***Literacy Activity Book*** page 24 focuses on *go, see, do, run,* and *come.* Page 25 focuses on *give, write, eat, take,* and *grow.* Refer students to the Handbook at the back of the *Literacy Activity Book* for more examples.

Cooperative Learning: An Irregular Picnic Divide the class into teams. Each team cuts ten index cards to look like picnic food, such as apples or sandwiches, and writes a verb on each card.

  go   see   do   run   come   give   write   eat   take   grow

SKILL FINDER Reading-Writing Workshop, p. 91E

INTERACTIVE LEARNING (continued)

Each team places its cards in a lunch bag. A designated leader shakes the bag and allows teammates in turn to choose a card, read the verb, and write its past time form on the card. If the leader decides the answer is correct, the card is returned to the bag. If incorrect, the team supplies the two missing verbs and the card is taken out of play. If a card has the present and past form on it, the player gives the form used with *has, have,* or *had.* If correct, the player keeps the card and scores a point.

 Writing Application: A Description Suggest that students describe a new type of food or a tradition they have discovered. Ask students to use verbs they studied in this lesson.

Students' Writing Ask students to check their writing in process for correct use and spelling of special verbs.

Reteaching

Irregular Verbs

Write the three forms of each verb in this lesson on oaktag strips. Elicit that most verbs in past time end in *-ed.* Ask for examples. Then help students see that the spelling and use of other verbs must be memorized. Hold up one strip, and ask volunteers to say each verb and create a sentence for it. To complete each strip, ask the group to say all three verbs together.

Then draw a ticktacktoe on the chalkboard. One at a time, write a verb from this lesson in a square as a prompt. Have a volunteer complete the adjacent vertical or horizontal squares with the other two forms of that verb. If correct, the student draws a line through the row and is seated. When the grid is full, erase it. Begin again with new verb prompts.

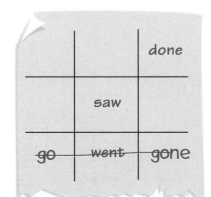 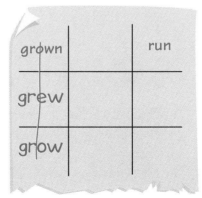

More Practice

Houghton Mifflin English Level 3
Workbook Plus, pp. 57–60
Reteaching Workbook, pp. 36–37

Write on Track
Write on Track SourceBook, pp. 89–90

Daily Language Practice

Focus Skills

Grammar: Irregular Verbs
Spelling: Words Ending with *er* or *le*

Each day write one sentence on the chalkboard. Have each student write the sentence correctly on paper. Tell students to check for correct use of verbs that show past time without an *-ed* ending. Ask them also to check for misspellings. Have students correct their own papers as a volunteer corrects the sentence on the chalkboard.

1. After a littel delay, the class gone to the park for a picnic.
   After a **little** delay, the class **went/had gone** to the park for a picnic.

2. Her grandmothre had took an apple for the child.
   Her **grandmother** had **taken** an apple for the child.

3. The peepul never seen such a great day for a picnic!
   The **people** never **saw/have seen** such a great day for a picnic!

4. The girl has ate the apple on the tabel.
   The girl has **eaten** the apple on the **table**.

5. Some people had wrote to Grandmother aftur the picnic.
   Some people had **written** to Grandmother **after** the picnic.

3

Communication Activities

Listening and Speaking

One, Two, Three, A-Lary
One, Two, Three, A-Lary
My first name is Mary;
If you think it's necessary,
Find it in the dictionary.

Jumping Jane and Jumping Joe
Jumping Jane and Jumping Joe
Jumped as high as they could go,
Jumped up to the moon and then
Jumped back down to Earth again.

Chanting Jump Rope Rhymes

Invite students outdoors to chant the rope rhyme made up by Yunmi's classmates on page 54. Then ask students to share their favorite jump rope jingles such as "One, Two, Three, A-Lary," "Teddy Bear, Teddy Bear," and "Jumping Jane and Jumping Joe." Use a rope long enough to allow several students to jump together.

Students Acquiring English Encourage students to teach their classmates jump rope rhymes in their primary language.

Greetings in Korean

Write the pronunciation for the Korean word for "Good morning" on the board and pronounce it with the class. Have students practice greeting one another in English and Korean. Encourage students who speak Korean to teach the class other phrases.

Good morning.	an-nyŏng-ha-shim-ni-ka
Thank you.	ko-map-sŭm-ni-da
See you later.	to poep-ke-ssŭm-ni-da
yes	ne
no	a-nyo

Visiting with Grandparents

Suggest that students invite their grandparents to class to talk about their experiences when they were the students' age. Some of them may be able to talk about customs in their birth country and how such customs are alike and different from those of the American culture.

Viewing

Chopsticks Demonstration

Ask a student volunteer in class who is proficient in the use of chopsticks to give a demonstration. The student should provide step-by-step instructions as other students observe the actions. Then let other students try their hands at using chopsticks. Remind students that the utensils are used to pick up bite-sized food only.

2 Add the second chopstick. Hold it like you hold a pencil. Hold the first chopstick in its original position.

1 Pick up the first chopstick. Tuck it under your thumb and hold it firmly.

3 Move the second chopstick up and down. Now pick up something.

A Video About Korean Americans

Cooperative Learning

Watch the video *Korean Americans.* Encourage students to explain why Koreans emigrated to the United States, where they settled, and which occupations many of them chose.

Korean Americans (Library Video Company)

Signs and Symbols

Have students look in their neighborhoods for special signs that use symbols instead of, or along with, words. Students may want to create new signs they think would help people who are learning English.

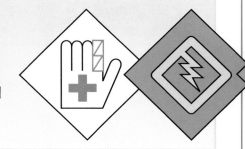

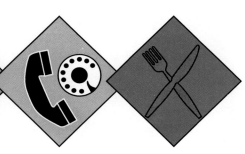

3

Instruct *and* Integrate

Cross-Curricular Activities

Book List

Health

Cooking the Korean Way
by Okwha Chung and Judy Monroe

Social Studies

Chi-Hoon: A Korean Girl
by Patricia McMahon

Look What We've Brought You from Korea: Crafts, Games, Recipes, Stories and Other Cultural Activities from Korean Americans
by Phyllis Shalant

Health

Making Kimbap

Some students might want to research and prepare kimbap. Once the food is prepared they can bring it to class and discuss the ingredients they used and the steps taken to prepare the kimbap.

Directions

1. Cook the rice according to the directions on the package.

2. Cook the spinach and carrot separately in cooking oil. Season with salt and pepper.

3. Spread out the seaweed.

4. Spread the cooked rice on a third of the seaweed.

5. Spread the cooked spinach and carrots on the rest of the seaweed.

6. Then roll up the seaweed and cut into small shapes.

Eat the kimbap with chopsticks, if available. *Mogobwa!* (Try it!)

Ingredients

- 1 cup of cooked rice
- ½ teaspoon of salt
- ½ teaspoon of pepper
- 1 cup of chopped spinach leaves
- 2 tablespoons of cooking oil
- 1 large carrot, chopped
- seaweed for wrapping ingredients

Math

Measuring Distances

Have students measure and compare distances from their city or town to Korea, San Francisco, and New York. Students need a ruler, a globe, a large wall map, or a small map in an atlas. Point out to students that they will need to understand and work with scales located on maps and globes. Let them

- estimate how many miles are represented in a 1-inch scale

- measure distances in inches and convert them to miles

Measuring Questions

- How far did Halmoni travel from Korea to New York City?

- If you wanted to visit Halmoni in New York City, how far would you have to travel?

- If you wanted to visit Korea, how far would you have to travel?

Choices for Social Studies

Charting Korean Exports

Challenge Encourage students to discover what products are made in Korea. Then have them list the products in a table under the following heads: *electronics, manufacturing, clothing, oil/chemicals,* and *other.* As an example, students would list telephones, video games, television sets, and radios under the heading *electronics.* Have them report their findings to the class.

Learning About Customs

Cooperative Learning

Explain to students that world travelers must adjust to the styles of living and the traditions of people in other countries. For example, in some cultures, you remove your shoes before entering a house because you are not supposed to show the soles of your shoes as you sit. Have students work together to make a handbook of customs. Encourage students acquiring English to take a lead role in this activity.

Portfolio Opportunity

Save the handbook to record students' understanding of various customs.

Spaghetti! Spaghetti!/I'd Never Eat a Beet

THEME: WHAT'S COOKING?

Spaghetti! Spaghetti!
I'd Never Eat a Beet

About the Poet

As a teenager, Jack Prelutsky was a promising opera student. Bob Dylan once observed that Prelutsky's voice sounded "like a cross between Woody Guthrie and Enrico Caruso." His musical influences are quite evident in his poetry. Prelutsky loves to engage his audience with clever wordplay.

Prior Knowledge

Ask if students like spaghetti. Make a chart like the following to prompt discussion.

Encourage them to quick-write a line or two telling what they think about spaghetti. Next, ask if students like beets. Again, encourage them to quick-write how they feel about beets.

Spaghetti		
What It Feels Like	**What You Add to It**	**How You Eat It**
• slippery	• meatballs	• Roll it around your fork.
• wet	• mushrooms	• Slurp it.

Explain that the poet Jack Prelutsky loves one of these foods but not the other. Ask if students can guess which food Prelutsky doesn't like.

Building Background

Have students read the titles of both poems and look at the illustrations. Ask if students think the poems will be serious or silly. How can they tell?

You may want to suggest that students listen as you read aloud the first verse of "Spaghetti! Spaghetti!" Then suggest that they read the poem with partners.

SPAGHETTI! SPAGHETTI!

Spaghetti! spaghetti!
you're wonderful stuff,
I love you, spaghetti,
I can't get enough.
You're covered with sauce
and you're sprinkled with cheese,
spaghetti! spaghetti!
oh, give me some more please.

Spaghetti! spaghetti!
piled high in a mound,
you wiggle, you wriggle,
you squiggle around.
There's slurpy spaghetti
all over my plate,
spaghetti! spaghetti!
I think you are great.

Spaghetti! spaghetti!
I love you a lot,
you're slishy, you're sloshy,
delicious and hot.
I gobble you down
oh, I can't get enough,
spaghetti! spaghetti!
you're wonderful stuff.

Jack Prelutsky

59

Challenge

Point out the poet's use of alliteration with the words *slurpy, slishy,* and *sloshy.* Invite students to think of other words that could be used to describe words that begin with the letter or letters shown below.

ch as in cheese	
• chewy	• chilly
• chunky	• choppy
sl as in slurpy	
• sloppy	• slushy
• slippery	• slivery
• slithery	
sp as in spaghetti	
• spicy	• spongy
• splashy	• spirally

Students Acquiring English

Word Meanings Discuss the meanings of *wiggle, wriggle,* and *squiggle.* Ask volunteers to pantomime these actions. Elicit that the words not only rhyme, they also mean almost the same thing. Ask students what they think the words *slishy* and *sloshy* mean. Point out that *slishy* is a made-up word, while *sloshy* describes the sound of splashing liquid.

Health Link

The cheese most often used on top of spaghetti is Parmesan, which originated in a small town near Parma, Italy. Parmesan is made from a mixture of whole and skim milk; its hard, granular texture makes it easy to grate.

Prior Knowledge/ Building Background

Take an informal survey of how many students have eaten beets, and what they think of them. Be sure students know that beets are vegetables that grow underground like carrots and potatoes.

Vocabulary

paddle: a flat, light wooden racket

talcum powder: a fine, often perfumed skin powder

chowder: a thick soup

Discussion

• If you had to, how would you try to persuade the poet to eat a beet?

• Why might someone like spaghetti more than beets?

Discuss the illustration with students. Ask what students expect this poem to be like, based on the one they just read.

Invite students to follow along as you read aloud the first verse. Then suggest that they read the poem independently or with partners.

Purpose Setting Suggest that students read to find out what the poet would rather eat than a beet.

I'd Never Eat a Beet

Jack Prelutsky

60

Vocabulary

Ask students to identify the several synonyms for *eat* used in the poem.

 Students Acquiring English

Explain that *would be wasted on my plate* means that the poet would not eat the beet. Also explain *fountain pen*, *Ping-Pong*, and *hockey puck*.

I'd never eat a beet, because
I could not stand the taste,
I'd rather nibble drinking straws,
or fountain pens, or paste,
I'd eat a window curtain
and perhaps a roller skate,
but a beet, you may be certain
would be wasted on my plate.

I would sooner chew on candles
or the laces from my shoes,
or a dozen suitcase handles
were I ever forced to choose,
I would eat a Ping-Pong paddle,
I would eat a Ping-Pong ball,
I might even eat a saddle,
but a beet? No! Not at all.

I would swallow talcum powder
and my little rubber duck,
I'd have doorknobs in my chowder,
I would eat a hockey puck,
I would eat my model rocket
and the socks right off my feet,
I would even eat my pocket,
but **I'd never eat a beet!**

61

Writing a Poem

Invite students to compose their own poems about a food they do or do not like. They might use the first verse of "Spaghetti! Spaghetti!" for a model. Or they could use this frame for a food they dislike:

I'd never eat _____, because

I cannot stand the taste;

I'd rather nibble _____,

or _____, or _____.

I would eat a _____,

I would eat a _____,

I might even eat a _____,

but a _____? No! Not at all.

Making a Menu

Invite students to make a menu for a restaurant that serves nothing but beets. Encourage them to emphasize different aspects of beets in their descriptions of each dish.

Health Link

Suggest that students create a bulletin board display of foods they like to eat that are also healthful. Encourage them to label each food—perhaps with two to four lines of rhyme (such as those Jack Prelutsky used to begin "Spaghetti! Spaghetti!").

★★★ Multicultural Link

Beets are always used in the Russian soup known as *borscht*. In Finland, beets are often combined with oranges in recipes for salads and sauces. In Scandinavia, pickled beets (*inkokta rödbetor*) are a popular dish for holiday smorgasbords.

SELECTION:

Henry and Beezus

by Beverly Cleary

Other Books by the Author

Henry and the Clubhouse

Otis Spofford

Ribsy

● **Best Books for Children**

Selection Summary

One dull Sunday afternoon, Henry Huggins takes Ribsy, his dog, and goes out to find his friend Robert. For want of anything better to do, the boys watch a neighbor, Mr. Grumbie, prepare a barbecue. When Mr. Grumbie brings out a large piece of raw meat, Ribsy notices. He dashes into the yard, grabs the roast, and runs.

A wild chase follows, and, to Henry's chagrin, the roast is finally salvaged by Scooter, the neighborhood show-off, who has the advantage of a bicycle that Henry has long envied.

Henry apologizes to the Grumbies, and Mr. Grumbie grudgingly throws the ruined meat to Ribsy. "Not that he deserves it," he says.

5-Day Planner

FIVE-DAY PLANS
See pages 32–33 of the
Five-Day Lesson Plans booklet.

Lesson Planning Guide

	Skill/Strategy Instruction	Meeting Individual Needs	Lesson Resources
1 Introduce *the* Literature *Pacing: 1 day*	**Preparing to Read and Write** Prior Knowledge/Building Background, 61C **Selection Vocabulary,** 61D • snickering • scoffed • triumphantly • modestly • reluctantly **Spelling Pretest,** 84I • happen • dinner • Sunday • invite • market • yellow • better • window	**Support in Advance,** 61C **Students Acquiring English,** 61C **Other Choices for Building Background,** 61C **Spelling Challenge Words:** • purpose • suggest • ignore • distance	*Literacy Activity Book,* Selection Vocabulary, p. 26 **Transparency:** Selection Vocabulary, 4–10 **Great Start** CD-ROM software, "What's Cooking?" CD
2 Interact *with* Literature *Pacing: 1–3 days*	**Reading Strategies** Predict/Infer, 62, 64 Think About Words, 62, 70 **Minilessons** Writer's Craft: Character Development, 65 Predicting Outcomes, 67 Following Directions, 69 Genre: Realistic Fiction, 71 ✓ Sequence of Events, 77 Library: Fiction Books, 79	**Choices for Reading,** 62 **Guided Reading,** 62 Comprehension/Critical Thinking, 68, 74, 80 **Students Acquiring English,** 62, 63, 65, 67, 68, 71, 73, 74, 75, 76, 77, 80, 84 **Extra Support,** 66, 70, 75, 81 **Challenge,** 65, 78	**Reading-Writing Workshop,** Research Report, 90–91F *Literacy Activity Book,* Selection Connections, p. 2; Comprehension Check, p. 27 **Audio Tape** for What's Cooking?: *Henry and Beezus* The Learning Company's Ultimate Writing & Creativity Center software
3 Instruct *and* Integrate *Pacing: 1–3 days*	✓ **Comprehension:** Sequence of Events, 84B ✓ **Writing:** Avoiding Stringy Sentences, 84D ✓ **Word Skills and Strategies:** The Prefixes *un-* and *re-*, 84F Think About Words Strategy, 84G **Building Vocabulary:** Vocabulary Activities, 84H ✓ **Spelling:** The VCCV Pattern, 84I ✓ **Grammar:** Punctuating Dialogue, 84J–84K **Communication Activities:** Listening and Speaking, 84L; Viewing, 84M **Cross-Curricular Activities:** Health, 84N; Science, 84O; Math, 84O	**Reteaching:** Sequence of Events, 84C **Activity Choices:** Personal Narrative, Sequel, Shared Writing: Write a List, 84E **Reteaching:** The Prefixes *un-* and *re-*, 84G **Activity Choices:** Analogies, Exact Words for *said*, Prefixes *bi-* and *tri-*, 84H **Challenge Words Practice,** 84I **Reteaching:** Punctuating Dialogue, 84K **Activity Choices:** Listening and Speaking, 84L; Viewing, 84M **Activity Choices:** Health, 84N; Science, 84O; Math, 84O	**Watch Me Read** *Help from Harry* **Reading-Writing Workshop,** Research Report, 90–91F **Transparencies:** Comprehension, 4–11; Writing, 4–12; Grammar, 4–13 *Literacy Activity Book,* Comprehension Skill, p. 29; Writing Skills, p. 31; Word Skills, p. 32; Building Vocabulary, p. 33; Spelling, pp. 34–35; Grammar, pp. 36–37 **Channel R.E.A.D.** videodisc: "Suspended in Space" **Spelling Spree** CD-ROM The Learning Company's Ultimate Writing & Creativity Center software **Audio Tape** for What's Cooking?: *Henry and Beezus*

✓ **Indicates Tested Skills.** *See page 16F for assessment options.*

Introduce *the* Literature

Preparing to Read and Write

Support in Advance

Use this activity with students who need extra support before participating in the whole-class activity.

Picture Walk Divide students into three groups to examine the illustrations at the beginning, middle, and end of the story. Ask students to make predictions about what they think is happening in each part of the story. Have them write their predictions and save them to check when they read.

Management Tip
Suggest that other students spend a few minutes writing in their journals about a pet they would like to have—if they could have any animal at all, real or imaginary.

Students Acquiring English
Word Wall On a large sheet of paper help students write words that describe the ways people talk. As they read, students can add colorful words from the story. (Examples: *cooed, yowl, whispered.*)

INTERACTIVE LEARNING

Prior Knowledge/Building Background

Key Concept
In the Doghouse

Semantic Web Tell students that a dog is one of the main characters in the next selection. Brainstorm with them the ways a dog can create trouble. Place responses in a semantic web like the following.

- chew furniture
- steal food
- get off leash
- WAYS DOGS CAN MAKE TROUBLE
- bark too loudly
- chase other dogs

Ask students who have dogs to tell about times when their pets got into mischief. Did students ever get into trouble because of something a pet did? How did they get into—and out of—trouble?

Other Choices for Building Background

Dog Debate

Extra Support Have students react to the following statements about dogs. Encourage them to cite examples from their own experience.

- Dogs make the best pets.
- A dog is a person's best friend.
- You can't teach an old dog new tricks.

Students Acquiring English You may need to discuss the characteristics of a good pet with students unfamiliar with this concept. Also have them share proverbs about pets from their cultures.

Quick Writing

Ask students to write what each of the following proverbs means:

- Every dog has his day.
- Love me, love my dog.
- Let sleeping dogs lie.

Word Web

Students Acquiring English Work with students to create a word web about dogs. Categories might include *Sounds Dogs Make; Foods They Love;* and *Things They Bark At.*

Great Start
For students needing extra support with key concepts and vocabulary, use the "What's Cooking?" CD.

Spelling

You may want to give the Spelling Pretest on page 84I before students read the selection.

Daily Language Practice

Use the activities on page 84K as a daily practice of the spelling and grammar skills taught with this selection.

INTERACTIVE LEARNING

Selection Vocabulary

Key Words

snickering

scoffed

triumphantly

modestly

reluctantly

Display Transparency 4–10. Work together with students to arrange each set of words according to the criteria shown. (All the words are from the story. Key Words are in bold type.) As each word is added to the map, ask students to define and pantomime it.

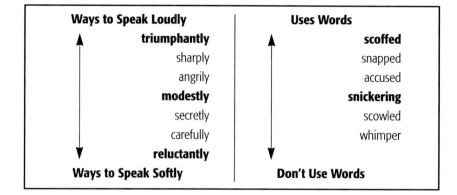

Ways to Speak Loudly	Uses Words
↑ **triumphantly**	↑ **scoffed**
sharply	snapped
angrily	accused
modestly	**snickering**
secretly	scowled
carefully	whimper
reluctantly ↓	↓
Ways to Speak Softly	Don't Use Words

Vocabulary Practice Have students work independently to complete page 26 of the *Literacy Activity Book.*

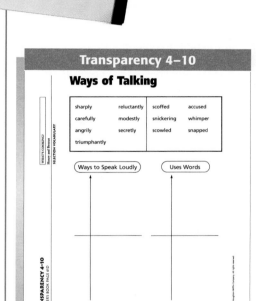

Social Studies

Teacher FactFile

1952

In the year *Henry and Beezus* was published:

- Dwight D. Eisenhower begins the first of two presidential terms.
- 4 out of 5 shirts sold in America are white.
- The top TV shows are *Dragnet* and *I Love Lucy.*
- In the Pacific the first H-bomb obliterates an entire island. Scientists observe from ships and planes fifty miles away.
- *Bwana Devil,* the first full-length 3-D movie, premieres in Los Angeles.

Literacy Activity Book, p. 26
A Girl and Her Dog

Use the words below the pictures to write the captions for the story about Kelly and her dog.

1. scoffed   snickering
2. reluctantly
3. triumphantly
4. modestly

26   What's Cooking?

Interact
with
Literature

Reading Strategies

▶ **Predict/Infer**
Think About Words

Student Application Ask students what strategies they think would be helpful with this selection. Suggest that, since the story appears to contain a lot of action, predicting and inferring might be useful. Also discuss how the Think About Words strategy can be applied in any selection in which there are unknown words or familiar words used in a new way.

Predicting/Purpose Setting

Have students review the illustrations of Ribsy and make predictions about how he will behave. Then have them read to see whether their predictions are correct.

Choices for Reading

Independent Reading	**Cooperative Reading**
Guided Reading	**Teacher Read Aloud**

 **Guided Reading**

Students using the Guided Reading option should read to the end of page 69. Comprehension questions can be found on page 68.

62

QuickREFERENCE

🏠 **Home Connection**

This selection contains details and language that reflect when it was written (1952). Encourage students to ask older family members to recall life in the '50s, and to share expressions they remember.

 Students Acquiring English

This story has many characters. As new characters are introduced, have students identify them from the illustrations and keep cluster diagrams telling what they learn about each one. Start them off with the title characters, Henry, Beezus, and Ribsy.

R I B S Y
and the Roast

HENRY HUGGINS stood by the front window of his
square white house on Klickitat Street and wondered
why Sunday afternoon seemed so much longer than
any other part of the week. Mrs. Huggins was
reading a magazine, and Mr. Huggins was reading
the funnies in the Sunday *Journal*.

Henry's dog, Ribsy, was asleep in the middle of
the living-room rug. As Henry looked at him, he
suddenly sat up, scratched hard behind his left ear
with his left hind foot, and flopped down again
without even bothering to open his eyes.

Henry pressed his nose against the windowpane
and looked out at Klickitat Street. The only person he
saw was Scooter McCarthy, who was riding up and
down the sidewalk on his bicycle.

"I sure wish I had a bike," remarked Henry to his
mother and father, as he watched Scooter.

"I wish you did, too," agreed his mother, "but
with prices and taxes going up all the time, I'm afraid
we can't get you one this year."

"Maybe things will be better next year," said Mr.
Huggins, dropping the funnies and picking up the
sport section.

Henry sighed. He wanted a bicycle now. He
could see himself riding up and down Klickitat
Street on a shiny red bike. He would wear his

63

Technology Link

In 1949, only one million homes in
the U.S. had TV sets; by 1950, the
number had increased to ten
million. A TV program in color was
broadcast in the U.S. for the first
time in 1951, a year before this
story was written.

**Students
Acquiring English**

Word Strategy If students know
what the word *funny* means, they
can use this knowledge to guess
which part of the Sunday newspaper
is sometimes called *the funnies*.

Interact
with
Literature

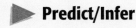

Reading Strategies

▶ **Predict/Infer**

Ask students what inferences they might make about Henry and Robert's friendship based on:

- giving white mice rides on electric trains

- Robert's question to Henry at the bottom of page 65 (When they are bored, they like to experiment and shake things up.)

Ask them to predict how the boys might work with "the only sign of life" next door.

genuine Daniel Boone coonskin cap with the snap-on tail, only he wouldn't wear the tail fastened to the hat. He would tie it to the handle bars so that it would wave in the breeze as he whizzed along.

"Henry," said Mrs. Huggins, interrupting his thoughts, "please don't rub your nose against my clean window."

"All right, Mom," said Henry. "I sure wish something would happen around here sometime."

"Why don't you go over to Robert's house? Maybe he can think of something to do," suggested Mrs. Huggins, as she turned a page of her magazine.

"O.K.," agreed Henry. Robert's mother said they couldn't give the white mice rides on Robert's electric train any more, but maybe they could think of something else. "Come on, Ribsy," said Henry.

Ribsy stood up and shook himself, scattering hair over the rug.

64

Quick REFERENCE

Media Literacy

Ask students how "genuine" they think Henry's cap is. Explain that the toy company used the name of Daniel Boone, a famous pioneer, to sell the cap. Discuss toys that are sold in the same way today and other brands that are popular with children.

"That dog," sighed Mrs. Huggins.

Henry thought he had better leave quickly. As he and Ribsy started down the front steps, Robert came around the corner.

"What's up, Doc?" said Robert.

"Hi," responded Henry.

"My dad said maybe if I came over to your house, you could think of something to do," said Robert.

The boys sat down on the front steps. "Here comes old Scooter," observed Robert. The two boys watched the older boy pumping down the street on his bicycle. He was whistling, and not only was he riding without touching the handle bars, he even had his hands in his pockets.

"Hi," said Scooter casually, without stopping.

"Big show-off," muttered Robert. "I bet he takes that bike to bed with him."

"He sure thinks he's smart," agreed Henry. "He's been riding up and down all afternoon. Come on, let's go around in the back yard, where we won't have to watch old Scooter show off all day. Maybe we can find something to do back there."

Ribsy followed at the boys' heels. Unfortunately, the back yard was no more interesting than the front. The only sign of life was next door. A large yellow cat was dozing on the Grumbies' back steps, and there was smoke coming from the barbecue pit.

Robert looked thoughtful. "Does Ribsy ever chase cats?"

"Not that old Fluffy." Henry, understanding what was on Robert's mind, explained that Mrs. Grumbie sprinkled something called Doggie-B-Gone

Writer's Craft
Character Development
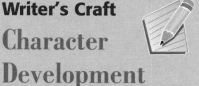

Teach/Model

Explain that sometimes authors tell their readers directly what their characters are like as people. More often, however, they use dialogue (what characters say) and action (what characters do) to develop their characters.

Help students use information from page 65 to complete this chart about Robert.

Dialogue	• calls Scooter a show-off
	• says he bets Scooter takes bike to bed
	• suggests they go to the back where they won't have to watch Scooter
	• asks if Ribsy chases cats
Actions	• comes over to Henry's house
	• sits on front steps with Henry; watches Scooter

Ask if students can tell anything about Robert from the chart. Elicit that he is bored, that he probably doesn't have a bike and is a bit jealous of Scooter, and that he has a mischievous side.

Practice/Apply

Suggest that students complete a similar chart for Henry (and/or another story character).

Writing Activities: Write a Sequel, p. 84E

Reading-Writing Workshop, pp. 90–91F

Students Acquiring English

Using Context If necessary, have students use context (what Scooter does; how Robert reacts to him) to figure out what a *show-off* is. This scene is a good one for students to role-play to help them focus on the action and characters.

Multicultural Link

Ask what other animals people keep as pets besides dogs and cats. In Japan, mice are popular. In some parts of China, cormorants (large sea birds) are kept as pets. Have students share other kinds of pets they know about.

Challenge

Nonsense Words Ask students if they think a product like Doggie-B-Gone actually exists. Challenge students to invent a word that might be used to describe a product that prevents a dog's hair from shedding.

on her side of the rosebushes. Ribsy disliked the smell of it and was careful to stay on his side of the bushes.

Robert was disappointed. "I thought Ribsy might . . ."

"No such luck," interrupted Henry, looking at his dog, who had settled himself by the back steps to continue his nap. Henry picked a blade of grass and started to blow through it when the squeak-slam of the Grumbies' screen door made him look up. "Jeepers!" he whispered.

Stepping carefully over Fluffy, Mr. Hector Grumbie walked down the back steps. He was

66

QuickREFERENCE

Background: FYI

Remind students that the title of this theme is on the hat: "What's Cooking?" Students may be interested to know that the word *cookout* did not enter the English language until 1953, the year after *Henry and Beezus* was published.

 Extra Support

Call attention to the ellipsis points at the end of the fifth line on this page. Ask how Robert might have finished this sentence—if Henry had not interrupted him.

wearing a chef's tall white hat and an immense white apron. *What's cooking?* was written across the hat, and on the apron was printed a recipe for *Bar X Ranch Bar-B-Q Sauce.* Mr. Grumbie carried a tray full of bowls, jars, bottles, and what appeared to be bunches of dried weeds.

"Is he really going to cook?" whispered Robert.

"Search me," answered Henry. The two boys edged closer to the rosebushes that divided the two yards.

"Hello, Mr. Grumbie," said Henry.

"Hello there, Henry." Mr. Grumbie crossed the lawn and set the tray on the edge of the barbecue pit in the corner of his yard. He peeled a small object which he put into a bowl, sprinkled with salt, and mashed with a little wooden stick. Then he broke off pieces of the dried weeds and mashed them, too.

Henry and Robert exchanged puzzled looks.

"Need any help, Mr. Grumbie?" asked Henry.

"No, thank you." Mr. Grumbie poured a few drops of something into the mixture.

"Is that something that's supposed to be good to eat?" asked Robert. Mr. Grumbie didn't answer.

"What's that stuff in the bowl?" asked Henry.

"Herbs and garlic," answered Mr. Grumbie. "Now run along and play, boys. I'm busy."

Henry and Robert did not move.

"Etta!" called Mr. Grumbie to his wife. "I forgot the vinegar." He coughed as a breeze blew smoke in his face.

"I'll go get it for you," offered Henry, but his neighbor ignored him.

Students Acquiring English

Use Mr. Grumbie's actions here and the illustration on page 68 to define *barbecue*, noting its spelling on the recipe. Also, have students discuss whether people in their native countries barbecue. If so, what kinds of foods are barbecued?

Health Link

Explain that herbs are valued for their flavoring, medicinal, and aromatic qualities. Garlic, when divided into cloves, is a common seasoning. Ask students if they have ever tasted these ingredients. If possible, bring in samples for students.

Students Acquiring English

Explain that when Henry says "*Search me,*" he means "I don't know." Let students guess what body language Henry uses when he says this. You might want to have students role-play Henry, Robert, and Mr. Grumbie in this scene.

MINILESSON

Predicting Outcomes

REVIEW & MAINTAIN

Teach/Model

Use a chart like the following to discuss the clues a reader might use to think of a possible outcome for the situation on pages 66–67.

What's in the Story:
- Mr. Grumbie has brought food outside. He is making a meat sauce.
- Ribsy is asleep.
- Mr. Grumbie wants to be left alone.
- Henry offers to help Mr. Grumbie.

What I Know:
- Dogs have a good sense of smell.
- Dogs love meat.
- The story is funny.
- When people looking to make trouble offer help, they're usually up to no good.

Possible Outcome:
Ribsy will be attracted to what Mr. Grumbie is cooking.

Practice/Apply

Invite students to list additional reasons why this outcome could be predicted such as:

- The fact that smoke is in the air.

- Henry and Robert are up in the cherry tree and so are unable to stop Ribsy.

- The Grumbies are nowhere in sight when Ribsy trots over.

SKILL FINDER

Full lesson/Reteaching, pp. 58B–58C

Minilessons, p. 53; Theme 1, p. 79

Interact *with* Literature

Guided Reading

Comprehension/Critical Thinking

1. What was Henry and Robert's problem? (They were both bored and unhappy that they didn't have a bike like Scooter did.)

2. What was going on at the Grumbie's? (Mr. Grumbie was preparing for a barbecue although Mrs. Grumbie argued against it—she wanted to take their guests out to dinner.)

3. Do you agree that anyone who can read a recipe can cook? (Encourage differing points of view and discussion.)

Predicting/Purpose Setting

Ask students if their predictions about Ribsy were correct. Have them revise or make new predictions if needed. Suggest that they predict what will happen to Mr. Grumbie's roast. Then have students read to the end of page 74.

Informal Assessment

If students' responses show that they understand the story, have them finish reading it independently or cooperatively.

Squeak-slam went the screen. Mrs. Grumbie stepped over Fluffy and walked across the yard with a bottle in her hand. "Hector, can't we take your friends out to dinner instead of going to all this trouble?" she asked, as she fanned smoke out of her eyes.

"This is no trouble at all." Mr. Grumbie added a few drops of vinegar to the mixture in the bowl.

Henry thought Mrs. Grumbie looked cross, as she said, "Hector, why don't you let me cook the meat in the house? It would be so much easier and then we could bring it outside to eat."

"Now, Etta, I know what I'm doing." Mr. Grumbie poured a few drops from another bottle and mashed some more.

"But I don't like to see you spoil the flavor of a perfectly good piece of meat with all that seasoning. It

QuickREFERENCE

Students Acquiring English

Using Context Remind students that some words have more than one meaning. Have them find the word *cross* on page 67 (*Mr. Grumbie crossed the lawn*) and again on page 68 (*Mrs. Grumbie looked cross*). Help them use context to figure out the two meanings. Suggest that they pantomime the two meanings.

would be different if you really knew how to cook." Mrs. Grumbie frowned, as she swatted at a bug circling over the sauce.

Mr. Grumbie frowned even more. "Anyone who can read a recipe can cook."

Mrs. Grumbie's face turned red, as she clapped the bug between her hands, and said sharply, "Oh, is that so? What about the time you cut up tulip bulbs in the hamburgers because you thought they were onions?"

"That," said Mr. Grumbie, even more sharply, "was different."

Mrs. Grumbie angrily fanned smoke with her apron. "Just remember when we try to eat this mess you're fixing that it wasn't my idea. Even if the recipe is any good, the meat will probably be burned on the outside and raw inside. Smoke will get in our eyes and we'll be eaten alive by mosquitoes and . . ."

Mr. Grumbie interrupted. "Etta, we won't argue about it any more. I invited my friends to a barbecue and we're going to have a barbecue."

Henry and Robert were disappointed. They hoped the Grumbies would argue about it a lot more.

Then Mr. Grumbie looked at the recipe printed on his apron. Because he was looking down at it, the words were upside down for him. "What does it say here?" he asked, pointing to his stomach.

Henry and Robert could not help snickering.

"Now, boys, run along and don't bother us. We're busy," said Mrs. Grumbie.

"Come on, Robert."

Henry turned away from the rosebushes. He felt uncomfortable around Mrs. Grumbie, because he thought she didn't like him. At least, she didn't like

69

Vocabulary

Exaggeration Point out the use of exaggeration in the phrase *eaten alive by mosquitoes*. Ask if students have ever gotten mosquito bites. How did the bites make them feel?

MINILESSON

Following Directions

REVIEW & MAINTAIN

Teach/Model

Discuss what might happen if Mr. Grumbie fails to follow the directions for making a barbecue sauce correctly. Review with students that in order to follow directions well a reader must:

- be sure to have all the ingredients or material ready before beginning
- pay attention to the sequence of steps in the directions
- look for words that tell the sequence, such as *first, next,* and *last*

Work with students to begin trying to reconstruct how Mr. Grumbie was making his sauce. Use information from page 67 to list the ingredients.

• salt	• garlic
• herbs	• vinegar

Practice/Apply

Have students reread pages 67–68 to find out how Mr. Grumbie was making his barbecue sauce. Then ask them to discuss what might be needed to complete the sauce. If possible, have a complete set of directions for making a sauce available for this discussion.

SKILL FINDER

Full lesson/Reteaching, pp. 37C–37D

Minilessons, p. 31; Theme 2, p. 171

Reading Strategies

▶ **Think About Words**

Discuss how both the illustration and the text on page 70 provide clues to the meanings of the word *baton*. Ask students to find the sentence that tells what the baton looked like. (*The boys examined the metal rod, which was about two and a half feet long with a rubber knob at each end.*) Ask what clues would help a reader know how a baton works and what a *drum majorette* is.

Clues for *baton*:

- Beezus says she is learning how to twirl it.

- She tries to turn it around in her hand.

Clue for *drum majorette*:

- Beezus says she wants to be a drum majorette in a parade, so this must be someone who twirls a baton in a parade.

Students Acquiring English

If possible, bring in a baton or pictures of parades with majorettes to help reinforce this concept.

Ribsy and that was the same as not liking Henry. He didn't want to make her any crosser than she was already, although secretly he couldn't see why she minded Ribsy's burying a bone in her pansy bed once in a while.

Henry tried standing on his hands just to show Mrs. Grumbie he wasn't paying any attention to what she was doing. Then he heard someone coming up his driveway. It was his friend Beezus and her little sister Ramona, who lived in the next block on Klickitat Street. Beezus' real name was Beatrice, but Ramona called her Beezus, and so did everyone else. Beezus was carrying a baton and Ramona was riding a shiny new tricycle.

"Whoa!" yelled Ramona to her tricycle. Then she got off and tied it to a bush with a jumping rope.

"Hello," said Beezus. "See my baton."

The boys examined the metal rod, which was about two and a half feet long with a rubber knob at each end.

70

Extra Support

Ask if students knew right away what Ramona was pretending when she tied her tricycle to a bush with her jumping rope. Point out the explanation on page 71, when Beezus says, *"Come on, Ramona, untie your horse."*

"What are you going to do with it?" asked Henry.

"Twirl it," said Beezus.

"I'll bet," scoffed Robert.

"I am too," said Beezus. "I take lessons every Saturday. By June I'll be good enough so I can twirl it in the Junior Rose Festival parade, and some day I'm going to be a drum majorette."

"June is only a couple of months away," said Henry, wondering what he would do in the parade this year. "Let's see you twirl it."

Beezus held the baton over her head and started to turn it with her right hand. It slipped from her fingers and hit her on the head.

"Boi-i-ing!" shouted the two boys together.

"You keep quiet," said Beezus crossly.

"Let me try," said Henry.

"No," answered Beezus, whose feelings were hurt.

"I didn't want to anyway." Henry started across the yard. "Come on, Robert, let's climb the cherry tree."

"All right for you, Henry Huggins!" shouted Beezus, as the boys scrambled up through the branches. "I'm going home. Come on, Ramona, untie your horse."

But Ramona had seen Ribsy and she began to pat him on the head. Ribsy groaned in his sleep and sat up to scratch. Suddenly he was wide awake, sniffing the air.

"Wuf!" said Ribsy.

71

Students Acquiring English

Have students say the sound word *boi-i-ing* aloud. Encourage groups of students to act out this scene.

Science Link

Dog Sense Smell is a dog's most highly developed sense. A gland inside a dog's nose releases a fluid that makes the tip moist, and this moisture helps a dog pick up odors that are hundreds of times too faint for people to detect.

Genre

Realistic Fiction

Teach/Model

Ask students what kind of story *Henry and Beezus* is—fiction or nonfiction. Then ask them to name fiction stories they have read recently. List titles on the board and work together to sort them into these categories: historical fiction, fantasy, and folktale.

For the titles that remain, ask students to identify which stories seem the most real to them and why they seem so real. Use these prompts to start:

- Which stories have characters that look or act like someone you know?

- Which stories have settings that remind you of places you have been?

Explain that fiction that accurately reflects life as it was lived in the past or today is called *realistic fiction*.

Practice/Apply

Invite students to review *Henry and Beezus* and list the characteristics that make it a work of realistic fiction.

Challenge Ask students to imagine the plot of the story if it were a work of historical fiction or fantasy.

Interact
with
Literature

Henry could tell by the sound of the bark that Ribsy was excited about something. He peered out through the leaves of the cherry tree, but could see nothing unusual in his back yard. He saw Ribsy stand up, shake himself, and trot purposefully toward the Grumbies' back yard, with Ramona running after him.

Henry looked across the rosebushes and groaned at what he saw. On a platter beside the barbecue pit was a large piece of raw meat. The Grumbies were nowhere in sight.

"Here, Ribsy! Come here, boy!" called Henry frantically, but Ribsy did not stop. "Catch him, Beezus!"

Ramona, who was trying to follow Ribsy through the rosebushes, shrieked.

"Hold still," directed Beezus, struggling with her little sister. "I can't get you loose from all these thorns when you wiggle that way."

"Come on, we better be getting out of here." Henry slipped and slid down the tree. "I bet the rain washed off the Doggie-B-Gone."

QuickREFERENCE

Science Link

Thorns Ask if students have ever tried to pick a rose. Did they feel the prick of a thorn? Roses are not the only plants with thorns; thorns protect many trees and shrubs from damage by grazing animals.

"I guess we better," agreed Robert cheerfully. After all, Ribsy wasn't his dog.

Henry hit the ground and tried to run through the rosebushes. Thorns clawed at his jeans and held him fast. "Here, Ribsy," he yelled. "Here, Ribs, old boy!"

Ribsy jumped for the roast.

With one desperate jerk, Henry tried to free himself from the roses. The thorns dug deeper into his legs.

Ribsy sank his teeth into the meat and pulled it to the ground.

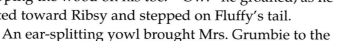

Mr. Grumbie came through the back door with an armload of kindling. "Hey, stop that dog!" he yelled, dropping the wood on his toe. "Ow!" he groaned, as he started toward Ribsy and stepped on Fluffy's tail.

An ear-splitting yowl brought Mrs. Grumbie to the back porch. "Fluffy," she cooed, "did the man step on the precious pussycat's tail?"

73

Interact *with* **Literature**

 **Guided Reading**

Comprehension/Critical Thinking

1. How do Beezus and Henry feel about one another? (Beezus wants to impress Henry with her baton-twirling. Henry is interested, but after Beezus refuses to let him try twirling, he acts like he isn't.)

2. What was the purpose of the Doggie-B-Gone on the rose-bushes? Did it work? Why or why not? (It was supposed to keep Ribsy away from the Grumbies' yard, but it had washed away during a rain.)

3. Do you like stories with chases in them? Why or why not? (Answers will vary.)

Predicting/Purpose Setting

Ask students to discuss their predictions about what would happen to Mr. Grumbie's roast. What clues did they use to make them? Before students read to the end of the story, have them predict how the roast will be retrieved.

Ribsy paused to take a firmer grip on the roast.

"If that cat hasn't any more sense than to sleep on the steps . . ." snapped Mr. Grumbie. "Hey, make that dog come back here!"

"Oh, my goodness!" exclaimed Mrs. Grumbie, when she saw what had happened. "Here, Ribsy, here, Ribsy!"

That was just what Ribsy needed to make him start running. He didn't like Mrs. Grumbie. He knew she sprinkled Doggie-B-Gone on the shrubbery to keep him away.

With one final yank and the sound of ripping cloth, Henry jerked away from the bushes.

"Tackle him," yelled Robert, who was still trying to untangle himself from the thorns.

Henry flung himself at his dog, but Ribsy raced on. Henry picked himself up off the Grumbies' driveway and ran after him.

Around the Grumbies' house he ran and on down Klickitat Street. He could hear Robert's and Mr. Grumbie's feet pounding down the sidewalk after him.

"Ribsy!" yelled Henry.

"Hey, come back here," shouted Robert.

74

QuickREFERENCE

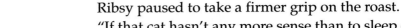 **Students Acquiring English**

Include the terms *picked himself up* and *feet pounding* in an enactment of this action-packed scene. You might add *snapped, exclaimed,* and *bellowed* to a list of words that describe ways of speaking.

"Stop thief!" bellowed Mr. Grumbie, holding onto his tall white hat with one hand.

Doors and windows began to open. "What's cooking, Grumbie?" someone called out.

Henry heard his mother say, "Oh, that dog!"

"Henry!" shouted Mr. Huggins.

"Go get 'em, Grumbie," yelled the man across the street.

Mr. Grumbie paused for breath. "Somebody head him off," he directed.

Ribsy ran into the street. A car turned the corner.

"Ribsy," wailed Henry, afraid to look.

"Hey, look out," warned Robert.

The car slammed on its brakes. Ribsy ran back to the sidewalk.

If only Henry could put on a burst of speed and make a really good flying tackle. But no matter how fast he ran, Ribsy was just out of his reach. He glanced over his shoulder and saw that Mr. Grumbie's face was red and he had lost his hat.

"Come . . . here . . . sir!" panted Mr. Grumbie. He wasn't used to running. Then his footsteps grew slower and slower until they stopped altogether.

Henry ran on, with Robert close behind. Their friend Mary Jane came out of her house and

---

Students Acquiring English

Explain that when Mr. Grumbie said *"Somebody head him off,"* he meant to get in front of Ribsy and block his way. Point out that when the man yells *"Go get 'em,"* he means *them.* (The apostrophe takes the place of *th.*)

Social Studies Link

You may want to discuss with students why most communities have laws that apply to dogs. Do students think "leash laws" are a good idea? How do these laws help protect dogs as well as people?

Extra Support

Ask what a *flying tackle* might be. Have a volunteer paraphrase this sentence from page 75: *If only Henry could put on a burst of speed and make a really good flying tackle.* Then discuss why he could not.

started down the sidewalk toward them. If only she would stop Ribsy. "Catch him!" yelled Henry.

When Ribsy was only a few feet from Mary Jane, he dropped the meat on the sidewalk. Here was her chance. "Get it, Mary Jane," Henry shouted, with almost all the breath he had left. "Get the meat!"

Mary Jane stood staring at Ribsy. "Pick up the meat, you dope!" yelled Robert.

Still Mary Jane did not move. Ribsy waited until Henry was almost within tackling distance before taking a firm grip on the roast and starting to run again.

"Mary Jane," panted Henry, "head him off."

Mary Jane stepped aside and Ribsy ran on. Henry felt as if he could not move another step. "Why didn't you grab the meat?" he demanded, as he paused to catch his breath.

"You could have caught him if you wanted to," accused Robert.

"I couldn't either stop your dirty old dog," said Mary Jane. "Can't you see I'm wearing my Sunday School dress?"

"Mary Jane, you give me a pain." Henry glared at her.

"You're a poet and don't know it," said Mary Jane, twirling around to show off her full skirt.

Robert and Henry looked at one another. Girls!

76

Informal Assessment

Oral Reading In order to check oral reading fluency, ask selected students to read aloud pages 76–77. If possible, tape-record their readings. Students should be allowed to first reread these pages silently. Use the Oral Reading Checklist in the *Teacher's Assessment Handbook* as a guide for assessment.

QuickREFERENCE

MEETING INDIVIDUAL NEEDS
Students Acquiring English

Have students use the illustration to help them figure out what a *Sunday School dress* is. Explain that it is a nice dress that a girl or woman might wear to church on Sunday or to Sunday School for religious instruction.

Robert clutched Henry's arm and pointed in the direction from which Ribsy had come. "Look!"

A police dog, a fox terrier, and a sort of collie were running down Klickitat Street toward Ribsy. Now there would be a dog fight, and the roast would be torn to pieces, and the two big dogs would chew up Ribsy. They would probably chew the fox terrier, too, and Henry knew the lady who owned him was very particular about keeping him out of dog fights. Henry would be blamed because the big dogs bit the little dog and . . . Suddenly Henry found he was too tired to do much of anything. He picked up a clod of dirt and threw it at the dogs as they passed him. "Beat it," he said, but he didn't bother to shout. He knew it was no use.

"Boy, a dog fight!" Robert was delighted. "This is going to be keen."

"Aw, keep quiet," said Henry. Robert wouldn't feel that way if Ribsy were his dog. The sort of collie was gaining on Ribsy, and the police dog was not far behind. Poor Ribsy! Henry shut his eyes. He couldn't stand seeing Ribsy chewed to pieces.

"Gangway everybody!" It was Scooter's voice. Leaning over his handle bars and pumping as hard as he could, he tore down the street behind the three dogs. He passed Henry and Robert and, swerving to avoid the dogs, caught up with Ribsy. He didn't stop for the curb, but rode right over it with a tremendous bump. Then he flung himself off the bicycle and on top of Ribsy before the dog knew what was happening.

Ribsy dropped the meat and Scooter snatched it. He sprang on his bicycle, wheeled around in the middle of the street, and started back toward the Grumbies' house, holding the meat above his head with one

77

Background: FYI

Kinds of Dogs Explain that at the time this story was written, German shepherds were known as police dogs. Today, other breeds are also used as police dogs. Ask students to describe what *"a sort of collie"* looks like.

Students Acquiring English

Ask what word kids today might use instead of *keen*. Explain that *gangway* in this context means "move aside." Discuss the meaning of *tore down [the street]*.

Sequence of Events

TESTED SKILL

Teach/Model

Discuss the sequence of events after Ribsy grabs the roast. Use a graphic like the following to review the first part of the chase.

| Henry Robert Mr. Grumbie | → Ribsy |

Then use this Think Aloud to model how to keep track of the sequence.

Think Aloud

After Mr. Grumbie quit the chase, I remember it got crazier because three dogs joined the chase. I think I'll alter my drawing to help me remember this fact.

| Henry Robert 3 dogs | → Ribsy |

Point out that drawing a diagram of a scene is sometimes a good way to help remember the sequence and show the action.

Practice/Apply

Have students draw diagrams to show what happens after Scooter gets the meat from Ribsy. Point out that they will need to reread pages 77–80 carefully.

SKILL FINDER

Full lesson/Reteaching, pp. 84B–84C

Minilessons, pp. 33, 117; Theme 1, p. 107

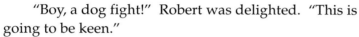

hand. The three other dogs and Ribsy all chased after Scooter, barking and growling as they jumped up and tried to snap at the meat.

Eluding them all, Scooter pedaled triumphantly back down Klickitat Street. "Hi," he said briefly to Henry and Robert, as he passed them.

"Hey, give me that meat," demanded Henry. Scooter ignored him.

"How do you like that!" said Robert. "He sure thinks he's smart."

Henry ran after Scooter, who pedaled even faster. Henry put on a burst of speed. So did Scooter. So did the dogs. Henry could hear the neighbors laughing. He tried to run faster, but Scooter stayed just out of his reach.

When Scooter reached the Grumbies' house, he handed the meat to its owner. "There you are, Mr. Grumbie," he said.

 78

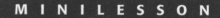

Mr. Grumbie took the battered roast. "Thank you, Scooter. That was mighty quick thinking on your part."

"It wasn't anything," said Scooter modestly. "It was easy to catch up with him on my bike."

The other dogs lost interest and ran away, but Ribsy continued to whimper and jump for the meat. Then even he gave up and sat panting, with his long pink tongue hanging out.

Poor Ribsy, thought Henry. He wanted that meat so much. Maybe he's tired of horse meat. Henry wished he dared to pet his dog, even though he had been cross with him.

"He's a dumb dog," said Scooter. "It's a good thing I came along and saved him from those other dogs when I did."

"I think you're mean, Scooter McCarthy," said Beezus. "Poor Ribsy."

"Why don't you go home?" said Henry to Scooter.

Health Link

Diet Explain that an adult dog like Ribsy requires only one meal a day. Veterinarians recommend that dogs also have something safe to chew on, such as a dog biscuit or a bone, to keep their gums and teeth healthy.

MINILESSON

Study Skill
Library: Fiction Books

Teach/Model

Ask students what kind of story *Ribsy and the Roast* is. (fiction) Discuss where books by Beverly Cleary can be found in a library. Have students name other kinds of books and where they might be found in a library. Be sure the following books and parts of the library are mentioned:

Fiction:
- Made up by authors
- Arranged alphabetically by author's last name

Nonfiction:
- Tells about real people and events
- Kept in separate part of library; books are grouped by subject and given numbers

Reference Books:
- Books of information such as atlases and encyclopedias
- Kept in separate part of library

Practice/Apply

Randomly display several fiction and nonfiction books and several reference books from your classroom library. Invite students to work to arrange the books the way a librarian would. You might like to invite your school librarian to class to assist in this activity.

 SKILL FINDER Full lesson, p. H3

Interact with Literature

Guided Reading

Comprehension/Critical Thinking

1. How did the roast finally get returned to Mr. Grumbie? (Scooter managed to catch Ribsy and get the meat. He returned it to the Grumbies, but it was ruined.)

2. Why do you think Henry and Scooter seem to dislike one another? (Answers will vary, but as much as possible have students cite evidence from the story.)

3. What did Mr. Huggins mean when he said that Henry *"wanted something to happen"*? (Henry had complained about being bored, so his father thought he secretly wanted something exciting to happen that day.)

"Now, children," said Mrs. Huggins. Then she said to Mrs. Grumbie, "You must let us buy you another roast. Henry can help pay for it out of his allowance. He knows he is supposed to keep his dog out of your yard."

"Gee, my mother says roasts are expensive," said Scooter.

"You keep quiet." Henry scowled at Scooter. Why was Scooter always around when things happened to him? "Jeepers, I'm sorry, Mrs. Grumbie," said Henry. "I don't know what got into Ribsy. He was just hungry, I guess."

"He always is," observed Mr. Huggins.

Meat markets were closed on Sunday, but Henry knew that the delicatessen counter in the Supermarket was open. "Delicatessens have wienies, don't they?" he asked. "I could run down to the Supermarket and get some for you, if you'd like."

"I could go faster on my bike," said Scooter.

Mrs. Grumbie smiled. "Thank you, Henry. That won't be necessary. I think we'll go out to dinner." She looked at Mr. Grumbie, who had started toward the house with the roast. "Just between you and me," she whispered, "I don't think the meat would have been fit to eat with that sauce Mr. Grumbie was going to put on it." Then she called to her husband, "Hector, what are you going to do with that dirty piece of meat?"

"I suppose he might as well have it," said Mr. Grumbie reluctantly. "Not that he deserves it." He threw the remains to Ribsy.

Mrs. Grumbie paused in the doorway. "Henry, I'm going to bake cookies tomorrow. If you'll stop by on your way home from school tomorrow, I'll give you some."

80

Self-Assessment

Ask students to use questions like these to assess their reading.

- Did making predictions keep me interested in the story?
- When I thought about words I didn't know, was I able to use clues to find their meaning?
- Did I enjoy the chase in this story?

QuickREFERENCE

Vocabulary

Word Origins *Delicatessen* comes from a German word meaning "delicacies." The word *wiener* is short for *wienerwurst*, also from the German, meaning "Vienna sausage." Wieners are a type of pork or beef sausage.

Students Acquiring English

Give students opportunities to use newly acquired vocabulary in meaningful ways. You might, for example, have students make a story map identifying the most important events in the story and then use the map to retell the story.

"Thank you, Mrs. Grumbie," answered Henry. She seemed almost glad Ribsy had stolen the roast. At least, she wasn't cross any more.

"Here, Ribsy, it isn't time for you to eat yet." Henry tugged at the roast, but Ribsy hung on and growled. "Come on, Dad, give me a hand."

Mr. Huggins took hold of the meat and together they got it away from Ribsy. "I'll put it in the refrigerator for him," said Mr. Huggins, "and I'll have a talk with you later."

"Aw, gee, Dad," protested Henry. "I wasn't doing anything."

"You wanted something to happen, didn't you?" said Mr. Huggins, as he carried the meat into the house.

Henry did not answer. He just sighed and sat down on the steps. Why did these things always have to happen to him, anyway?

81

Interact *with* Literature

More About the Author

Beverly Cleary

Born in 1916, Beverly Cleary grew up in Portland, Oregon. When Beverly started first grade, she couldn't wait to learn to read. But the experience that she approached so joyfully turned out to be an ordeal. She was placed in the Blackbird reading group, and did much less reading than she had hoped.

In third grade, she picked up a book called *The Dutch Twins* and, out of boredom, began to read. Much to her delight, her pleasure in reading was reawakened.

Today Beverly Cleary looks back on over forty years of writing books for children. She has received more than fifty prestigious honors and awards. But her greatest satisfaction has been "the number of people who tell me of a child who didn't enjoy reading until my books came along."

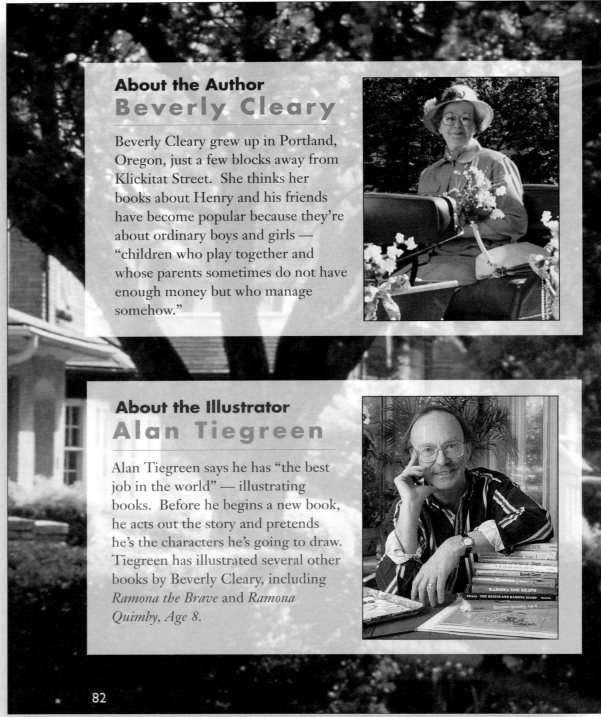

About the Author
Beverly Cleary

Beverly Cleary grew up in Portland, Oregon, just a few blocks away from Klickitat Street. She thinks her books about Henry and his friends have become popular because they're about ordinary boys and girls — "children who play together and whose parents sometimes do not have enough money but who manage somehow."

About the Illustrator
Alan Tiegreen

Alan Tiegreen says he has "the best job in the world" — illustrating books. Before he begins a new book, he acts out the story and pretends he's the characters he's going to draw. Tiegreen has illustrated several other books by Beverly Cleary, including *Ramona the Brave* and *Ramona Quimby, Age 8*.

82

If you're ever in Beverly Cleary's hometown of Portland, Oregon, be sure to visit Grant Park. There you'll find life-size statues of Henry, Ribsy, and Ramona. Above, the bronze figures are shown in the studio of sculptor Lee Hunt. Hunt says she modeled Ramona after a photograph of Beverly Cleary at age five.

83

More About the Illustrator

Alan Tiegreen

Alan Tiegreen is looking forward to the day when he can devote all of his time to illustration instead of dividing it up with his duties as an instructor in illustration at Georgia State University.

When Tiegreen is working on a children's story, he likes to get into character. "I act out the story myself," he says. "I pretend that I am the character. This makes it more personal. I work from memory rather than using models."

His advice to aspiring artists? "Do a lot of reading and a lot of drawing," he advises. "And use your imagination!"

Interact
with
Literature

Responding Activities

 Personal Response

- Ask students to write about the character in the story they liked best, and why. (Allow them to choose Ribsy, if they wish.)

- Allow students to choose their own way of responding to the selection.

Anthology Activities

Choose—or have students choose—an activity from page 84.

RESPONDING

Where's the Beef?

Draw a Map

Ribsy on the Run

Ribsy takes us on an adventure through Henry's neighborhood. Make a map that shows Ribsy's route. Be sure to include all the houses and streets that appear in the story.

Retell the Story

What Would Ribsy Say?

Retell the events of the story from another character's point of view. How might Ribsy tell the story? What about Mr. Grumbie?

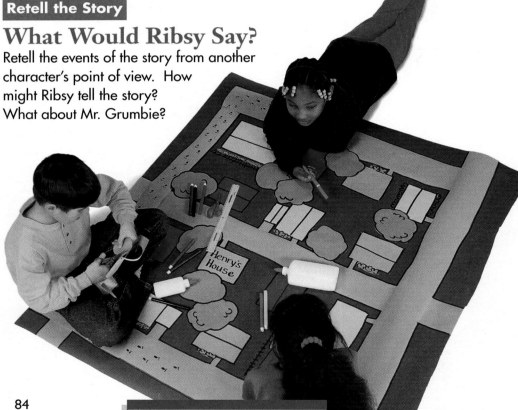

Henry's House

84

Informal Assessment

Responses should indicate general understanding of the story and appreciation of the author's style.

Additional Support:
- Use the Guided Reading questions to check comprehension.
- Reread confusing sections aloud.
- Use story illustrations and/or text to support opinions.

QuickREFERENCE

 Home Connection

Suggest that students share a chapter from a Beverly Cleary book with family members. (There are Spanish editions such as *Henry Huggins* and *Ramona la chinche.*)

Students Acquiring English

For the activity "Ribsy on the Run," you may want to have students acquiring English add labels to the map. They might also draw figures on the map to show where the three dogs joined the chase and where Scooter came along.

More Choices for Responding

Literature Discussion

- How might the chase have ended if Scooter hadn't come along?

- Would you like to own a dog like Ribsy? Why or why not?

- What do you think Mr. Grumbie was going to do with the roast at the end before he threw it back to Ribsy?

- What can the Huggins family do to show the Grumbies that Ribsy will behave from now on?

✍ Ribsy Speaks Up

Have students write letters of apology to the Grumbies from Ribsy, as written by Henry, of course. They might write their apologies on sheets of construction paper cut into the following shapes: a dog bone, doghouse, dog tag, or food dish.

No Bones About It—I Goofed!

I'm So Doggone Sorry!

Help Get Me Out of the Doghouse!

Selection Connections
LAB, p. 2

Remind students to complete the part of the chart on *Literacy Activity Book* page 2 that refers to *Henry and Beezus.*

What's Cooking? Hats

Suggest that students make chef's hats like the one Mr. Grumbie wears. Cardboard could be rolled to form the stem and a wide variety of colorful fabrics could be stapled to the top. Encourage students to invent their own cooking slogans for the hats, such as *Come and Get It!* or *Soup's On!*

Reader's Theater
Cooperative Learning

Have students work in small groups to prepare a dramatic rereading of a favorite scene from the story. Suggest these scenes:

- Henry and Robert watching Mr. Grumbie prepare the sauce

- Ramona waking up Ribsy and then Ribsy grabbing the roast

- The return of the roast to the Grumbies

Comprehension Check

Use these questions and/or *Literacy Activity Book* page 27 to discuss the selection.

1. Why was Ribsy able to grab the roast? (Robert and Henry were up in a tree and the Doggie-B-Gone had washed off the bushes. Also, Mr. Grumbie wasn't there.)

2. How do you know Ribsy was hard to catch? (Several people, such as Mr. Grumbie and Henry, gave up the chase because they were tired.)

3. Why might Henry's parents have been unhappy with him? (They probably suspected he intentionally started the whole situation.)

Literacy Activity Book, p. 27

Ribsy in the Movies
Complete the summary for the movie version of *Henry and Beezus.*

The Race for Ribsy

Main Characters: _____

Setting: _____

Background: Mr. Grumbie is cooking a roast because _____

The Chase: _____

The Recovery: _____

What's Cooking? 27

Portfolio Opportunity

- Selection comprehension: Save *Literacy Activity Book*, p. 27.

- Writing samples: Save responses to the writing activities.

Instruct and Integrate

Comprehension

Transparency 4–11

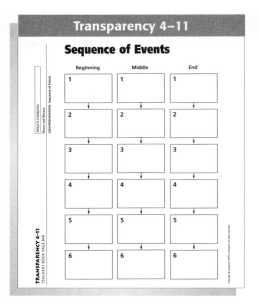

Sequence of Events

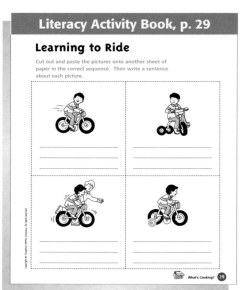

Literacy Activity Book, p. 29

Learning to Ride

Cut out and paste the pictures onto another sheet of paper in the correct sequence. Then write a sentence about each picture.

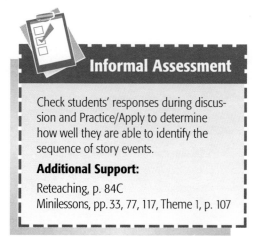

What's Cooking? 29

Informal Assessment

Check students' responses during discussion and Practice/Apply to determine how well they are able to identify the sequence of story events.

Additional Support:

Reteaching, p. 84C
Minilessons, pp. 33, 77, 117, Theme 1, p. 107

INTERACTIVE LEARNING

Sequence of Events

TESTED SKILL

LAB, p. 29

Teach/Model

Ask students why sequencing the events in a story is important when doing a summary. Then display Transparency 4–11. Read this jumbled summary of the first part of *Henry and Beezus* aloud, and then use the Think Aloud to model how to correct the sequence in the summary.

> **Beginning**
>
> Beezus and Ramona approached Henry and Robert. First Beezus tried to twirl her baton, but she was unsuccessful. Then Ramona chased Ribsy and got caught in the rosebushes. Next Mr. Grumbie dropped his kindling and stepped on the cat. Ribsy woke from his nap and smelled the roast. Then he trotted up to the pit and grabbed the roast. Finally Henry and Robert slid down the tree.

Think Aloud

Everything sounded OK until I came to the sentence describing Ribsy waking up. I know that happened before he ran into the bushes. I also know that Mr. Grumbie dropped the kindling after he saw Ribsy take the roast, so that sentence is out of order too.

Work with students to write the sentences in order on the transparency. Then ask a volunteer to use the transparency to give the summary again aloud, this time in the proper sequence. Then complete the transparency by having students give summaries of the middle and end of the story.

Practice/Apply

- Have students complete *Literacy Activity Book* page 29.

- Have students draw pictures to show the sequence of events in a familiar story, such as a fable or folktale.

SKILL FINDER
Minilessons, pp. 33, 77, 117; Theme 1, p. 107

Reteaching

Sequence of Events

Divide a bulletin board into four sections that are prominently numbered. Then write the names of the following characters on index cards and mix them up in a hat: *Henry, Ribsy, Mr. Grumbie,* and *Scooter.* Have students pick a name from the hat and pin it on the board according to when the character is introduced in the story.

Then make up cards that describe three things each of the characters did. Mix those cards in a hat. Ask students to select a card and pin it in its proper position next to the character's name. Encourage students to check the story to confirm that they have arranged the events correctly.

Students can use the **Channel R.E.A.D.** videodisc "Suspended in Space" for additional support with Sequence.

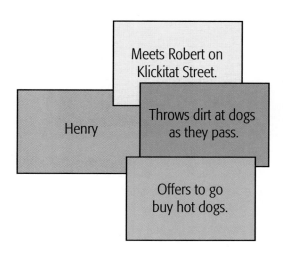

Henry
- Meets Robert on Klickitat Street.
- Throws dirt at dogs as they pass.
- Offers to go buy hot dogs.

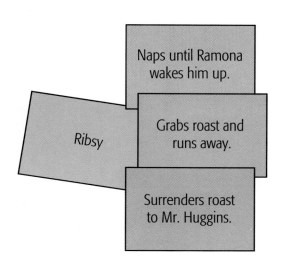

Ribsy
- Naps until Ramona wakes him up.
- Grabs roast and runs away.
- Surrenders roast to Mr. Huggins.

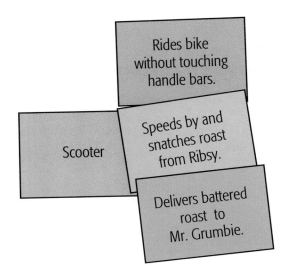

Scooter
- Rides bike without touching handle bars.
- Speeds by and snatches roast from Ribsy.
- Delivers battered roast to Mr. Grumbie.

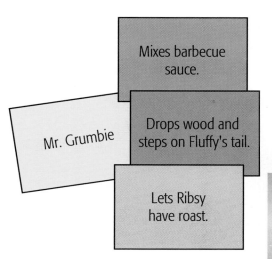

Mr. Grumbie
- Mixes barbecue sauce.
- Drops wood and steps on Fluffy's tail.
- Lets Ribsy have roast.

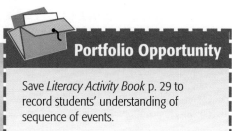

Portfolio Opportunity

Save *Literacy Activity Book* p. 29 to record students' understanding of sequence of events.

Instruct *and* Integrate

Writing Skills and Activities

Transparency 4–12

Avoiding Stringy Sentences

Which paragraph is easier to read? Why?

Mr. Grumbie crossed the lawn and set the tray on the edge of the barbecue pit in the corner of his yard and he peeled a small object into a bowl, sprinkled it with salt, and mashed it with a little wooden stick and then he broke off pieces of the dried weeds and mashed them, too.

OR

Mr. Grumbie crossed the lawn and set the tray on the edge of the barbecue pit in the corner of his yard. He peeled a small object which he put into a bowl, sprinkled it with salt, and mashed it with a little wooden stick. Then he broke off pieces of the dried weeds and mashed them, too.

Henry put on a burst of speed. So did Scooter. So did the dogs. Henry could hear the neighbors laughing. He tried to run faster, but Scooter stayed just out of his reach.

OR

Henry put on a burst of speed and so did Scooter but so did the dogs and Henry could hear the neighbors laughing and so he tried to run faster, but Scooter stayed just out of his reach.

Literacy Activity Book, p. 31

Doggie Data

Rewrite each stringy sentence.

1. Dogs have two kinds of teeth and the front teeth are used for nibbling and the canine teeth, or fangs, are used for tougher food and fighting.

2. Some dogs have pointed ears and the ears of other dogs may be heavy and long so they droop and other dogs get their ears cropped.

3. Dogs have four toes and they also have a fifth toe and this toe is called a dewclaw.

4. Most dogs shed their coats once a year and when they shed depends on how much sunlight they get and as days grow longer, dogs begin to shed.

What's Cooking? **31**

Informal Assessment

Check students' writing for fluency and the ability to communicate ideas, as well as to see if they have corrected any stringy sentences. For additional support, you may want to schedule more time for self-selected writing.

INTERACTIVE LEARNING

TESTED SKILL

Avoiding Stringy Sentences
LAB p. 31

Teach/Model   Write these sentences on the board.

1. Unfortunately, the back yard was no more interesting than the front and the only sign of life was next door and a large yellow cat was dozing on the Grumbies' back steps and there was smoke coming from the barbecue pit.
2. Unfortunately, the back yard was no more interesting than the front. The only sign of life was next door. A large yellow cat was dozing on the Grumbies' back steps, and there was smoke coming from the barbecue pit.

Ask which statement is easier to read. (the second) Elicit that the first one contains so many ideas that it is confusing. The second statement is easier to read because it uses three sentences instead of one to express the same ideas. Discuss another way the first statement might have been corrected. (by breaking it into four separate sentences)

Explain that sentences that contain too many ideas connected with *and, so, and/so,* and *but* are called stringy sentences. Writers can correct stringy sentences by making them into separate sentences.

Display Transparency 4–12. Work together with students to rewrite the stringy sentences. Encourage them to describe in their own words how they corrected each sentence.

Practice/Apply   Assign the activity Write a Personal Narrative. Remind students to avoid using stringy sentences in their writing.

SKILL FINDER → Reading-Writing Workshop, pp. 90–91F

Writing Activities

Write a Personal Narrative

Henry Huggins and Robert unexpectedly get into trouble. Invite students to remember a time when they got into trouble without meaning to. Have them write brief descriptions of what happened. Encourage them to avoid stringy sentences in their personal narratives.

Write a Sequel

Invite students to write a sequel about Henry Huggins. Encourage them to brainstorm ideas in small groups. If necessary, suggest these:

- As Mr. Huggins is having his talk with Henry, Ribsy starts barking. Someone is at the door!

- Beezus comes by the next day looking for Henry. Beezus is all upset because her baton is missing.

- Ribsy gets a new leash, which he doesn't like one bit.

Encourage students to work with partners or in small groups to write their sequels. Explain that they should include as much dialogue as they can—just as Beverly Cleary did. (*See Writer's Craft Minilesson page 65.*)

Shared Writing: Write a List

Remind students that Henry and Beezus was written in 1952. Have them recall how Henry was looking for something to do at the start of the selection. Ask students: If this story took place today, what might Henry do to cure his boredom? Then work together with the class to write a list of activities and why Henry might find them interesting.

What Henry Could Do

Activity	Why Henry Would Like It
Watch TV.	There are lots of different shows on.
Go to the video store and rent a movie.	You can pick from lots of movies rather than just watching what's on TV.

Portfolio Opportunity

Save responses to activities on this page for writing samples.

Instruct *and* Integrate

Word Skills and Strategies

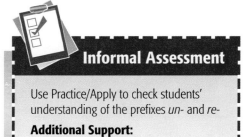

Literacy Activity Book, p. 32

Not Again!

Write the word from the box that fits each meaning. Each word has the prefix *un-* or *re-*. Then solve the riddle by unscrambling the letters in each shape.

| reenter | unscramble | unfinished | unhurt |
| recapture | untidy | reforest | reelect |

1 vote back into office
2 catch again
3 plant again with trees
4 not complete
5 not harmed
6 go back into
7 not neat
8 opposite of "mix up"

RIDDLE: What do you call a dog that steals the neighbors' meat?

ANSWER: ◯◯◯◯ ▢▢▢▢▢

32 What's Cooking?

INTERACTIVE LEARNING

TESTED SKILL

Structural Analysis
The Prefixes *un-* and *re-*
LAB, p. 32

> Henry got tangled in the rosebush but soon got himself <u>untangled</u>.

Teach/Model

Write this sentence on the chalkboard. Have a volunteer read it.

Ask students what the difference is between the meanings of the two underlined words (*Untangled* is the opposite of *tangled*.) and between the spellings of the two words. (*Untangled* begins with *un*.) Introduce the term *prefix*, a word part that is added to the beginning of a word or word part to change its meaning. Elicit that

* the prefix *un-* means "not" or "opposite of;"
* *untangled* means "not tangled."

Have students find other *un-* words in the story. (*unfortunately*, p. 65; *uncomfortable*, p. 69; *unusual*, p. 72) Discuss the meaning of the words, combining the meaning of each prefix with its base word.

Write this sentence on the board, and have a student read it aloud.

> Scooter reappears at the end of the story.

Ask students to find a word made up of a prefix and a base word. (*reappear*) Call on a volunteer to underline it. Elicit that

* the prefix *re-* adds the meaning "again" or "back" to a base word;
* *reappear* means "appear again;"
* *re* and *un* are not always prefixes. Examples: *realize /uncle*.

Note also that it is not always possible to figure out meaning by separating the prefix from the rest of the word. For example, *remind* does not mean "mind again" but rather "call to mind again;" *return* means "arrive back" or "give back" as well as "turn back."

retell	tell again
replace	place back
unfair	not fair
refresh	make fresh again
unlike	not like
unbutton	opposite of button
unclear	not clear
rebuild	build again
unexpected	not expected
recycle	cycle again
unhealthy	not healthy
uncover	opposite of cover
refill	fill again
reassemble	assemble again
reclaim	claim back
unfriendly	not friendly

Practice/Apply

Have students form small groups to define each word in the box, using the base word and the meaning "not" or "opposite of" for *un-* and "again" or "back" for *re-*. Sample answers are given.

SKILL FINDER Spelling, Theme 6

Informal Assessment

Use Practice/Apply to check students' understanding of the prefixes *un-* and *re-*

Additional Support:
Reteaching, p. 84G

Reteaching

The Prefixes *un-* and *re-*

Write the words at right on the chalkboard.

Take a long ribbon; tie it into a bow. Ask students which word describes what you did. *(tie)* Undo the bow; ask the same question. *(untie)* Tie another bow; ask it again. *(retie)* Elicit the definition of *prefix* and that *un-* and *re-* are prefixes. Call on volunteers to say what meaning *un-* adds to tie *("opposite of")* and to circle *un-* on the board. Do the same for *re-*. *(again)*

MINILESSON

Think About Words

Teach/Model

Review the Think About Words Strategy. Then have students locate the sentence in their book, and use the Think Aloud that follows.

page 65 A large yellow cat was dozing on the Grumbies' back steps, and there was smoke coming from the barbecue pit.

Think Aloud

I sound out the word *barbecue* because once I hear it, I might recognize it. I look for familiar patterns of letters.

• The first three letters are the same as in the word *bar*;

• The last two letters are the same as the last two letters in *blue*.

I look for clues in pictures, words, or phrases near the word.

• Words such as *apron, recipe, tray, bowls, salt,* and *smoke* hint that a barbecue has something to do with cooking;

• The setting is outdoors, so it may deal with outdoor cooking.

Practice/Apply

Have students form groups to find these words in the story. Ask for strategies to use if the word is not familiar. Sample answers are given.

casually, p. 65	Familiar pattern of letters: *-ally*; clues: *whistling, hands in his pockets, without stopping*; exact understanding not needed.
immense, p. 67	Familiar pattern of letters: *im-, -ense* as in *sense*; clues: picture on page 66, *tall white hat*; exact understanding not needed.
majorette, p. 71	Familiar pattern of letters: *major-, -ette* as in *barrette*; clues: picture on page 70, *baton, twirl, parade*; exact understanding not needed.

Word Skills Practice

Cumulative Skill Practice
Help from Harry
by Anne Viking

WATCH **ME READ**

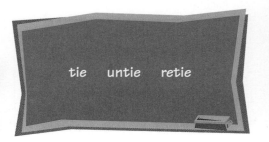

tie   untie   retie

Think About Words Strategy

Ask yourself this question: Is this word important to your understanding of what you are reading?

If the answer is yes, follow these steps:

• Try to pronounce the word.

• Think of other words that remind you of this one.

• Look for context clues.

• Look for familiar prefixes, base words, roots, or suffixes.

• Use a dictionary.

Portfolio Opportunity

Save *Literacy Activity Book* page 32 to record students' understanding of the prefixes *un-* and *re-*.

3

Instruct *and* Integrate

Building Vocabulary

High-Frequency Vocabulary Practice

Cumulative Skill Practice
Help from Harry
by Anne Viking

1. Collie is to dog as oak is to tree.
2. Hot is to cold as big is to little.
3. Up is to down as awake is to asleep.
4. Windowpane is to glass as sidewalk is to cement.
5. Jump is to leap as spin is to twirl.
6. Good is to bad as interesting is to boring.
7. Nose is to smell as ear is to hear.
8. Cooking is to recipe as traveling is to map.
9. Laugh is to snicker as cry is to weep.
10. Brakes are to stop as handlebars are to steer.

Literacy Activity Book, p. 33

No Bones About It!

Fill in each list with words from the box and your own words. Sample answers shown.

| immense | modestly | reluctantly | snickering |
| scoff | scowl | tremendous | triumphantly |

How a Dog Might Approach You
1
2
3
4
5

How to Describe a Large Dog
1
2
3
4
5

What Angry People Might Do
1
2
3
4
5

Ways People Laugh
1
2
3
4
5

What's Cooking? 33

Use this page to review Selection Vocabulary.

Vocabulary Activities

Analogies

Students may recall that one of the dogs that chased Ribsy was a collie. Write the following sentences on the board: *A collie is a kind of dog. A robin is a kind of bird.* Explain that the first sentence expresses the relationship between the words *collie* and *dog.* Then point out that in the second sentence the words *robin* and *bird* have the same relationship to each other as the words *collie* and *dog.*

Next, write the following sentence on the board, and tell students that this kind of sentence, called an *analogy,* is a way of saying that the two pairs of words have the same relationship: *Collie is to dog as robin is to bird.*

Discuss the relationship between the first two underlined words in each of the analogies listed, and have students suggest a word to complete the sentence.

Exact Words for *said*

Write the following sentence on the board: *"I sure wish I had a bike,"* *remarked Henry to his mother and father.* Circle the word *remarked* and tell students that one way writers make their dialogue clear and vivid is by replacing the word *said* with a more exact word.

Have students search through dialogue in the story to find other examples of exact words for *said.* For especially colorful words, ask volunteers to read the quotations with the proper expression. *(remarked, suggested, responded, observed, muttered, whispered, offered, added, yelled, scoffed, groaned, exclaimed, bellowed, wailed, warned, demanded, accused, protested)*

Prefixes *bi-* and *tri-*

Challenge Remind students that Scooter rode a bicycle and Ramona rode a tricycle. Ask students what the difference is between a bicycle and a tricycle. (A bicycle has two wheels; a tricycle has three wheels.) Explain that the prefix *bi-* means "two" and the prefix *tri-* means "three." Tell students that many other words also begin with the prefixes *bi-* and *tri-*. Then list the words to the right on the board. Have students discuss the words they know and look up any they don't know.

bisect	triangle
binoculars	trio
biannual	triple
bimonthly	triplets
bicuspid	triathlon
bilingual	tripod

Spelling

FIVE-DAY PLAN

DAY 1	DAY 2	DAY 3	DAY 4	DAY 5
Pretest; Minilesson; Challenge Words/ Additional Words (opt.); Take-Home Word Lists (LAB)	First LAB page; Challenge Words Practice (opt.)	Check first LAB page; Second LAB page (except writing application)	Check second LAB page; writing application (LAB)	Test

Teaching CHOICES

MINILESSON

 TESTED SKILL

The VCCV Pattern

LAB, pp. 34–35

Spelling Words

* happen
* dinner
* Sunday
* invite
* market
* yellow
* better
* window

Challenge Words

* purpose
* suggest
* ignore
* distance

Additional Spelling Words

carry
Monday
forget
order

*Starred words or forms of the words appear in *Henry and Beezus*.

- Write *dinner* and *Sunday* on the board, and have students say them. Ask how many vowel sounds there are in *dinner*. (two) Write *V* above each vowel. Ask what consonants appear between the vowels. (n, n) Label each with a C. Explain that *VCCV* stands for *vowel-consonant-consonant-vowel*.

- Ask if *dinner* is divided into syllables between vowels or consonants. (consonants) Explain that a word with the VCCV pattern is often divided into syllables between the two consonants.

- Ask students where the word *Sunday* should be divided into syllables. (Sun/day) Then ask what spelling patterns they see in *Sunday*. (the short vowel pattern in the first syllable and the /ā/ spelled *ay* in the second syllable) Tell students that one way to remember the spelling of a VCCV word is to divide the word into syllables and look for spelling patterns.

Spelling Assessment

Spelling Assessment

Pretest

Say each underlined word, read the sentence, and then repeat the word. Have students write only the underlined words.

1. I wish something exciting would happen!
2. What are we having for dinner?
3. That store is closed on Sunday.
4. Who did you invite to the barbecue?
5. My brother works at the market.
6. I got a yellow racing bike for my birthday.
7. My dog behaves better than yours.
8. We broke a window playing baseball.

Test

Spelling Words Use the Pretest sentences.

Challenge Words

9. Long distance calls are expensive.
10. Mom said to ignore my brother when he teases me.
11. I suggest you read this book.
12. We didn't break it on purpose.

SKILL FINDER

Daily Language Practice, p. 84K
Reading-Writing Workshop, p. 91E

Literacy Activity Book, p. 34

Ribsy's Roast

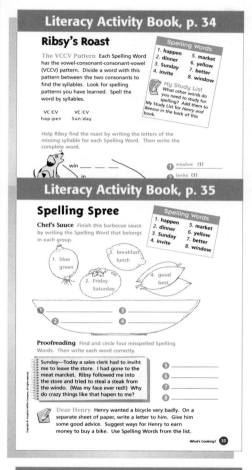

The VCCV Pattern Each Spelling Word has the vowel-consonant-consonant-vowel (VCCV) pattern. Divide a word with this pattern between the two consonants to find the syllables. Look for spelling patterns you have learned. Spell the word by syllables.

Spelling Words
1. happen
2. dinner
3. Sunday
4. invite
5. market
6. yellow
7. better
8. window

My Study List What other words do you need to study for spelling? Add them to My Study List for *Henry and Beezus* in the back of this book.

Help Ribsy find the roast by writing the letters of the missing syllable for each Spelling Word. Then write the complete word.

VC|CV   VC|CV
hap|pen   Sun|day

win _____
in

1 window (1)
2 invite (1)

Literacy Activity Book, p. 35

Spelling Spree

Chef's Sauce Finish this barbecue sauce by writing the Spelling Word that belongs in each group.

1. blue green
2. Friday Saturday
3. breakfast lunch
4. good best

Spelling Words
1. happen
2. dinner
3. Sunday
4. invite
5. market
6. yellow
7. better
8. window

1 _____ 3 _____
2 _____ 4 _____

Proofreading Find and circle four misspelled Spelling Words. Then write each word correctly.

Sunday—Today a sales clerk had to invitt me to leave the store. I had gone to the meat market. Ribsy followed me into the store and tried to steal a steak from the windo. (Was my face ever red!) Why do crazy things like that hapen to me?

5 _____
6 _____
7 _____
8 _____

 Dear Henry Henry wanted a bicycle very badly. On a separate sheet of paper, write a letter to him. Give him some good advice. Suggest ways for Henry to earn money to buy a bike. Use Spelling Words from the list.

What's Cooking? 35

Literacy Activity Book

Take-Home Word Lists: pp. 171–172

 Students can use the **Spelling Spree CD-ROM** for extra practice with the spelling principles taught in this selection.

 MEETING INDIVIDUAL NEEDS

Challenge

Challenge Words Practice Have students use the Challenge Words to write tips for teaching pets how to behave.

Grammar

5-Day Planner

FIVE-DAY PLAN

DAY 1	DAY 2	DAY 3	DAY 4	DAY 5
Daily Language Practice 1; Teach/Model; First LAB page	Daily Language Practice 2; Check first LAB page; Cooperative Learning	Daily Language Practice 3; Writing Application	Daily Language Practice 4; Reteaching (opt.); Second LAB page	Daily Language Practice 5; Check second LAB page; Students' Writing

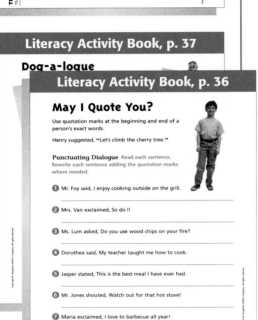

Transparency 4–13

Punctuating Dialogue

Robert shouted, "Hey, come back here!"
He asked, "What should we feed Ribsy?"
Henry suggested, "Let's see you twirl the baton."
Mr. Grumbie said, "Anyone who can read a recipe can cook."

Mrs. Huggins said don't touch my clean window

Robert asked what do you want to do

Henry replied let's go around to the back yard

He screamed your dog has the roast

Mrs. Grumbie asked do you want a cookie

Mrs. Huggins said please keep Ribsy in his own yard

Mr. Huggins shouted stop that dog

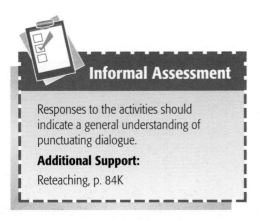

Literacy Activity Book, p. 37

Dog-a-logue

Literacy Activity Book, p. 36

May I Quote You?

Use quotation marks at the beginning and end of a person's exact words.

Henry suggested, "Let's climb the cherry tree."

Punctuating Dialogue Read each sentence. Rewrite each sentence adding the quotation marks where needed.

1. Mr. Foy said, I enjoy cooking outside on the grill.

2. Mrs. Van exclaimed, So do I!

3. Ms. Lum asked, Do you use wood chips on your fire?

4. Dorothea said, My teacher taught me how to cook.

5. Jasper stated, This is the best meal I have ever had.

6. Mr. Jones shouted, Watch out for that hot stove!

7. Maria exclaimed, I love to barbecue all year!

36 What's Cooking?

Informal Assessment

Responses to the activities should indicate a general understanding of punctuating dialogue.

Additional Support:
Reteaching, p. 84K

INTERACTIVE LEARNING

Punctuating Dialogue

LAB, pp. 36–37

TESTED SKILL

Quotation marks show you the exact words that a person says.

- Use quotation marks at the beginning and end of a person's exact words.
- Use a comma to separate the speaker's exact words from the rest of the sentence.
- Begin a quotation with a capital letter.
- Put the end mark before the last quotation mark.

Teach/Model

Have students find the passage on page 63 that begins *Henry pressed his nose. . . .* Have volunteers play the parts of Henry, Mr. and Mrs. Huggins, and Ribsy. Elicit that players read only the exact words their character says. Point out that a speaker's words are inside quotations marks. Then take the role of narrator, and begin the action. Have the class follow in their books, ending with *"That dog," sighed Mrs. Huggins.*

Write this simple quotation on the chalkboard: *Mr. Huggins said, "Things will be better next year."* Use it to make observations and generalizations on the use of quotation marks, capital letters, commas, and end marks. Remind students that a comma tells a reader to pause.

Display Transparency 4–13. Use the models to show how to punctuate dialogue. Then complete the first practice sentence together as a class. Call on two volunteers for each remaining sentence—one to add quotation marks, the other to mark the capital letter, comma, and end mark.

Practice/Apply

Literacy Activity Book page 36 focuses on quotation marks. Page 37 deals with capitalization and other punctuation in a quote.

Cooperative Learning: **Team Quotations** Remind students that at the end of the story Mr. Huggins tells Henry, ". . . I'll have a talk with you later." Have students work in teams to create that conversation. Each team writes a dialogue, using sentences with quotation marks, commas, and end

SKILL FINDER

Reading-Writing Workshop, p. 91E

INTERACTIVE LEARNING (continued)

marks. Ask teams to distribute their script so others can follow along with the play.

 Writing Application: Personal Narrative Suggest that students write a story about a barbecue, a neighbor, a bad day—anything from their own experience. Urge them to enliven their stories with quotations.

 Students' Writing Ask students to check their recent writing for correctly punctuated quotations.

Reteaching

Punctuating Dialogue

Cut a simple cartoon or comic strip from the newspaper to model how to write a conversation. Show the cartoon. Ask students to say the exact words each character says and tell how they know. (speech balloons) Choose a sentence from one speech balloon, and ask a volunteer to write it on the chalkboard. Elicit that quotation marks, like speech balloons, signal the speaker's exact words. Draw quotation marks in. Then step-by-step, add the "said" part and the comma. Check the end mark before the last quotation mark. Have students change the other balloons into quotations. Extend this activity by starting with cartoons they create together.

More Practice

Houghton Mifflin English Level 3
Workbook Plus, pp. 101–104
Reteaching Workbook, pp. 66–67

Write on Track
Write on Track SourceBook, pp. 21–24, 105, 110

Daily Language Practice
Focus Skills

Grammar: Punctuating Dialogue
Spelling: The VCCV Pattern

Each day write one sentence on the chalkboard. Have each student write the sentence correctly on a sheet of paper. Tell students to correct any errors in writing quotations as well as any misspelled words. Have students correct their own paper as a volunteer corrects the sentence on the chalkboard.

1. Mrs. Huggins said, "You had better not dirty my windo.
   Mrs. Huggins said, "You had better not dirty my **window**."

2. Mrs. Grumbie answered, We can invite your friends to dinner on Sonday."
   Mrs. Grumbie answered, **"**We can invite your friends to dinner on **Sunday**."

3. Robert asked, "will Ribsy chase the yelow cat after dinner?"
   Robert asked, "**W**ill Ribsy chase the **yellow** cat after dinner?"

4. Henry sighed "Nothing exciting had bettar happen again very soon."
   Henry sighed**,** "Nothing exciting had **better** happen again very soon."

5. Mr. Grumbie said, "The meat markit is closed on Sunday"
   Mr. Grumbie said, "The meat **market** is closed on Sunday**.**"

3

Instruct *and* Integrate

Communication Activities

Listening and Speaking

Making Apologies

Invite students to work in small groups to role-play a scene in which Henry apologizes to the Grumbies for Ribsy's bad behavior. Have students think about the characters and what they are like.

Challenge Encourage students to research how people in other countries make restitution when they do something wrong.

Listening to Dogs Howl

Urge interested students to listen to dog sounds in their neighborhoods. Then discuss the kinds of sounds dogs make when they are hurt, mad, happy, and tired. Suggest that students tape dog sounds in their neighborhoods and play the tapes for the class.

Selecting Music for Chase Scenes

Have students reread the chase scene in the story. If the scene were in a movie, what kind of music might be played during the chase? Explain that the "William Tell Overture" was used for *The Lone Ranger* TV series. If possible, share the music. Then challenge students to pick music from TV shows and movies that would be good in the background during the chase scene. If possible, play the songs while a student rereads the scene aloud.

Informal Assessment

Use the Guidelines for Making Apologies to evaluate students' presentations.

Additional Support:
- Review the guidelines.
- Have students work in pairs to practice.

Viewing

Watching a Video About Dogs

Let students view the video *Best Friends,* available from the American Kennel Club, Public Education Department, 51 Madison Avenue, New York, NY 10010. Discuss with students the characteristics of the different breeds of dogs in the video. Have students identify as many of the breeds as possible.

Resources
Best Friends from the American Kennel Club

Collecting Animal Comic Strips

Remind students that many comic strips have dog or other animal characters. Ask students to find and cut out comic strips with animals in them to bring to class. Compare the strips. Which one is the funniest? How are the strips alike? Different? Invite students to draw a new animal cartoon character they would like to see in a strip.

Observing Dogs in the Community

Invite students to take a survey of the dogs that live on their block. Students can focus on questions such as these:

- Which dogs are friendly and which are not?
- How many dogs were on leashes?
- How many dogs live outdoors? Inside?
- Were any of the dogs wearing special clothing?
- Which dog was their favorite? Why?

Cross-Curricular Activities

Bicycle Safety Rules
• Always wear a helmet.
• Ride single file and always in the same direction as traffic.
• Be aware of turning cars and opened doors.
• Check brake cables and tire pressure for safe riding.

Choices for Health

Riding It Right: Bicycle Safety

Review bicycle safety rules with students. Remind them that each year thousands of children are injured while riding their bicycles.

Suggest that students make handbooks and posters illustrating bike safety rules. Let some students plan a bike inspection day and invite a local police officer to assist in the safety program.

right turn

stop

left turn

Making Barbecue Sauce

Challenge Have students research the ingredients used for making barbecue sauce. Then have them calculate the amount of ingredients that would be necessary to fill up 8-ounce bottles for the whole class so each student could take one home. Remind students to keep ingredients simple to keep costs down and to allow a short preparation time. Have a group decide on what cooking utensils are necessary.

Science

Parts of a Bicycle

Have students observe the parts of a bicycle. Remind them that a bike is a complex machine made up of different kinds of simple machines: gears, levers, and wheels and axles. Other simple machines include screws, pulleys, and the inclined plane. Let students locate and name each of the simple machines on a bike. Ask some students to make a list of other complex machines in their homes and which simple machines go into each.

lever

screws

wheel and axle

pulley/gears

Math

Compiling Dog Statistics

Have students research the top ten most popular dog breeds in the United States this year and in the past. Ask students to compile statistics for each breed, such as height, weight, and length.

Challenge Invite some students to make a graph showing the number of times each breed has been in the top ten list. Which breed has been chosen most often?

Resource
American Kennel Club
Public Education
Department
51 Madison Avenue
New York, NY 10010

Portfolio Opportunity

Save safety posters and handbooks in a portfolio for class safety projects.

Get the Facts on Fast Foods

Activating Prior Knowledge

Chart Take an informal survey. Ask students how many hamburgers and servings of French fries they have eaten in the past week. Then ask students to identify the foods pictured on page 85. Work together to fill out a chart showing where these foods originate and how they are prepared.

How It Starts	How It Is Prepared	How It Ends
potatoes	Potatoes are cut, then fried. Sometimes salt is added.	French fries
onions	Onions are cut in circular pattern, then breaded and deep-fried.	onion rings
chicken	Chicken parts are separated, then breaded and deep-fried.	fried chicken

Tell students that the food in the third column is called *fast food* because the person buying it has to do little or no preparation.

Selection Vocabulary

Ask students to bring wrappers or food labels to class. Use them to discuss the following vocabulary:

calories: a unit of heat used for measuring the amount of heat energy in food

diet: the usual food and drink taken in by a person

protein: a substance that contains nitrogen, occurs in all living plant and animal tissue, and is necessary to life

fat: an oily substance found in plant and animal tissues

Building Background

Suggest that students survey the selection with partners. Be sure they understand that a *survey* is a preview in which they look at titles, pictures, illustrations, and captions.

Purpose Setting Suggest that students read to find out about fast foods and the part they play in our daily diets.

Get the Facts On

FAST FOODS

You're watching TV when a commercial comes on. A popular fast-food restaurant tempts you with one of its specials. The camera closes in on a big, juicy burger — two meat patties layered with bacon and oozing with melted cheese.

Your mouth starts watering. You suddenly feel hungry. How could anyone resist?

People buy fast foods for several reasons. They're tasty, quick, convenient, and don't cost too much. It's easy to pick up a sausage biscuit on your way to school or grab a cheeseburger when you don't have time for a regular meal.

But there are some important things you should know about fast food and the part it plays in your daily diet.

85

Background: FYI

Tell students that the canning and refrigeration of food only began in the United States in the 1800s. Ask them to speculate how people ate before then.

Explain that colonial and pioneer Americans used salt, spices, and pickling and brine mixtures to preserve their food. Later, the Civil War and the growth of cities made the need for easier means of preserving food more immediate.

By the 1950s, Americans were storing most of their food in refrigerators. The food had changed drastically too. Thanks to the growth of food technology, Americans could now enjoy all sorts of fruits and vegetables all year round.

Media Literacy

Ask students to tell about food commercials they have seen on TV recently. How often was the commercial about something other than the food itself?

Interact with Literature

MEETING INDIVIDUAL NEEDS
Students Acquiring English

Explain that *specials* are offers made only on certain occasions. Ask students how a restaurant might let a customer know about its specials. Tell them that *patties* are small, flat pieces of meat. Pantomime how to make a patty as you discuss how this word may have come about.

Discussion

Discuss the Food Guide Pyramid with students. Point out that the foods shown at the base of the pyramid are those we should eat the most of. Help students identify the foods pictured.

Work your way up the pyramid. Be sure students understand that dairy foods such as milk and yogurt contain some fats and sugars, and that protein foods such as meat and poultry also contain some fats; this explains why these foods are near the top of the pyramid.

Think About Words

Discuss how a reader might figure out what *pasta* means. Lead students to see that the process of elimination would work well—if a reader knows what bread, cereal, and rice look like, then he or she can easily find the pasta at the base of the pyramid.

Vocabulary

servings: portions of food

fillets: strips of boneless meat or fish

nuggets: small, compact portions

processed: prepared or treated by a special process: *Milk is processed to kill certain germs.*

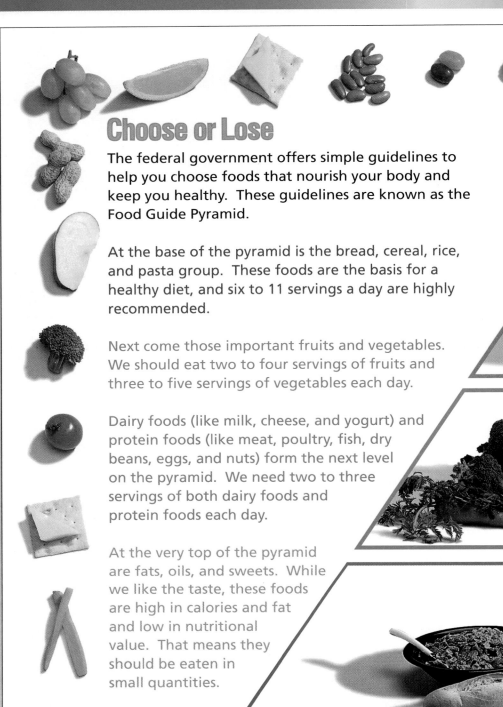

Choose or Lose

The federal government offers simple guidelines to help you choose foods that nourish your body and keep you healthy. These guidelines are known as the Food Guide Pyramid.

At the base of the pyramid is the bread, cereal, rice, and pasta group. These foods are the basis for a healthy diet, and six to 11 servings a day are highly recommended.

Next come those important fruits and vegetables. We should eat two to four servings of fruits and three to five servings of vegetables each day.

Dairy foods (like milk, cheese, and yogurt) and protein foods (like meat, poultry, fish, dry beans, eggs, and nuts) form the next level on the pyramid. We need two to three servings of both dairy foods and protein foods each day.

At the very top of the pyramid are fats, oils, and sweets. While we like the taste, these foods are high in calories and fat and low in nutritional value. That means they should be eaten in small quantities.

86

 Students Acquiring English

Be sure students know that to *nourish* means "to feed" and that *servings* are "portions" or "helpings." Ask them to share foods they enjoy that contain ingredients shown in the pyramid.

And that's where we run into a problem with fast foods. Many of the most popular are very high in fat. Deep-frying foods, like potatoes or onion rings, chicken pieces or chicken nuggets, and fish fillets adds fats. Adding cheese and processed meats, like bacon and sausage, also adds a lot of fat.

87

Instruct and Integrate

MINILESSON

Study Skill
Reading a Chart

Teach/Model

Explain that charts are a way of organizing a mass of information. Discuss how the chart on pages 86–87 organizes information. Lead them to see it organizes the information in two ways.

- *types of food:* It sorts food into categories.

- *recommended serving sizes:* It arranges categories according to the recommended daily serving sizes.

Bring in other examples of charts and have students look for examples in their textbooks. Discuss the ways information is presented.

Practice/Apply

Have students work together to think of ways of presenting the following information in a chart.

- Recommended daily calories for children ages 1–3: 1,300; ages 4–6: 1,800; ages 7–10: 2,000

- Calories per pound: broccoli, 69; grapes, 196; raw steak, 1,585

- Grams of fat in: an onion ring, 2.5; a tbsp. of mayonnaise, 11; a 4 oz. cheeseburger, 3

SKILL FINDER Full lesson, p. H4

Interact with Literature

Health Link

Explain that eating too much deep-fried food is unhealthy because the food absorbs much of the fat it is being boiled in.

Math Link

You may want to compare the number of calories in the following meal with the number in the fast-food meal described on page 88.

Food	Calories
2 slices white bread	140
½ cup tuna salad	175
8 oz. whole milk	150
1 banana	125

Science Link

Use a chart or diagram of the circulatory system to show students how blood travels in *arteries* through the human body. Discuss the importance of blood: It carries nutrients to all the cells of the body and it carries away waste products.

Also discuss the meaning of cholesterol. (a waxy substance found in animal foods) Explain that cholesterol can collect on the inner walls of the body's arteries (blood vessels) and cause them to harden.

Discussion

- Why do you think fast-food restaurants offer healthful foods?

- Do you think it is easy or hard to eat healthful foods? Why?

The Fault of Fat

The problem with the fat in fast foods is that it is usually *saturated* (sat´-ū-rāt-ed) — the kind of fat that can increase the cholesterol level in your blood. Many studies have shown that can cause arteries to clog and get in the way of normal blood flow.

What's more, many fast foods contain a great deal of sodium (salt) and sugar.

Let's say you order a quarter-pound cheeseburger, large order of fries, chocolate shake, and apple pie. That meal contains 1,560 calories, 17 teaspoons of fat, and 1,640 milligrams of sodium. This is far more than anyone needs — especially at one meal.

That fast-food meal contains more than half of the total calories needed for the whole day.

So, does this mean that we have to cut out all fast foods if we want to be healthy and fit?

Of course not. You don't have to cut out the fun, convenience, and taste of fast foods — if you learn to make smart choices. And many fast-food restaurants now offer more healthy foods.

Vocabulary

Use a chart like the following to discuss the different ways meat and fish can be cooked.

Term	Meaning
broil	cook under or over a heat source
grill	cook on a grill
roast	cook with dry heat, as in an oven
deep-fry	cook in hot oil or fat

Fast-Food Good News

You can choose healthy fast foods. Here are some tips:

- Stay away from regularly eating deep-fried foods. Choose broiled, grilled, or roasted sandwiches instead of breaded and deep-fried.
- Hold the sauces. Hidden fat and calories hide in the mayo, tartar sauce, and dressings.
- Watch your toppings. A good choice in fast food is a baked potato. But go easy on the cheese, butter, and sour cream.
- Stay away from processed meats. Shift to plain burgers, and try pizza with veggies like mushrooms, green peppers, and onions.
- Head for the salad bar. Load up on lettuce, spinach, tomatoes, carrots, broccoli, and mushrooms. Skip the croutons and bacon bits.
- Instead of a regular shake or sugary soda, order low-fat milk or fruit juice.
- End with a winner. Top off your meal with frozen yogurt.

   Get in the habit of healthy eating. It's one habit you'll never want to break!

89

Instruct *and* Integrate

Health Link

Suggest that students keep track of *all* the foods they eat for a period of one day. Then have them compare their lists with the recommendations on the Food Guide Pyramid. Encourage students to identify any food groups they may need to pay more attention to in the future.

Science Link

Demonstrate for students a simple way to test foods for fat. Cut a few squares from a brown paper bag. Then rub a piece of food on a square of paper, and let the paper dry. Hold the paper up to a source of light (such as a light bulb). The light will show through if fat is present. Encourage students to work in small groups to perform the test on a few common foods (such as a slice of apple or banana, a hot dog, a wedge of cheese).

🏠 Home Connection

Suggest that students make copies of the Food Guide Pyramid to share with their families. They can make pyramids from heavy construction paper and then paste onto the appropriate sections several pictures of foods clipped from magazines. Or, they can draw their own food pictures.

Interact *with* Literature

📖 MEETING INDIVIDUAL NEEDS Students Acquiring English

Point out that *mayo* is short for mayonnaise; *veggie*, for vegetable. Also discuss the meanings of these idiomatic expressions: *hold the sauce, watch your toppings, head for the salad bar,* and *breaking a habit.*

Reading-Writing Workshop

A Research Report

About the Workshop

This workshop includes suggestions and activities to help you guide students to write research reports. Workshop minilessons focus on topic sentences, supporting details, and introductions and conclusions. These elements form the assessment criteria at the end of the workshop.

Recommendations:

- Consider linking report writing to a class theme. Finding resources, targeting questions, and directing discussions is more manageable.

- Assemble resource materials that students can read from home, school, and community libraries to make information easily accessible. Enlist the help of parents.

  Students Acquiring English Provide resources in these students' primary languages, if possible.

Connecting to "Get the Facts on Fast Foods"

Define *facts*, and then discuss which facts students found most surprising.

Introducing the Student Model

Ask students what they know about oranges. Invite them to read the report third grader Cristina Vela wrote for her social studies class. Discuss the questions on page 91.

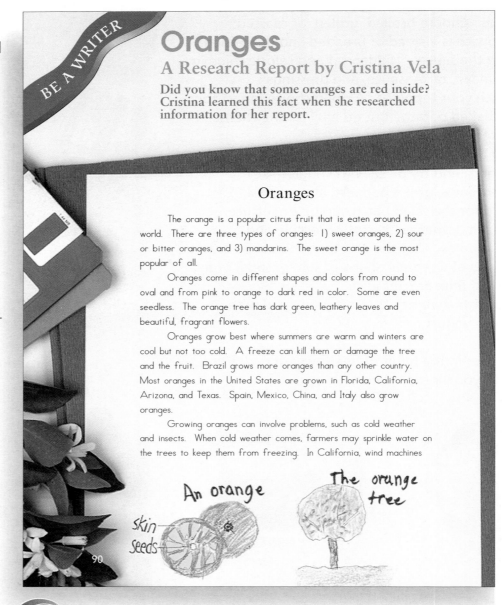

BE A WRITER

Oranges

A Research Report by Cristina Vela

Did you know that some oranges are red inside? Cristina learned this fact when she researched information for her report.

Oranges

The orange is a popular citrus fruit that is eaten around the world. There are three types of oranges: 1) sweet oranges, 2) sour or bitter oranges, and 3) mandarins. The sweet orange is the most popular of all.

Oranges come in different shapes and colors from round to oval and from pink to orange to dark red in color. Some are even seedless. The orange tree has dark green, leathery leaves and beautiful, fragrant flowers.

Oranges grow best where summers are warm and winters are cool but not too cold. A freeze can kill them or damage the tree and the fruit. Brazil grows more oranges than any other country. Most oranges in the United States are grown in Florida, California, Arizona, and Texas. Spain, Mexico, China, and Italy also grow oranges.

Growing oranges can involve problems, such as cold weather and insects. When cold weather comes, farmers may sprinkle water on the trees to keep them from freezing. In California, wind machines

An orange
skin
seeds

The orange tree

90

SKILL FINDER

PREWRITING/DRAFTING

Workshop Minilessons	Theme Resources
• Topic Sentences, p. 91A	*Writing*
• Supporting Details, p. 91B	• Avoiding Stringy Sentences, p. 84D
• Introductions and Conclusions, p. 91C	
Resource Lessons	
• Taking Notes, p. H5	
• Library: Nonfiction Books, p. H6	

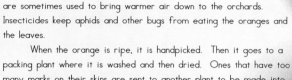

are sometimes used to bring warmer air down to the orchards. Insecticides keep aphids and other bugs from eating the oranges and the leaves.

When the orange is ripe, it is handpicked. Then it goes to a packing plant where it is washed and then dried. Ones that have too many marks on their skins are sent to another plant to be made into juice. The very best oranges are waxed and dried again. Then they pass through machines that stamp them and separate them by size. Finally, they are put into boxes.

It takes a lot of work to produce the oranges that people like to eat.

Bibliography

"Orange." Britannica Junior Encyclopedia. 1979 ed.

"Orange." The World Book Encyclopedia. 1993 ed.

Rogow, Zack. Oranges. New York: Orchard, 1988.

Silverstein, Alvin and Virginia B. Oranges: All About Them. Englewood Cliffs: Prentice, 1975.

Cristina Vela
E. A. Jones Elementary School
Missouri City, Texas

Cristina wrote this report in her third grade social studies class. She also likes to write stories. Cristina enjoys reading, math, and social studies. For fun she likes to play with her younger brother and watch television. Someday Cristina wants to be a teacher.

91

SKILL
FINDER

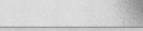

PROOFREADING

Theme Resources

Grammar

- Helping Verbs, pp. 37K–37L
- Irregular Verbs, pp. 58J–58K
- Punctuating Dialogue, pp. 84J–84K
- Commas in a Series, pp. 121K–121L

Theme Resources

Spelling

- The First Sound in *city* and *just*, p. 37J
- Words Ending with *er* or *le*, p. 58I
- The VCCV Pattern, p. 84I
- Words Often Misspelled, p. 91E
- Homophones, p. 121J

Discussing the Model

Reading and Responding

- What facts did you learn about oranges that you didn't know?
- What do you like about this report?

Reading As a Writer

- Why is the first sentence a good way to begin? (It introduces the topic.)
- What is each paragraph about? (kinds of oranges, appearance, where grown, growing problems, how picked and shipped)
- What is the fourth paragraph about? (problems growing oranges) Which sentence tells you what the paragraph is about? (first)
- What supporting facts are given about problems caused by cold weather? (trees might freeze; farmers sprinkle water on them or use wind machines to bring warm air) by insects? (eat oranges and leaves; farmers use insecticides)
- Why is the last sentence a good ending? (sums up the report)

Characteristics of Reports

Help students list these characteristics:

- *Purpose*: to present facts
- Topic sentences with supporting details
- An introduction and a conclusion

Reading-Writing Workshop (continued)
A Research Report

Topic Sentences

Resource: Anthology pp. 85–89

- Review the *topic* of "Get the Facts on Fast Foods." (facts about fast foods) Be sure students understand that the whole article is about that one topic.

- Invite a volunteer to read aloud the third paragraph on page 85. Ask students what the paragraph is about. (why people buy fast foods) Elicit that this is the *main idea* of the paragraph.

- Ask students to identify the sentence that states that main idea. (*People buy fast foods for several reasons.*) Explain that this sentence is a *topic sentence* and all other sentences in the paragraph give information about the main idea. Point out that the topic sentence is often the first sentence so that the reader will know what the paragraph will be about.

- Invite students to suggest topic sentences for this paragraph:

  Most of the world peanut crop is used to make peanut oil. In the U.S., most peanuts are eaten as peanut butter. Peanuts are also used for animal feed, soap, and plastics. (Sample: Peanuts have many different uses.)

Warm-up

Shared Writing

Write the question and notes below on the chalkboard.

What does a pineapple plant look like?	
grows 2 to 3 feet tall	blue-green, sword-shaped leaves
greenish-orange, yellowish-green, or dark green outer skin of fruit	crown—the group of small leaves at the top of the fruit
sign of welcome	Thailand grows the most

Help the class select which notes to use to answer the question. (Notes about Thailand and being a sign of welcome should be omitted.) Work with students to write a paragraph with a topic sentence and supporting details.

Prewriting

LAB, pp. 38–39

Choose a Report Topic

Students list topic ideas as a class, and then choose individual topics.

- **List and Discuss** As a class, create a list of topics related to a theme of study. Display the list, and add to it over a few days. Allow "incubation time" for research ideas to take hold. Discuss what information students might research about each topic.

- **Think** Have each student select two or three topics and ask these questions about each one: Why am I interested in this topic? What do I want to find out? Can I find enough facts?

Help with Topics

Chart

To help them select or narrow a research topic, have students make K-W-L charts. Encourage students to consider several topics that interest them. Have students fill in the last column when they finish their reports.

What I Know	What I Want to Know	What I Learned
Topic potatoes	How are they grown?	
round or oval shaped brown, white, red		

Prewriting *(continued)*

Plan the Report

Students research facts and plan their report.

- **Write Questions** Have students use the questions from their K-W-L charts to focus their research. Help them adjust their questions if they cannot find enough facts or if they become interested in other facts.
- **Take Notes** Remind students to write only key words.

Help with Planning

Research Logs

Provide stapled booklets of lined paper with construction paper covers. Students write their questions on separate pages. As they do their research, they write notes that answer the questions and also record their sources.

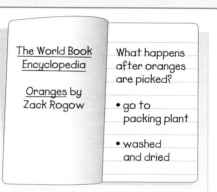

The World Book Encyclopedia

Oranges by Zack Rogow

What happens after oranges are picked?

- go to packing plant
- washed and dried

Literacy Activity Book, p. 38

What Do I Want to Learn About?

Write the theme your class has chosen to research.

Our theme is _____

If your class has not chosen a theme, do any of these themes interest you? Write a theme you want to research on the line above.

Native Americans	stars and planets	Australian animals
sports	weather	American heroes
insects		and heroines

In the boxes, list topics about your theme that you would like to research.

Ask yourself these questions about each topic.

What do I want to find out?

Why am I interested in this topic?

Can I find enough facts?

Which topics would you most like to research? Circle them.

38 What's Cooking?

Literacy Activity Book, p. 39

Ask Some Questions

Write what you know about two topics you want to research. Next, write questions you would like to answer about each one. Think about each topic. Then put a check mark next to the one you will research. (You will fill in the last column later.)

What I **K**now	What I **W**ant to Know	What I **L**earned
Topic:		
Topic:		

What's Cooking? 39

Supporting Details

Resource: Anthology pp. 85–89, 90–91

- Recall with students the main idea of the third paragraph on page 85: why people buy fast foods. Ask students what details are given that tell why people buy fast foods. *(tasty, quick, convenient, don't cost too much)* Remind students that details that support the main idea are called *supporting details.* Emphasize that only those supporting details that tell about the main idea of the paragraph should be included in that paragraph.

- Have students reread the paragraph on page 87 and identify the topic sentence, main idea, and supporting details. (*main idea:* fast foods are high in fat; *topic sentence:* second sentence; *supporting details:* deep-fried foods add fat; cheese and processed meats add fat)

- Have students look at Cristina's report on pages 90–91. Ask students if she could have added these facts to any paragraphs:

  People have grown oranges for over 4000 years. (no, would need new paragraph)

  Bitter oranges are used to make jam and perfume. (yes, first paragraph)

Reading-Writing Workshop *(continued)*
A Research Report

M I N I L E S S O N

Introductions and Conclusions

Resource: Anthology pp. 85–89, 90–91

- Read aloud page 85 of "Get the Facts on Fast Foods." Discuss with students why it catches their interest. (describes a familiar situation; makes them wonder what they should know about fast food) Explain that an *introduction* presents the topic and makes the reader want to read on.

- Have students reread the first sentence of Cristina's report on page 90. Discuss with them how it introduces her topic by giving some general information about oranges.

- Explain that a report also needs an ending, or *conclusion*. Review with students the last sentences on pages 89 and 91. Elicit that a conclusion finishes the report by summing up a main idea. It might also show the writer's new understanding about the topic, as in Cristina's conclusion.

Self-Assessment

Have students revise their reports, using the Revising Checklist.

Drafting

Students use their questions and notes to help them write their drafts.

Help with Drafting

Drafting Strategy

Students might find it easier to write the body of the report first.

Topic Sentences

Have students use their questions as topic sentences, or show them how to turn their questions into topic sentences. Explain that they should look at their notes for each question to find the main idea.

Coding Details

Suggest that students use color codes to group details.

What are the problems in growing oranges?

- bugs eat leaves
- freezing temperatures
- insecticides used

research question	topic sentence
Where do oranges grow?	Where do oranges grow?
	or
	Oranges grow best where summers are warm and winters are cool but not too cold.

Revising

LAB, p. 40

Students revise their drafts and discuss them in writing conferences.

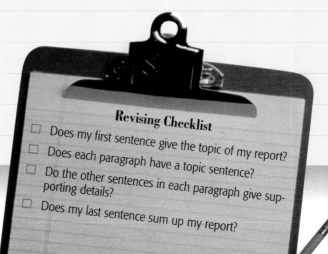

Revising Checklist

☐ Does my first sentence give the topic of my report?

☐ Does each paragraph have a topic sentence?

☐ Do the other sentences in each paragraph give supporting details?

☐ Does my last sentence sum up my report?

Revising (continued)

Writing Conference

Cooperative Learning Have students discuss their reports with you or one or more classmates. They can use the Questions for a Writing Conference to guide the discussion.

Questions for a Writing Conference

- Which facts are the most interesting?
- What other facts could be added?
- Are any parts unclear? Why?
- Are any facts out of place? Where should they go?
- Does the first sentence tell the topic?
- Does the last sentence finish the report?

Help with Revising

Revising Strategies

TECH TIPS Students can boldface each topic sentence and underline each sentence that supports the topic sentence.

Suggest that students do these things in each paragraph.

- Underline each topic sentence.
- Put a check mark next to each sentence that supports the topic sentence.
- Put an X next to any sentence that does not support the topic sentence.

Then have them do these things.

- Write a topic sentence for any paragraph that needs one.
- Move sentences that do not belong to other paragraphs or take them out.
- Add more supporting details, if necessary.

Additional Questions for Writing Conferences

These questions may be useful during teacher-student conferences.

- Tell me more about [main idea]. Can you add those facts?
- What is this paragraph about? Let's brainstorm a topic sentence together.
- What does [word] mean? Can you include its meaning?
- [This fact] does not seem right. Let's check your notes and your source again.
- What will I learn from your report? Can you use those ideas in your introduction?
- What did you learn? Can you use that information to conclude your report?

Students can use The Learning Company's new elementary writing center to write the first drafts of their reports.

Literacy Activity Book, p. 40

Take Another Look

Read your report to yourself. Then revise your report.

Revising Checklist

Ask yourself these questions about your research report.

☐ Does my first sentence give the topic of my report?
☐ Does each paragraph have a topic sentence?
☐ Do the other sentences in each paragraph give supporting details?
☐ Does my last sentence sum up my report?

Questions for a Writing Conference

Use these questions to help you discuss your report with a classmate.

- Which facts are the most interesting?
- What other facts could be added?
- Are any parts unclear? Why?
- Are any facts out of place? Where should they go?
- Does the first sentence tell the topic?
- Does the last sentence finish the report?

My Notes

I can make my report better by _____

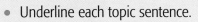

40 What's Cooking?

Reading-Writing Workshop (continued)
A Research Report

 Students can use the newsletter format in **The Learning Company's Ultimate Writing & Creativity Center** to publish their reports.

Proofreading

Students proofread their reports, using the Proofreading Checklist and the proofreading marks in the Handbook of the *Literacy Activity Book*. Encourage them to make as many changes on their own as they can.

Grammar/ Spelling Connections

- **Checking Verbs and Commas** Remind students to check that they have used helping verbs and irregular verbs correctly. Ask them to double-check that they have used commas correctly with items in a series. *pp. 37K–37L, 58J–58K, 84J–84K, 121K–121L*

- **Spelling** Have students double-check that they have correctly spelled words with the spelling principles they have studied in this theme as well as the Words Often Misspelled. *pp. 37J, 58I, 84I, 91E, 121J*

Publishing and Sharing

Students title their reports, choose a way to share them, and make neat final copies.

Ideas for Publishing and Sharing

Poster

Students can create posters that present their information visually.

- Students determine the best way to illustrate information in the report: a picture? a map? a graph? a chart?

- They draw rough layouts showing where the text and illustrations will go. Explain that the arrangement usually is top to bottom and left to right.

- They place their typed or handwritten paragraphs on the poster and make adjustments before attaching.

- They add their illustrations.

Materials
- poster board
- magazines
- reference materials (atlas; models of charts, graphs)
- scissors
- markers, pens, crayons
- glue

M I N I L E S S O N

Spelling
Words Often Misspelled

Write the Spelling Words on the board, say them, and have students repeat them. Work with students to identify the part of each word that is likely to be misspelled.

Spelling Words

girl	was	our
they	into	new
want	who	

Challenge Words

wouldn't	through
world	while

Additional Spelling Words

would	a lot
could	buy

S E E

5-Day Planner

Spelling Plan p. 84I

Spelling Assessment

Pretest

1. Is that <u>girl</u> picking oranges?
2. Are <u>they</u> ripe?
3. Do you <u>want</u> one?
4. It <u>was</u> juicy!
5. The washed oranges are put <u>into</u> boxes.
6. Do you know <u>who</u> grows oranges?
7. This is <u>our</u> orange grove.
8. We planted <u>new</u> orange trees.

Test Use the Pretest sentences.

Challenge Words

9. Oranges are eaten around the <u>world</u>.
10. My brother <u>wouldn't</u> eat fruit.
11. Please wait <u>while</u> I peel this orange.
12. Let's walk <u>through</u> the orchard.

Challenge Words Practice Have students write the Challenge Words in ABC order and then write a sentence for each word.

Literacy Activity Book

Spelling Practice: pp. 137–138
Take-Home Word Lists: pp. 173–174

More Ideas for Publishing and Sharing

Dioramas

Students can create dioramas that show information in their reports. Challenge students to work with larger boxes than shoe boxes and to use a wide variety of materials.

Videotaping

Videotape students presenting their reports. Use the videotape as a teaching tool the next time students prepare for an oral presentation.

Reflecting/Self-Assessment

Use the Self-Assessment questions, or others of your own, to help your students reflect on and evaluate their experience writing a report. Students can discuss their thoughts or share them in writing.

Evaluating Writing

Use the criteria below to evaluate students' reports.

Criteria for Evaluating Research Reports

- The report includes several paragraphs with topic sentences and supporting details.
- An introduction presents the topic.
- A conclusion sums up and closes the report.

Self-Assessment

- Did you learn what you wanted to know?
- What parts of your report do you think are the best? Explain.
- What task was most difficult? finding the facts? putting the facts together? writing the report?
- What did you enjoy about writing a report?
- What might you do differently the next time you write a report?

Portfolio Opportunity

- Save students' final copies to show their understanding of writing research reports.
- Save students' Research Logs and drafts to show their application of study skills as well as their use of the writing process.
- Take photos of accompanying projects or include the videotape of students' oral presentation.

Sample Scoring Rubric

1	2	3	4
This paper is not a research report, or it meets the criteria only minimally. There is one paragraph with little factual content.	The report has a clear topic and includes facts about it, but the report is somewhat disorganized and unclear. Most paragraphs do not have a clear topic sentence, and supporting details are not consistently organized by main idea.	The report includes paragraphs with topic sentences and supporting details; more details would be helpful. There is a simplistic introduction (*My paper is about . . .*) and conclusion. Significant usage, mechanics, and spelling errors might keep it from rating a 4.	The report successfully meets all the evaluation criteria with few usage, mechanics, and spelling errors. Paragraphs are well-organized, with well-written topic sentences and supporting details and an interesting introduction and conclusion.

SELECTION:
Chicken Sunday

by Patricia Polacco

Other Books by the Author
Firetalking
Just Plain Fancy
The Keeping Quilt
Thunder Cake

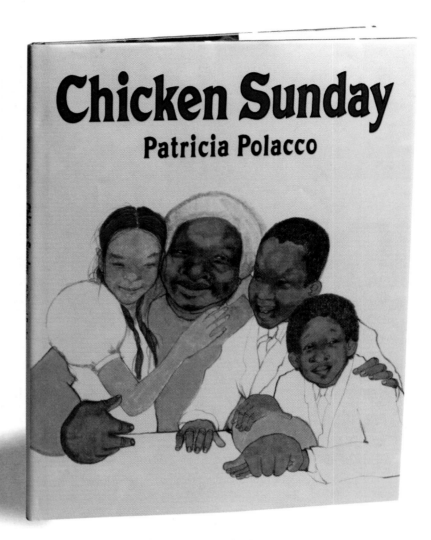

- **Notable Children's Trade Book in the Field of Social Studies**
- **Booklist Editors' Choice**

Selection Summary

Tricia and her neighbors Stewart and Winston share a love for the boys' grandmother. Longing to buy Miss Eula a hat, the children decide to ask Mr. Kodinski, who owns the hat shop, if they can do chores to earn money. But when they arrive at his shop, some older boys have just thrown eggs at his door, and Mr. Kodinski blames them. To win his trust, they bring Mr. Kodinski Ukrainian eggs they have decorated. Reminded of his homeland, Mr. Kodinski is touched. Why not sell your eggs in my shop? he says. Soon the children have earned enough money for the hat—but Mr. Kodinski gives it to them as a gift. On Easter, Miss Eula wears her new hat to church.

Lesson Planning Guide

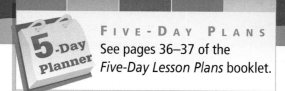

FIVE-DAY PLANS
See pages 36–37 of the
Five-Day Lesson Plans booklet.

	Skill/Strategy Instruction	Meeting Individual Needs	Lesson Resources
1 Introduce *the* Literature *Pacing: 1 day*	**Preparing to Read and Write** Prior Knowledge/Building Background, 91I **Selection Vocabulary,** 91J • solemn • decent • glared • sputtered • glowered • apologized **Spelling Pretest,** 121J • hear • here • to • two • too • there • their • they're	**Support in Advance,** 91I **Students Acquiring English,** 91I **Other Choices for Building Background,** 91I **Spelling Challenge Words,** 121J • die • dye • hole • whole	*Literacy Activity Book,* Selection Vocabulary, p. 41 **Transparency:** Selection Vocabulary, 4–14 **Great Start** CD-ROM software, "What's Cooking?" CD
2 Interact *with* Literature *Pacing: 1–3 days*	**Reading Strategies** Evaluate, 94, 114 Summarize, 94, 102, 112 Think About Words, 104 **Minilessons** Writer's Craft: Poetic Language, 95 Author's Viewpoint, 97 ✓ Problem Solving/Decision Making, 99 Sequence of Events, 117	**Choices for Reading,** 94 **Guided Reading,** 94 Comprehension/Critical Thinking, 100, 106, 120 **Students Acquiring English,** 95, 97, 99, 100, 102, 105, 107, 108, 111, 112, 114, 116, 120, 121 **Extra Support,** 94, 106 **Challenge,** 98	**Reading-Writing Workshop,** Research Report, 90–91F *Literacy Activity Book,* Selection Connections, p. 2; Comprehension Check, p. 43 **Audio Tape** for What's Cooking?: *Chicken Sunday* The Learning Company's Ultimate Writing & Creativity Center software
3 Instruct *and* Integrate *Pacing: 1–3 days*	✓ **Comprehension:** Problem Solving/Decision Making, 121C **Writing:** Poem, 121E ✓ **Word Skills and Strategies:** Homophones, 121G Phonics: Phonograms, 121H **Building Vocabulary:** Vocabulary Activities, 121I ✓ **Spelling:** Homophones, 121J ✓ **Grammar:** Commas in a Series, 121K–121L **Communication Activities:** Listening and Speaking, 121M; Viewing, 121N **Cross-Curricular Activities:** Art, 121O; Science, 121P; Math, 121P	**Reteaching:** Problem Solving/ Decision Making, 121D **Activity Choices:** Poem, Character Sketch, Essay, 121F **Reteaching:** Homophones, 121H **Activity Choices:** "Wonderful" Words, Word Family for *decorate,* Words for Hats, 121I **Challenge Words Practice,** 121J **Reteaching:** Commas in a Series, 121L **Activity Choices:** Listening and Speaking, 121M; Viewing, 121N **Activity Choices:** Art, 121O; Science, 121P; Math, 121P	**Watch Me Read** *Mother's Day Special* **Reading-Writing Workshop,** Research Report, 90–91F **Transparencies:** Comprehension, 4–15; Writing, 4–16; Grammar, 4–17 *Literacy Activity Book,* Comprehension, p. 44; Writing Skills, p. 45; Word Skills, p. 46; Building Vocabulary, p. 47; Spelling, pp. 48–49; Grammar, pp. 50–51 **Spelling Spree** CD-ROM The Learning Company's Ultimate Writing & Creativity Center software **Audio Tape** for What's Cooking?: *Chicken Sunday*

✓ *Indicates Tested Skills. See page 16F for assessment options.*

1

Introduce *the* Literature

Preparing to Read and Write

Support in Advance

Use this activity with students who need extra support before participating in the whole-class activity.

Defining Gifts Use these prompts to open a discussion about gifts and presents:

- What do you think makes a nice gift?

- Is a gift necessarily an object, or can a gift be an action?

- Is a gift something you buy, or can a gift be homemade?

Management Tip Suggest that other students spend a few minutes writing in their journals about special times they have spent with friends or neighbors.

Students Acquiring English
Easter Customs Depending on students' backgrounds, you may need to introduce customs associated with Easter. Explain that on Easter Sunday some people:

- dye Easter eggs

- receive Easter baskets

- wear new clothes (including Easter bonnets) to church

Ask students if they use eggs for other kinds of celebrations in their native countries.

Great Start
For students needing extra support with key concepts and vocabulary, use the "What's Cooking?" CD.

Prior Knowledge/Building Background

Key Concept
Gift Giving

Ask students to discuss gifts they have given to someone. Encourage them to tell what the gift was, how they knew the person wanted this thing, and how they felt about giving the gift. Map responses.

```
                        GIFTS
     who you give them to          how you feel when you
                                        give them
              why you give them
```

Then have students imagine that they've had a misunderstanding with someone. What can they do to change this person's feelings about them? Is there any kind of gift they can give?

Other Choices for Building Background

Penny Power

Challenge Ask students to quick-write about times when they needed to earn extra money to buy something—either for themselves or as a gift for someone else.

Meet the Characters

Students Acquiring English Use page 93 to introduce young Patricia Polacco (who was called Tricia as a child), the Washington boys (Stewart and Winston), and their grandmother (Eula Mae Walker). Tell students that this is a story told in the first person by the author.

Pysanky Eggs

Extra Support Share with students the book *Rechenka's Eggs,* also by Patricia Polacco. This story, set in Moskva (Old Moscow), will familiarize students with the tradition of *Pysanky* (Ukrainian-style Easter eggs)—without giving away what happens in *Chicken Sunday.*

Selection Vocabulary

Key Words

solemn

decent

glared

sputtered

glowered

apologized

Display Transparency 4–14 and have students read the dialogue at the top silently. Then have volunteers read it aloud. After discussing the meaning of each underlined word, have students group the words into the categories at the bottom of the transparency. Suggest that students add other words to the categories as they read the story.

words about being angry	
words about being serious	
words about being sorry	
words about being confused	

Vocabulary Practice Have students work in small groups to complete *Literacy Activity Book* page 41.

Spelling
You may want to give the Spelling Pretest on page 121J before students read the selection.

Daily Language Practice
Use the activities on page 121L as a daily practice of the spelling and grammar skills taught with this selection.

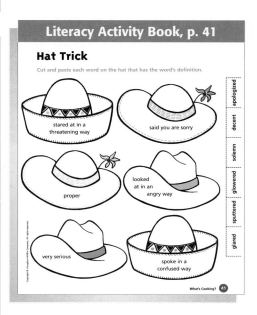

Transparency 4–14

Saying You're Sorry

"Who broke this vase?" asked Mother. She was angry. She glared at us children.

"I didn't," stammered Mark.

"And I didn't," sputtered Amy.

"What about you, Tom?" Mother asked. She glowered at me.

"I promise I did not," I said in my most solemn voice.

Just then our new puppy crawled out from under a chair. In her mouth was a big red bow.

Mother apologized. "I'm sorry," she said. "I should have known. You are all decent children. If you had broken the vase, you would have told me so."

words about being angry	
words about being serious	
words about being sorry	
words about being confused	

Social Studies

Teacher FactFile
Ukrainian *Pysanky* Eggs

Pysanky is a craft that has been passed down from generation to generation of Ukrainians. Pysanky artists use a writing instrument called a *kistka,* as well as beeswax, a lighted candle, and brilliant dyes to decorate their eggs, which are given as Easter gifts. Their intricate designs are based on symbols. (The fish, cross, triangle, and eight-pointed star, for example, are symbols associated with Christ. The egg itself is a symbol of new life.)

Literacy Activity Book, p. 41

Hat Trick

Cut and paste each word on the hat that has the word's definition.

stared at in a threatening way

said you are sorry

proper

looked at in an angry way

very serious

spoke in a confused way

apologized · decent · solemn · glowered · sputtered · glared

What's Cooking? 41

Interact *with* Literature

More About the Author-Illustrator

Patricia Polacco

Patricia Polacco's fondest memories growing up are of sitting in front of the fireplace listening to her family "tell glorious stories about the past." It was from them that she learned the art of storytelling. But while she felt embraced by a warm family life, school was isolating. Polacco struggled with dyslexia, and the problems it caused her in reading and math set her apart from the other children. However, her artistic talent gave her an oasis of self-confidence.

Today Polacco has written and illustrated more than a dozen children's books. Many of her best-loved books are based on her family. *The Keeping Quilt* is the story of how her mother's family preserved their Russian-Jewish heritage after emigrating to the United States. Polacco still has the treasured heirloom, the "keeping quilt," which she brings out on special occasions. *Thunder Cake* recalls how young Polacco overcame her fear of thunder with help from her grandmother—her *babushka*.

In all her stories, Polacco conveys a strong appreciation for family, community, and especially for older people. "If I have a mission," she says, "it's to say that old people have value; that we should listen to them."

Meet Patricia Polacco

As a young girl, Patricia Polacco spent many evenings in front of the fireplace, popping corn and listening to her grandmother's stories. Her family called this "firetalking."

Today Polacco writes and illustrates her own stories, many of which are based on family memories. *Chicken Sunday* is about her friendship with Stewart and Winston, two neighborhood boys who are still her best friends today.

On this page, Patricia Polacco in her art studio. **At right**, the finished book with original artwork from the story.

92

93

Visual Literacy

Draw students' attention to the finished piece of artwork shown under the cover of *Chicken Sunday*. Suggest that students keep an eye out for the illustration, which appears later in the story (pages 110–111).

Interact *with* Literature

HATS BY

94

Reading Strategies

▶ **Evaluate**
Summarize

Student Application Ask students what reading strategies they think they will use to read *Chicken Sunday*. Have volunteers model how they would use these strategies. If necessary, suggest that students summarize as they read and evaluate what the author is trying to say through this story.

Predicting/Purpose Setting

Have students set their own purposes for reading and make predictions about what they are going to read. Suggest that they read to find answers to their questions.

Choices for Reading

Independent Reading	**Cooperative Reading**
Guided Reading	**Teacher Read Aloud**

Guided Reading

Have students who are using the Guided Reading option read to the end of page 101 to see if they find answers to their purpose-setting questions. Questions for checking comprehension can be found on page 100.

QuickREFERENCE

Journal

Strategies Have students apply reading strategies by writing

- any questions they have
- how the story is affecting them
- any predictions they make

Extra Support

First Person Ask students who the narrator of the story is. As necessary, remind them that the author, Patricia Polacco, is telling this story about her childhood.

Visual Literacy

Viewpoint Discuss the interesting viewpoint of the illustration on pages 94–95: The reader is inside the hat shop looking out. Ask students to point out details that tell them this. (palms pressed against the "glass"; the backward lettering of the store name)

Stewart and Winston were my neighbors. They were my brothers by a <u>solemn</u> ceremony we had performed in their backyard one summer. They weren't the same religion as I was. They were Baptists. Their gramma, Eula Mae Walker, was my gramma now. My babushka had died two summers before.

Sometimes my mother let me go to church on Sunday with them. How we loved to hear Miss Eula sing. She had a voice like slow thunder and sweet rain.

We'd walk to church and back. She'd take my hand as we crossed College Avenue. "Even though we've been churchin' up like <u>decent</u> folks ought to," she'd say, "I don't want you to step in front of one of those too fast cars. You'll be as flat as a hen's tongue." She squeezed my hand.

When we passed Mr. Kodinski's hat shop, Miss Eula would always stop and look in the window at the wonderful hats. Then she'd sigh and we'd walk on.

95

MINILESSON

Writer's Craft
Poetic Language

Teach/Model

Ask students to find the words telling what Miss Eula's voice sounded like when she sang. (*like slow thunder and sweet rain*) Encourage them to tell how singing could be like thunder. Is thunder always loud (and scary)? How could singing be like rain? Have volunteers demonstrate.

Remind students that this kind of comparison is called a *simile*. Discuss how using similes and other devices can add to the poetic language of a story:

- comparisons using *like* or *as* (simile): *flat as a hen's tongue*

- repetition of beginning sounds (alliteration): *solemn ceremony*

- words with the same last sound (rhyme)

- use of human characteristics to describe something that is not human (personification)

Practice/Apply

Encourage students to look and listen for other examples of poetic language in the story. Students might revise their own writing to incorporate these devices.

SKILL FINDER

Writing Activities: Write a Poem, p. 121F

Reading-Writing Workshop, pp. 90–91F

Students Acquiring English

Slang Ask volunteers who know what a church is to guess what the phrase *churchin' up* might mean. ("going to church") Help students see that they can often figure out unfamiliar words by looking for word parts they do know.

Vocabulary

Develop the meaning of *ceremony* by giving examples: wedding, bar mitzvah, baptism. Ask students to suggest others. Point out that the children performed a ceremony they had made up, not a real one.

★★★ Multicultural Link

Grandparents Ask students what they call their grandparents. Compare with *gramma* and *babushka*, a word that also refers to a scarf worn by Russian women. On page 107, the author also calls her grandmother *bubbie*, for short.

Interact *with* Literature

96

QuickREFERENCE

Art Link

Actual photographs of family and friends often find their way into Patricia Polacco's books. Ask who students think the people are in the photos on page 96. Have them find another illustration that includes a photograph. (page 102) Polacco creates these images by drawing a layout in pencil first, adding color with markers and acrylic paints, and then gluing on cutout photographs. Students might enjoy trying this technique in their own artwork.

We called those Sundays "Chicken Sundays" because Miss Eula almost always fried chicken for dinner. There'd be collard greens with bacon, a big pot of hoppin' john, corn on the cob, and fried spoon bread.

One Sunday at the table we watched her paper fan flutter back and forth, pulling moist chicken-fried air along with it. She took a deep breath. Her skin glowed as she smiled. Then she told us something we already knew. "That Easter bonnet in Mr. Kodinski's window is the most beautiful I ever did see," she said thoughtfully.

The three of us exchanged looks. We wanted to get her that hat more than anything in the world.

97

Author's Viewpoint

REVIEW & MAINTAIN

Teach/Model

Remind students that an author's viewpoint is what the author thinks or feels about the subject he or she is writing about. Students should recall that *Chicken Sunday* is a true story about Patricia Polacco's childhood. How does Polacco feel about Stewart and Winston? Discuss the details on pages 95 and 97 that reveal her viewpoint toward them.

Stewart and Winston
• She performed a solemn ceremony with them.
• She went to church with them.
• She ate Sunday dinner with them.

Students should conclude that the author loved the boys like brothers and enjoyed spending time with them.

Practice/Apply

Have students work with a partner to analyze the author's feelings toward Miss Eula.

Miss Eula
• She loved to hear Miss Eula sing.
• She referred to Miss Eula as her *gramma*.
• She wanted to buy Miss Eula a new hat.

SKILL FINDER

Full lesson/Reteaching, Theme 2, pp. 180B–180C

Minilessons, Theme 2, pp. 153, 205

Health Link

Food *Collard greens* are a leafy green vegetable rich in calcium and vitamin A. *Hoppin' john* is made from black-eyed peas cooked with onions and pigs' knuckles. *Spoon bread* is made from corn meal, eggs, and buttermilk.

Students Acquiring English

Word Meaning Have students find Miss Eula's paper fan in the illustration. Ask how *fluttering* it could "pull" chicken-fried air along with it. Ask two or more volunteers to demonstrate the meaning of *the three of us exchanged looks.*

★★★ Multicultural Link

Is Sunday dinner an important custom in any students' families? Are there any other occasions on which their families celebrate by eating a special meal together? Invite students to share the importance of special dinners in their culture.

Interact
with
Literature

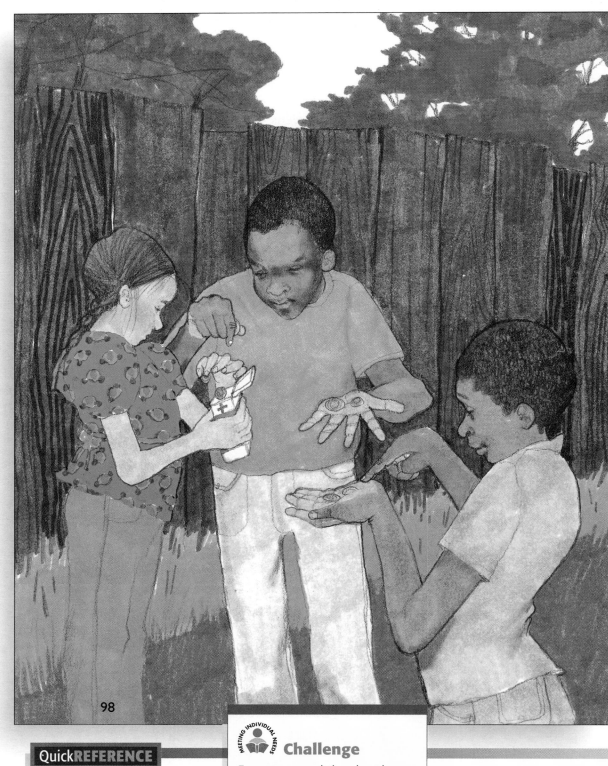

98

QuickREFERENCE

MEETING INDIVIDUAL NEEDS
Challenge

Encourage speculation about how much money the children have. (a few silver coins, which might be quarters; pennies) In the 1950s, one might have been able to buy a hat for $10. Have students write word problems about the purchase of the bonnet.

Stewart reached into the hole in the trunk of our "wish tree" in the backyard. He pulled out a rusty Band-Aid tin. The three of us held our breath as we counted the money inside that we had been saving for weeks.

"If we are going to get that hat for Miss Eula in time for Easter, we are going to need a lot more than this," I announced.

"Maybe we should ask Mr. Kodinski if we could sweep up his shop or something to earn the rest of the money," Stewart said.

"I don't know," Winnie said fearfully. "He's such a strange old man. He never smiles at anyone. He always looks so mean!" We all agreed that it was worth a try anyway.

MEETING INDIVIDUAL NEEDS
Students Acquiring English

Have students discuss why the children call the tree their *wish tree*. (They hide their money there; it is money for things wished for.) If necessary, point out that *Winnie* is a nickname for *Winston*.

Also, ask students if Easter is celebrated in their native countries and, if so, what it is called. Encourage them to share these terms with the rest of the class.

Problem Solving/ Decision Making

Teach/Model

TESTED SKILL

Ask students what the children's problem is on page 99. (They do not have enough money to buy the hat.) Point out that one way to solve a problem is to think about the pros and cons of alternative solutions. The pros and cons can then be used to make a good decision. Share this model:

Problem:	
Children don't have enough money to buy the hat.	
Possible Solutions	**Pros (+) and Cons (−)**
1. Work for Mr. Kodinski.	(+) Could earn money quickly. (−) Mr. Kodinski seems mean.
2. Save money from allowances.	(+) Would not take any extra time. (−) Might not save enough by Easter.
Decision:	

Discuss the pros and cons of each alternative. Ask students to decide on the better alternative.

Practice/Apply

Have students work in small groups to suggest a third alternative, as well as pros and cons for that alternative.

SKILL FINDER

Full lesson/Reteaching, pp. 121C–121D

Minilessons, p. 49; Theme 2, p. 141

Interact *with* Literature

Guided Reading

Comprehension/Critical Thinking

1. How did the children know Miss Eula wanted the Easter bonnet? (She looked longingly at it in the window; she commented on how beautiful it was.)

2. What did the children think of Mr. Kodinski before their encounter with him? (They thought he was strange and mean.)

3. Do you think their opinion of him was fair? Why or why not? (Encourage discussion. Students might note that the children didn't really seem to know Mr. Kodinski.)

4. Do you think it was fair of Mr. Kodinski to accuse the children of throwing eggs at his shop? Why or why not? (Encourage discussion. Students might say that the evidence seemed to lead to that conclusion.)

Predicting/Purpose Setting

Ask students if any of their purpose-setting questions have been answered. Then ask if they want to revise or add to their questions, now that the children have another problem to solve. Have students read to the end of page 107. Use the questions on page 106 to check comprehension.

Informal Assessment

If students' responses indicate that they understand the children's problem, you may wish to have them finish reading the story independently.

The next day we took a shortcut down the alley in back of the hat shop. Bigger boys were there. They were yelling. Eggs flew past us and pelted Mr. Kodinski's back door.

Just as the boys ran away the door flew open. Mr. Kodinski glared straight at us! "You there," he yelled. "Why do you kids do things like this?"

"It wasn't us," Stewart tried to say, but Mr. Kodinski wouldn't listen to us.

"All I want to do is live my life in peace. I'm calling your grandmother," he shouted as he wagged his finger in Stewart's face.

100

QuickREFERENCE

Social Studies Link

Community Take the opportunity to talk with students about the need for respecting other people in the community—and their property. Encourage them to discuss what they can do to show such respect.

Students Acquiring English

If students do not know what a *shortcut* is ("a shorter route"), remind them to break the word into parts to see if that helps them. Discuss what Mr. Kodinski means when he says, "I'm calling your grandmother." (He'll call her on the telephone.)

101

Interact
with
Literature

Reading Strategies

▶ **Summarize**

Ask volunteers how they would summarize what has happened in the story thus far. If necessary, provide this sample summary:

The children loved Miss Eula and wanted to buy an Easter bonnet for her, but they didn't have enough money. They went to Mr. Kodinski's hat shop to ask for some small jobs, but some boys had just thrown eggs at the shop door. When Mr. Kodinski saw the children, he accused them of doing it. Upset, they wanted to do something to change his mind about them.

Miss Eula was waiting in her living room for us. "Miss Eula, we didn't throw those eggs," I sobbed.

"Some big boys did," Stewart <u>sputtered</u>.

"What were you doing at the back of his shop in the first place?" she asked. We knew that we couldn't tell her the truth, so we just stood there and cried.

She looked at us for a long while. "Baby dears, I want to believe you. Heaven knows that I brought you children up to always tell the truth. If you say you didn't do it, then I believe you."

"It is too bad though," she went on to say. "That poor man has suffered so much in his life, he deserves more than eggs thrown at him. You know, he thinks *you* threw the eggs. You'll have to show him that you are good people. You'll have to change his mind somehow."

102

Students Acquiring English

MEETING INDIVIDUAL NEEDS

Ask why Miss Eula calls the children *Baby dears*. Invite students to share terms of affection used for *children* in their primary language. Be sure students understand that *to change his mind* means to make Mr. Kodinski change his opinion.

Visual Literacy

Body Language Discuss how the body language of the characters shows their feelings of sadness and shame. You may want to have students compare this illustration with the one on pages 116–117, which exudes happiness.

Interact *with* Literature

Reading Strategies

▶ **Think About Words**

Ask if the illustration on these pages provides any clues to the meanings of the words *beeswax*, *funnel*, and *dye*. (no) Without picture clues, ask how students might be able to figure out the meanings of these words. (Read on; the next illustration shows the items and how they are used.)

Informal Assessment

Oral Reading To check oral reading fluency, have small groups read aloud pages 102 and 105. Allow students time to first reread the pages silently. The Oral Reading Checklist in the *Teacher's Assessment Handbook* provides criteria for assessment.

Quick REFERENCE

Art Link

Icons Patricia Polacco holds a Ph.D. in art history; her specialty is Russian and Greek painting and iconographic history. She still paints and restores ancient Russian and Greek icons for museums. These often find their way into her illustrations.

In my kitchen the next day we thought and thought.

"How can we win him over when he thinks that we threw those eggs?" Stewart asked.

"He doesn't even like us," Winston chirped.

"Eggs," I said quietly.

"Eggs?" Stewart asked.

"Eggs!" I screamed.

I went to the kitchen drawer and took out a lump of beeswax, a candle, a small funnel with a wooden handle, and some packets of yellow, red, and black dye.

105

Health Link

Eggs The good news: Chicken eggs are an excellent source of protein, iron, and vitamins A, D, and B. The bad news: Chicken eggs also contain cholesterol, too much of which may contribute to heart disease.

MEETING INDIVIDUAL NEEDS Students Acquiring English

Have students review the illustrations on pages 102–103 and 104–105 to look for different ways the characters' culture and religion are represented. As necessary, assist with vocabulary and explain what the items are.

Interact
with
Literature

Guided Reading

Comprehension/Critical Thinking

1. Why didn't the children tell Miss Eula their reason for being at Mr. Kodinski's shop? (They didn't want to spoil the surprise.)

2. Do you think the children should have told Miss Eula why they were there? Explain. (Encourage discussion. Students may feel that they should have told her at that point.)

3. What do you think of Tricia's idea of decorating eggs for Mr. Kodinski? (Answers will vary. Some may feel the gift is appropriate, since eggs got the children into trouble.)

Predicting/Purpose Setting

Invite students to make predictions about what will happen between Mr. Kodinski and the children. Have students finish reading the story. Questions for checking comprehension can be found on page 120.

QuickREFERENCE

Art Link

The instrument Tricia is using is called a *kistka*. The funnel part is heated over the candle, and then the larger end is used to scoop up beeswax. The wax melts and flows to the pointed end. Designs are drawn as the melted wax pours out.

Extra Support

Setting Ask students how they were able to tell that the setting of the story has changed—that the children are now at Tricia's house. (The room looks different; a new character is present.)

Mom helped me show the boys how to decorate eggs the way my bubbie had taught us. The way they do it in the old country. We made designs on the egg shells with hot wax, then dyed them and finally melted the wax patterns off.

We put the eggs in a basket and, even though we were afraid, marched into Mr. Kodinski's shop and put them on the counter.

107

Social Studies Link

Ukraine *The old country* referred to is Ukraine, where Polacco's ancestors are from. Egg decoration has been an art form in Ukraine for many years; the eggs are often called *Ukrainian eggs*. Using an up-to-date map, locate Ukraine.

He raised his eyebrows and <u>glowered</u> at us. Then his eyes dropped to the basket.

"Spaseeba," he said softly. That means "thank you" in Russian. "Pysanky eggs!" he said as he looked closely. "I haven't seen these since I left my homeland."

"We didn't throw those eggs at your door, Mr. Kodinski," we told him.

He looked at us for a minute. "Well, then, you have great courage to be here. Chutzpah, you have chutzpah!" Then his eyes glistened and his mouth curled into a warm smile. "Come, have some tea with me."

108

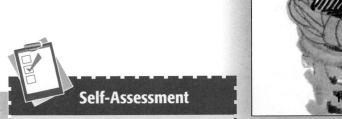

Self-Assessment

Have students assess how well they've enjoyed and understood the story thus far:

- If they've had difficulty understanding the events, have they stopped to summarize what they have read?
- How have they been able to figure out any new words they've encountered?
- Has the story surprised them in any way?

Quick REFERENCE

Vocabulary

Pronunciations

- *spaseeba:* spuh SEE buh
- *chutzpah:* KHUTS puh

Students Acquiring English

MEETING INDIVIDUAL NEEDS

Expressions Be sure students understand that the expression *his eyes dropped* means that Mr. Kodinski looked down. You may want to have students pantomime the actions described in the first sentence.

109

Yiddish The word *chutzpah* is from the Yiddish language, which is spoken primarily in eastern European Jewish communities and by emigrants from these communities. Yiddish is based primarily on German but incorporates usages from any place its speakers live. The word *Yiddish* literally means "Jewish." Written Yiddish uses Hebrew characters.

2

Interact
with
Literature

110

QuickREFERENCE

Background: FYI

Yarmulkes Mr. Kodinski wears a
yarmulke—a skullcap—under his hat.
Religious Jewish men cover their
heads at all times because they are
not permitted to walk more than 6
feet (1.83 m) without having their
heads covered. Often, they wear
both a hat and a yarmulke so that
the yarmulke is already on their
head when they take off the hat.

We spent the whole afternoon talking together, having poppy-seed cake and strong tea. He told us about his life. We told him about ours.

When we finally got the courage to ask about doing odd jobs to earn some extra money, he apologized and told us that there was no work. We didn't tell him what we wanted the money for. It didn't seem the right thing to do. Our hearts sank.

"I tell you this," he said thoughtfully. "These eggs are as beautiful as my hats."

Stewart, Winnie, and I looked at each other.

"It is almost Easter," he went on to say. "I'm sure that people would love these eggs. Set up a table and sell them right there in my shop!"

111

Journal

The story says, *He told us about his life. We told him about ours.* Invite students to write what they think Mr. Kodinski and the children told each other about their lives that afternoon as they shared tea and poppy-seed cake.

Interact
with
Literature

Reading Strategies

 Summarize

Invite volunteers to summarize what has happened in the story since the children were accused of throwing eggs at Mr. Kodinski's shop. Summaries might include the following events:

- Tricia showed the boys how to make *pysanky* eggs.

- The children brought the eggs to Mr. Kodinski to convince him that they really were good children.

- Mr. Kodinski suggested that the children sell the eggs in his shop to earn the money they needed.

- The children made many eggs and sold all of them in a day.

For the next few days we worked very hard. We made almost a dozen "Pysanky" eggs. When people came in, they picked them up and said things like, "Beautiful!" "Splendid!" "Intricate!" "Glorious!" We sold them all in one single day.

That afternoon when all the eggs were gone, we counted our money. We had more than enough for the hat.

112

QuickREFERENCE

Math Link

A Dozen The children made almost a dozen eggs. Ask students how many eggs there are in a dozen. (12) Can students think of other things that come in twelves? (numbers on a clock, months in a year, inches in a foot)

Students Acquiring English
MEETING INDIVIDUAL NEEDS

Synonyms Ask students how they would describe the eggs. Encourage them to make a web of words that mean "beautiful," including words from their primary language. Have students role-play the shoppers admiring the eggs.

Interact *with* Literature

Reading Strategies

 Evaluate

Encourage students to evaluate what they have been reading. You might suggest that they ponder the following:

- How has knowing that this is a true story from the author's life affected the way I have read and understood it? Has it made me look at the characters differently?

- Has reading about what happened to Mr. Kodinski changed the way I feel about people who seem different from me at first?

Just as we were about to tell Mr. Kodinski that we wanted to buy the hat, he came out from the back room holding a beautiful hatbox . . . gift-wrapped! "Keep your money, children," he said softly. "I have seen Miss Eula admire this. It is for her, isn't it? Tell her that I know you are very good children, such good children!"

114

QuickREFERENCE

Journal

Have students ever changed their mind about someone after getting to know that person? Encourage them to write about their experience by completing this statement: *I used to think _____ but now I _____.*

MEETING INDIVIDUAL NEEDS

Students Acquiring English

To build on comprehension for this scene, have students retell it by writing thought balloons for the characters in the illustration.

115

Background: ᶠʏɪ

The Holocaust Students may notice the numbers on Mr. Kodinski's left forearm (here and on page 110). Though the author never states it, it's apparent that Mr. Kodinski is a Holocaust survivor. Students may want more information about this subject. A good resource for discussion is *Remember Not to Forget: A Memory of the Holocaust* by Norman H. Finkelstein (Morrow 1993).

When Easter Sunday arrived, we thought our hearts would burst when we watched Miss Eula open the hatbox. She held us close, as big tears rolled down her cheeks.

Our hearts sang along with the choir that Sunday. She looked so beautiful in that hat. When it was time for her solo, we knew that she was singing just for us.

Her voice was like slow thunder and sweet rain.

116

QuickREFERENCE

Music Link

Gospel Music Invite volunteers to explain what a *choir* is. (a group of singers, especially in a church) Students might want to sing songs they know to demonstrate the difference between a choir and someone who sings a *solo*.

MEETING INDIVIDUAL NEEDS Students Acquiring English

Ask students to imagine how the children felt when Miss Eula opened the hatbox. (proud, happy) Use this context to develop meaning for *we thought our hearts would burst*, contrasting it with *our hearts sank* (page 111).

117

MINILESSON

Sequence of Events

Teach/Model

Stewart, Winston, and Tricia had a busy week leading up to Easter Sunday. With students, trace the events of the first couple of days of that week. Remind them to look for clue words such as *next* and *the next day* that reveal sequence.

Day	What Children Did
Sunday	decided to ask Mr. Kodinski for work
Monday	went to Mr. Kodinski's shop
Tuesday	made eggs; spent afternoon with Mr. Kodinski

Practice/Apply

Suggest that students work with partners to chart the events for the rest of the week. Point out that although it's not stated, the children probably sold their eggs in Mr. Kodinski's shop on Friday, not Saturday; as a religious Jew, Mr. Kodinski most likely closed his shop on Saturday, the Sabbath.

Day	What Children Did
Wednesday	made eggs
Thursday	made eggs
Friday	sold eggs in Mr. Kodinski's shop
Sunday	gave hat to Miss Eula; went to church

SKILL FINDER

Full lesson/Reteaching, pp. 84B–84C

Minilessons, pp. 33, 77; Theme 1, p. 107

Background: FYI

More About the Author

Although Patricia Polacco is Jewish, as a child she often shared the celebration of Christian holidays with her good friends and neighbors, the Washingtons. Stewart Washington later served as best man at the marriage of Patricia and Enzo-Mario Polacco, which was a Jewish ceremony. Enzo's family were Holocaust victims, and the author uses the name *Polacco* in their memory.

Interact
with
Literature

118

Later that day as Miss Eula sat at the head of the table she said, "Oh baby dears, I can die happy now. And after I'm dead, on Chicken Sundays, I want you to boil up some chicken — bones, gravy, and all — and pour it over my grave. So late at night when I'm hungry, I can reach right out and have me some."

Then she rolled her head back and laughed from a deep, holy place inside.

119

 Home Connection

Encourage students to ask parents and/or grandparents how they celebrated special days when they were growing up. Invite students to then share the family stories with classmates.

Interact *with* Literature

 Guided Reading

Comprehension/Critical Thinking

1. How did the *pysanky* eggs help change Mr. Kodinski's mind about the children? (The eggs reminded him of his homeland; he admired the children for having the courage to bring the eggs to him.)

2. How did your impression of Mr. Kodinski change over the course of the story? (Answers will vary, but should perhaps show an increased understanding and sympathy for him.)

3. What lesson did the children learn from what happened with Mr. Kodinski? (Sample response: They learned not to judge people they didn't know; they learned the importance of telling the truth.)

Winston, Stewart, and I are grown up now. Our old neighborhood has changed some, yet it's still familiar, too. The freeway rumbles over the spot where Mr. Kodinski's shop once stood. I think of him often and his glorious hats.

We lost Miss Eula some time back, but every year we take some chicken soup up to Mountain View Cemetery and do just as she asked.

Sometimes, when we are especially quiet inside, we can hear singing. A voice that sounds like slow thunder and sweet rain.

120

Self-Assessment

Use questions like the following to prompt students to reflect on their own reading:

- Did I use my reading strategies effectively to help me through this story?
- Was this story enjoyable to me? If not, did I evaluate why I felt this way?
- How does this story compare to other stories I have read by Patricia Polacco? To other stories in this theme?

QuickREFERENCE

Students Acquiring English

Using Context From context, students should be able to figure out that the expression *we lost Miss Eula* means that she died.

Beautiful! Splendid! Glorious!

Make an Advertisement

Eggs for Sale!
Make a poster for Mr. Kodinski's store that advertises the pysanky eggs. Include a picture of the eggs and use descriptive words like those found in the story.

Share a Memory

Show Me How
Patricia Polacco's bubbie taught her how to make pysanky eggs. Talk about something you learned how to do from a friend or family member.

FOR SALE
Beautiful Pysanky eggs
handmade
the perfe gift

Personal Response
- Invite students to write their reactions to the story *Chicken Sunday*. Were any parts of it uplifting? Sad? What would they say about it to someone who has never read it?
- Allow students to choose their own way of responding to the story.

Anthology Activities
Select—or have students select—an activity from page 121. You might suggest that they work with a partner on the "Eggs for Sale!" activity.

121

QuickREFERENCE

Home Connection
Encourage students to retell or read the story *Chicken Sunday* to family members. This is a good opportunity for students to discuss with a parent how Mr. Kodinski was treated in the community.

MEETING INDIVIDUAL NEEDS
Students Acquiring English
For the "Show Me How" activity, suggest that students ask their parents and other family members to describe crafts made in their homeland.

Informal Assessment
Students' responses should indicate a general understanding of the problem in the story and the intent of the author.

Responding **121**

2

Interact *with* **Literature**

Responding

More Choices for Responding

A "Chicken Sunday" Meal

Have students sit around a big table. Go around the table and ask each student to describe their favorite meal—their equivalent of Patricia Polacco's favorite meal at Miss Eula's. Encourage the use of adjectives and vivid details. Students may enjoy making paper fans to flutter back and forth as they talk.

1 Fold paper like an accordion.

2 Cut notches in the paper while it is still folded. Be careful not to cut across the paper!

3 Glue a strip of paper around one end of the folded paper. Open out the other end.

Students Acquiring English Students may want to draw or find a picture of their favorite meal to show the group and then describe it. Or, they could use the picture to make a fan!

Materials
- blank paper
- safety scissors
- glue

Informal Assessment

Check responses for a general understanding of the story.

Additional Support:
- Use the Guided Reading questions to review the story.
- Pair students and have them reread confusing parts of the story.
- Use story illustrations to retell the story.

Selection Connections
LAB, p. 2

Remind students to return to *Literacy Activity Book* page 2 to complete the part of the chart that refers to *Chicken Sunday.*

Making an Apology

Have small groups role-play a scene in which the children convince the bigger boys to apologize to Mr. Kodinski for throwing the eggs. Then have students act out the apology. (You may wish to review the Guidelines for Making Apologies on page 84L.)

More Choices for Responding

Literature Discussion

- What did you learn from reading this story?

- Patricia Polacco is still good friends with Stewart and Winston Washington. What do you think they talk about now? Do you think they like to share childhood memories?

- If you could spend time with Patricia Polacco, what would you talk about?

Writing an Epilogue

Invite students to write a scene set in the present in which the three friends—Winston, Stewart, and Patricia—go to Mountain View Cemetery to visit Miss Eula's grave. They might need to reread pages 119–120 first.

Pantomiming the Story

Have students work in small groups to choose a scene from the story to pantomime. As a narrator reads the scene, others can act it out. Remind students to be mindful of their movements and expressions.

In preparation, they might want to look at and discuss the illustrations on pages 102–103, 112–113, and 116–117.

- What emotions are being expressed in each of the illustrations?

- How can students pantomime these emotions?

Honoring the Author

Reading *Chicken Sunday* may interest students in reading other books by Patricia Polacco, especially those in which some of the same characters appear. Suggest that students host a tea party in honor of Polacco. Serve hot tea and poppy seed cake, like Mr. Kodinski did. Have students take turns reading aloud books by Polacco. You may wish to invite another class to join you.

Suggested books:

- *Firetalking* (Polacco's autobiography)

- *The Keeping Quilt*

- *Meteor*

- *Thunder Cake*

Comprehension Check

Use the following questions and/or *Literacy Activity Book* page 43 to check understanding of the story.

1. What was the main problem in the story, and how was it solved? (The children were accused of throwing eggs at Mr. Kodinski's shop; they made *pysanky* eggs for him.)

2. What memories does Patricia Polacco have of Miss Eula? (She loved having Sunday dinner at Miss Eula's; she loved Miss Eula's voice.)

Literacy Activity Book, p. 43

Hats for Sale

Fill in the chart to tell about *Chicken Sunday*.

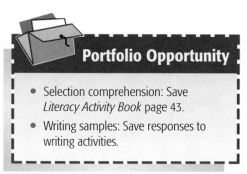

Portfolio Opportunity

- Selection comprehension: Save *Literacy Activity Book* page 43.

- Writing samples: Save responses to writing activities.

Instruct and Integrate

Comprehension

Transparency 4–15

Problem Solving/Decision Making

Problem:
Mr. Kodinski thinks we threw the eggs.

Possible Solutions	Pros (+) and Cons (-)
1. Write Mr. Kodinski a note saying that we didn't do it.	(+) This would be easy to do. (-) He might not believe us. (-) It's not special enough.
2. Ask Miss Eula to tell Mr. Kodinski what good children we are.	(+) He might believe Miss Eula. (-) Miss Eula might not want to do it. (-) She thinks we should find a way to change his mind.
3. Make Ukrainian eggs for Mr. Kodinski.	(+) Tricia knows this is a special gift. (-) The boys don't know how to make them. (+) Tricia can teach boys. (+) Mr. Kodinski is Russian; he'll know eggs are special. (-) It would take time; eggs might break.

Decision:
Sample: Make Ukrainian eggs for Mr. Kodinski.

TRANSPARENCY 4–15
TEACHER'S BOOK PAGE 121C

Problem Solving/Decision Making
LAB, p. 44

Teach/Model

Ask students to tell how they have gone about solving problems or making decisions in their own lives. Use these prompts:

- Did you consider several possible solutions?
- Did you make a list of pros and cons?
- Did your decision work out? Why or why not?

Then ask what problem the children in *Chicken Sunday* faced when Mr. Kodinski saw the eggs on his back door. (He thought they had thrown the eggs.) Review that the next day, the children thought about how to win him over. Display Transparency 4–15. Ask students to imagine that they are the children in the story. Help them use the chart to think about possible solutions to the problem:

Problem: Mr. Kodinski thinks we threw the eggs.	
Possible Solutions	**Pros (+) and Cons (-)**
1. Write Mr. Kodinski a note saying that we didn't do it.	(+) This would be easy to do. (-) He might not believe us. (-) It's not special enough.
2. Ask Miss Eula to tell Mr. Kodinski what good children we are.	(+) He might believe Miss Eula. (-) Miss Eula might not want to do it. (-) She thinks we should find a way to change his mind.
3. Make Ukrainian eggs for Mr. Kodinski.	(+) Tricia knows this is a special gift. (-) The boys don't know how to make them. (+) Tricia can teach boys. (+) Mr. Kodinski is Russian; he'll know eggs are special. (-) It would take time; eggs might break.

Informal Assessment

Check students' responses during discussion and Practice/Apply to determine how well they are able to use the decision-making model.

Additional Support:

Reteaching, p. 121D
Minilessons, pp. 49, 99; Theme 2, p. 141

SKILL FINDER
Minilessons, pp. 49, 99;
Theme 2, p. 141

Ask students why the third alternative is such a good one. (There are more pluses than minuses.) Then discuss why the children's decision worked so well. Ask if students think any of the other alternatives would have worked.

Practice/Apply

1. Have students solve the problem on *Literacy Activity Book* page 44.

2. Invite students to use the model to think of ways to solve a problem that your class or school is having.

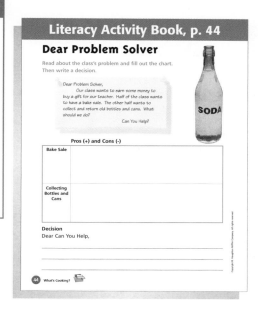

Literacy Activity Book, p. 44

Dear Problem Solver

Read about the class's problem and fill out the chart. Then write a decision.

> Dear Problem Solver,
>   Our class wants to earn some money to buy a gift for our teacher. Half of the class wants to have a bake sale. The other half wants to collect and return old bottles and cans. What should we do?
>   Can You Help?

Pros (+) and Cons (-)

Bake Sale	
Collecting Bottles and Cans	

Decision
Dear Can You Help,

44 What's Cooking?

Reteaching

Problem Solving/Decision Making

MEETING INDIVIDUAL NEEDS

Cooperative Learning Divide students into two debate teams: the Pros and the Cons. Have the teams sit facing each other. You might suggest that students make a sign for their team.

Announce that the two teams are going to debate possible solutions to a problem Henry Huggins had at the beginning of *Henry and Beezus*: It was Sunday afternoon and Henry was bored.

Suggest a possible solution for consideration, such as "Henry could ask his friend Beezus to come over and play." (Reuse Transparency 4–15 to keep track of the debate.)

- The Pros confer and give a reason in favor of this solution.
- The Cons then try to think of a reason the solution won't work.
- The debate continues until it's apparent that one side outweighs the other.
- Another solution is proposed, and the debate begins anew.

To end, both teams decide which solution seems the most reasonable. Students may enjoy role-playing the solution.

Possible Solutions

1. Henry could ask his friend Beezus to come over and play.
2. He could stay home and read the funnies.
3. He could go visit his neighbor Mr. Grumbie.
4. He could take Ribsy for a walk around the neighborhood.

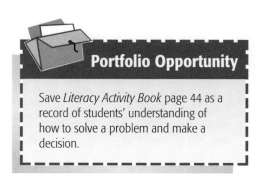

Portfolio Opportunity

Save *Literacy Activity Book* page 44 as a record of students' understanding of how to solve a problem and make a decision.

Writing Skills and Activities

INTERACTIVE LEARNING

Transparency 4–16

Writing a Poem

Easter
by Joyce Kilmer

The air is like a butterfly
  With frail blue wings.
The happy earth looks at the sky
  And sings.

At Home
by Christina Rossetti

Mix a pancake,
Stir a pancake,
  Pop it in the pan;
Fry the pancake,
Toss the pancake,—
  Catch it if you can.

TRANSPARENCY 4–16
TEACHER'S BOOK PAGE 121E

Writing a Poem
LAB, p. 45

Teach/Model

Ask students to recall what time of year *Chicken Sunday* takes place. (spring) Point out that many stories and poems are set in springtime, and ask students why that might be so. Elicit that spring is an exciting time of year—a time of rebirth and happiness.

Display Transparency 4–16. Read the first poem aloud, reading slowly enough so that students can savor the words. Explain that a poem is a description that is written in a special way. Use a chart to help students see how the poet describes spring in a special way.

Ordinary Way	Special Way
The air is breezy, and the sky is blue.	The air is like a butterfly With frail blue wings.
Things are starting to grow.	The happy earth looks at the sky And sings.

Then read the second poem aloud. Use both poems to discuss that poetry is broken into lines. A line might be part of a sentence—as in the case of "Easter"—or it could be a complete thought—as in "At Home." Discuss how the groups of words on each line highlight one thought or idea. You might also point out that poets sometimes indent lines.

Discuss these guidelines for writing a poem with students.

- Choose words that describe something in a special way.

- Put different thoughts on separate lines.

- A poem may or may not use rhyming words.

Practice/Apply Assign the activity Write a Poem.

Literacy Activity Book, p. 45

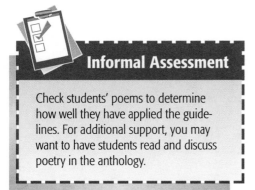

A Spring Fling Thing

Think about spring as you complete these sentences. Write the first thought that comes into your head. Answers will vary.

The color of spring is _____

Spring brings the smell of _____

In spring I like to _____

Now list some other people, places, things, or activities that make you think of spring.

_____
_____
_____

What's Cooking? **45**

Informal Assessment

Check students' poems to determine how well they have applied the guidelines. For additional support, you may want to have students read and discuss poetry in the anthology.

Writing Activities

Creative Writing: Write a Poem

Suggest that students write a poem about spring or some other annual holiday or activity, a food they enjoy, or a topic of their choice.

Students might want to model their poems on the ones on Transparency 4–16. Have students use the prewriting on *Literacy Activity Book* page 45 when writing their poems, or help them adapt it to their topics.

If students wish to model their poems after "Easter," suggest that they change the title to reflect the holiday they are writing about. Then they can tell what the world is like at that time of year. You might put a poetry frame on the board for students' reference. Encourage them to make up the last two lines to tell how the world looks or how they feel. (*See the Writer's Craft Minilesson on page 95.*)

Students can use The Learning Company's new elementary writing center for all their writing activities.

[Name of Holiday]
The air is like _____
With _____ .
_____
_____

Write a Character Sketch

Ask if students got a good picture of Miss Eula from the story. Suggest that each student write a character sketch of someone in his or her own family. It might be a grandparent–or perhaps even a great-grandparent. Encourage students to map out details before they begin to write, as in this example.

Grandma			
Her History	**Activities She Enjoys**	**Things She Says**	**What We Do Together**
• grew up in Japan	• gardening	• "Practice makes perfect."	• cook • go to movies

Write an Essay

Encourage students to write essays about their favorite meals. Prompt ideas about what to include by asking questions such as

- When do you eat this meal? On Friday night? On Sunday? On holidays?

- What foods are included? Which one(s) do you like best? Why?

- Who prepares the food? Who helps with the preparation?

Portfolio Opportunity

Save responses to activities on this page for writing samples.

3

Instruct *and* Integrate

Word Skills and Strategies

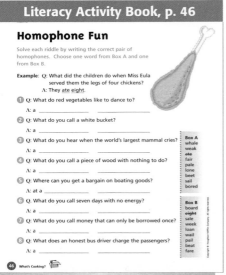

INTERACTIVE LEARNING

TESTED SKILL ✓ Homophones
LAB, p. 46

Teach/Model   Write this sentence on the chalkboard.

As they walked by the hat shop, the children wished they could buy a beautiful hat for Miss Eula.

Ask students to find the two words that sound exactly alike but are spelled differently and have different meanings. *(by, buy)* Have a volunteer circle them. Introduce the term *homophone* for words that sound alike but have different spellings and meanings. Then display the phrases below. Have volunteers read each phrase on the left, think of a homophone for the underlined word, and fill in the phrase on the right.

flowers <u>die</u>	to <u>dye</u> eggs	a <u>whole</u> pizza	a <u>hole</u> in the ground
to come <u>here</u>	to <u>hear</u> a sound	to <u>know</u> the answer	to have <u>no</u> idea

Practice/Apply   Write the phrases below on the board, and divide the class into teams. At the signal, have them hunt through the story for a homophone for each underlined word. Have each team write down the homophone and its page number. The first to find a homophone for each word is the winning team. Have members of that team read the sentence in which they found each homophone as the rest of the class reads along silently.

to have <u>won</u> a game	one (p. 95)
how <u>to</u> play	two, too (p. 95)
a ship at <u>sea</u>	see (p. 97)
to wait an <u>hour</u>	our (p. 99)
to <u>sew</u> a dress	so (p. 99)
to pet <u>their</u> puppy	there (p. 100)
a <u>piece</u> of chicken	peace (p. 100)
a <u>new</u> hat	knew (p. 102)
a <u>sum</u> of money	some (p. 102)
to <u>weigh</u> a pound	way (p. 107)
to <u>grate</u> cheese	great (p. 108)
to <u>groan</u> loudly	grown (p. 120)

SKILL FINDER Spelling, p. 121J

Informal Assessment

Use Practice/Apply to check students' understanding of homophones.

Additional Support:
Reteaching, p. 121H

Reteaching

Homophones

Review homophones by copying the drawings on the board. Tell students that each pair of drawings is a clue to a homophones pair. Work together to recall the definition of *homophones* and to complete the first clue. Ask a volunteer to write the two words as labels for the sketches. For the remaining pairs, invite students to guess the homophones and to label each picture.

Word Skills Practice

Cumulative Skill Practice
Mother's Day Special
by Claire Masurel

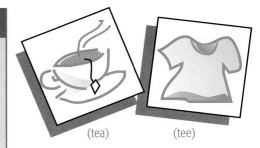

(tea)   (tee)

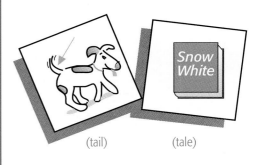

(tail)   (tale)

M I N I L E S S O N

Phonics Review
Phonograms

Teach/Model

Write this sentence on the chalkboard; have a volunteer read it.

They loved to walk to church and talk with Miss Eula.

Ask students which words end with the same sound and the same three letters. *(walk, talk)* Call on a volunteer to list the words on the board. Point out that *alk* is a familiar pattern of letters in the English language and is usually pronounced /ôk/. Ask students to add words to the list. *(stalk, chalk, balk)* Elicit that knowing common patterns of letters and their pronunciation can help students read unfamiliar words.

Write the word *end* on the board and follow the same procedure to brainstorm and list words that show this pattern. Add other words that students are not familiar with, such as *wend, vend,* or *rend*.

send	descend
recommend	tend
mend	fend
blend	offend
pretend	ascend
lend	defend
trend	amend

Practice/Apply

Have students work in groups, brainstorming for words that end with *ank* and *ing*. (Caution them not to include words with the suffix *-ing*, such as *going*.) Encourage the groups to use the words they generated to compose a funny poem. Ask each group to share their poem with the class.

bank	prank	thing	wring
blank	plank	fling	ring
crank	sank	cling	ping
shrank	frank	herring	zing
thank	rank	wing	sing
clank	flank	sting	sling
yank	tank	swing	earring
drank	stank	bring	

Portfolio Opportunity

Save *Literacy Activity Book* page 46 to record students' understanding of homophones.

Instruct *and* **Integrate**

Building Vocabulary

Vocabulary Activities

High-Frequency Vocabulary Practice

Cumulative Skill Practice
Mother's Day Special
by Claire Masurel

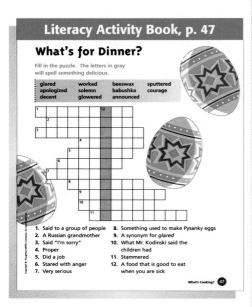

Literacy Activity Book, p. 47

What's for Dinner?

Fill in the puzzle. The letters in gray will spell something delicious.

glared	worked	beeswax	sputtered
apologized	solemn	babushka	courage
decent	glowered	announced	

1. Said to a group of people
2. A Russian grandmother
3. Said "I'm sorry"
4. Proper
5. Did a job
6. Stared with anger
7. Very serious
8. Something used to make Pysanky eggs
9. A synonym for *glared*
10. What Mr. Kodinski said the children had
11. Stammered
12. A food that is good to eat when you are sick

What's Cooking? 47

Use this page to review Selection Vocabulary.

"Wonderful" Words

Have students turn to page 112 of the story and read the words people said when they saw the eggs the children had decorated. *("Beautiful!" "Splendid!" "Intricate!" "Glorious!")* Point out that the words *beautiful, splendid,* and *glorious* are all ways of saying that something is wonderful. Have the class brainstorm other words that mean "wonderful." List their words on the board, and add others.

awesome	superior
fantastic	admirable
outstanding	great
superb	super
remarkable	heavenly
terrific	incredible
fabulous	stupendous
perfect	marvelous

Words for Hats

Have the class brainstorm names for different kinds of hats and headgear. Discuss what each item looks like and have volunteers illustrate each kind of hat. Use the pictures to create a "Hat Shop" bulletin-board display. (Sample answers: bonnet, baseball cap, turban, derby, beret, yarmulke, crown, helmet, sombrero, Panama hat, cowboy hat, hood, kaffiyeh, ski cap, beanie, scarf)

bonnet
baseball cap
yarmulke
kaffiyeh
helmet
beanie

Word Family for *decorate*

Challenge Ask students what it means to *decorate* something, like the eggs were decorated. (to add something to it to make it beautiful) Explain that several words belong to the same word family as *decorate,* and each is related to making something beautiful. Write the underlined words at right on the board and ask the questions that follow.

- decor: What would you mention if you were describing the decor of a room?
- redecorate: What would you do if you decided to redecorate your room?
- decorator: Why might a family with a new home hire a decorator?
- decorations: What decorations have you seen on Christmas trees?
- decorative: If a bowl of fruit is placed on a table for decorative purposes only, should you eat a piece?

Spelling

5-Day Planner

FIVE-DAY PLAN

DAY 1	DAY 2	DAY 3	DAY 4	DAY 5
Pretest; Minilesson; Challenge Words/ Additional Words (opt.); Take-Home Word Lists (LAB)	First LAB page; Challenge Words Practice (opt.)	Check first LAB page; Second LAB page (except writing application)	Check second LAB page; writing application (LAB)	Test

Teaching CHOICES

MINILESSON

Spelling Words

*hear	*too
*here	*there
*to	*their
*two	they're

Challenge Words

*die	*hole
*dye	*whole

Additional Spelling Words

meet	sale
meat	sail

*Starred words or forms of the words appear in *Chicken Sunday*.

TESTED SKILL

Homophones

LAB, pp. 48–49

- Write the words *two* and *too* on the board. Have students listen to these words as you say them.

- Ask students if these words sound alike. (yes) Ask if the words have the same meaning. (no) Elicit that *two* means "the number after one" and *too* means "also." Then ask if the words have the same spelling. (no) Tell students that words that sound alike but have different meanings and spellings are called *homophones*.

- Write the Spelling Words on the board. Tell students that each Spelling Word is a homophone. Say the words and have students repeat them.

Spelling Assessment

Pretest

Say each underlined word, read the sentence, and then repeat the word. Have students write only the underlined words.

1. We went to hear her sing in the choir.
2. They used to sell hats here in this shop.
3. Come over to our house for dinner.
4. I have two best friends.
5. They live on my street, too.
6. That's my house over there.
7. This is their house right here.
8. I think they're lots of fun to play with.

Test

Spelling Words Use the Pretest sentences.

Challenge Words

9. This sweater has a hole in it.
10. Water your plant or it will die.
11. The whole class went outside for recess.
12. It's fun and easy to dye eggs.

SKILL FINDER

Daily Language Practice, p. 121L
Reading-Writing Workshop, p. 91E

Literacy Activity Book

Take-Home Word Lists: pp. 173–174

Students can use the **Spelling Spree CD-ROM** for extra practice with the spelling principles taught in this selection.

MEETING INDIVIDUAL NEEDS

Challenge

Challenge Words Practice Have students use the Challenge Words to make pictionaries, in which they illustrate the meaning of the word and use it in a sentence.

Instruct and Integrate

Grammar

5-Day Planner

FIVE-DAY PLAN

DAY 1	DAY 2	DAY 3	DAY 4	DAY 5
Daily Language Practice 1; Teach/Model; First LAB page	Daily Language Practice 2; Check first LAB page; Cooperative Learning	Daily Language Practice 3; Writing Application	Daily Language Practice 4; Reteaching (opt.); Second LAB page	Daily Language Practice 5; Check second LAB page; Students' Writing

Transparency 4–17

Commas in a Series

Grandmother, Jessie, and Joe have new hats.
The eggs were boiled, cooled, and painted with great care.
The children approached the door quietly, happily, and quickly.
We used a candle, beeswax, and dye.

Gloria had a voice like _____ _____ and _____.

_____ _____ and _____ were on the Sunday menu.

What did they eat on _____ _____ and _____?

_____ _____ and _____ decorated eggs.

Mr. Hammell invited them in for _____ _____ and _____.

The children saved their _____ _____ and _____.

Her grandmother _____ _____ and _____ her hat.

The _____ _____ and _____ eggs are on the shelf.

TRANSPARENCY 4–17
TEACHER'S BOOK PAGE 121L

WHAT'S COOKING
Chicken Sunday
GRAMMAR Commas in a Series

Literacy Activity Book, p. 51

Oh, That Hat!

Literacy Activity Book, p. 50

Who's Coming to Dinner?

Commas in a Series Here is part of a play. Fix the script by adding commas where needed.

Sunday Dinner Menu
corn   potatoes   chicken
We will make corn, potatoes, and chicken for Sunday dinner.

Max: Let's invite Miss Lara Mr. Spellman and the choir for dinner.
Sue: We can have the chicken broiled fried or baked.
Willy: I will peel wash and boil these potatoes.
Max: Good. I will clean cut and cook the corn on the cob.

Complete the rest of the script, using words in a series. Remember to use commas correctly.

Max: Sure. We will also _____ _____ and _____ the dishes.
Willy: How can we make _____ _____ and _____ with the leftover chicken?
Max: You always think about _____ and _____!
Sue: Afterward we can _____ _____ and _____ together.
Max: What a _____ _____ and _____ idea this is!

50   What's Cooking?

Informal Assessment

Responses to the activities should indicate a general understanding of how to use commas in a series.

Additional Support:

Reteaching, p. 121L

INTERACTIVE LEARNING

TESTED SKILL

Commas in a Series

LAB, pp. 50–51

> A **series** is a list of three or more words.
> Use commas to separate words in a series.

Teach/Model

Write this sentence on the chalkboard, omitting the commas.

This story is about Easter, eggs, and chicken.

Ask a volunteer how many things this story is about, according to this sentence. (two) Then add commas, and ask the question again. Students should recognize that the sentence is about three things. Explain that three or more words listed together are a *series*. Guide them to recall that without the commas, the sentence seems to be about two things. Commas make the meaning of the sentence clear.

Prepare a set of index cards, writing one category on each card, such as foods, colors, pets, wild animals, cities, or articles of clothing. Then invite the class to play a game of Category Cards. Let students take turns drawing a card and writing a sentence on the chalkboard that includes three or more items in the category.

Lions, tigers, and bears are very large mammals.

Display Transparency 4–17. Use the example sentences to review the concept of a series and the need for commas between items. Have volunteers complete the sentences by writing items in the spaces and separating them with commas.

SKILL FINDER Reading-Writing Workshop, p. 91E

INTERACTIVE LEARNING (continued)

More Practice

Houghton Mifflin English Level 3
Workbook Plus, pp. 99–100
Reteaching Workbook, p. 65

Write on Track
Write on Track SourceBook, pp. 9–10, 65–66, 105

Practice/Apply

Cooperative Learning: **Creating a Menu** Divide the class into five teams, one for each weekday. Invite teammates to work together to prepare a menu for breakfast, lunch, and dinner for their day. Encourage them to offer three items at each meal and to write complete sentences naming those foods. Show students a model. Have them cut their menus in different shapes and decorate them.

Menu for Monday
Breakfast
The cold buffet will offer juice, cereal, and fruit.
Lunch
Noodles, salad, and apples are our low-fat choices.
Dinner
The main course includes chicken, potatoes, and beans.

Daily Language Practice
Focus Skills

Grammar: Commas in a Series
Spelling: Homophones

Each day write one sentence on the chalkboard. Have each student write the sentence correctly on a sheet of paper. Tell students to correct any errors in the use of commas in a series as well as any misspelled words. Have students correct their own paper as a volunteer corrects the sentence on the chalkboard.

Writing Application: Memory Book Suggest that students write one or more paragraphs about an event in their lives that has special meaning. Ask them to use a series of three or more words in some sentences.

Students' Writing Suggest that students check recent pieces of their writing to find commas used in a series. Remind them that these commas add clarity to their writing.

1. Susan James, and Pat went to two churches with there grandmother.
   Susan**,** James, and Pat went to two churches with **their** grandmother.

2. I here thunder, rain, and, love in her voice too.
   I **hear** thunder, rain, and love in her voice too.

3. There pleased with the milk tea, and cake here.
   They're pleased with the milk**,** tea, and cake here.

4. Yellow red, and black are they're favorite colors.
   Yellow**,** red, and black are **their** favorite colors.

5. Pat met me their on Monday Wednesday, and Friday.
   Pat met me **there** on Monday**,** Wednesday, and Friday.

Reteaching

Commas in a Series

MEETING INDIVIDUAL NEEDS

Write this sentence on the chalkboard, omitting the first comma.

Our group includes Mary, Elizabeth, Kwanzi, and Juanita.

Ask students to tell how many are in the group (three) and to name the members. (Mary Elizabeth, Kwanzi, Juanita) Have them also name the kind of punctuation that separates the names. Then erase the commas. Work together to punctuate the sentence so that the group now has four people.

Ask students to write their first name or their first and middle names on a name tag and to pin it on their clothes. Form teams of three, and ask them to write a sentence about their team, using all three teammates' names. Invite one teammate to write the sentence on the chalkboard; have teams check to see if commas are used correctly.

3

Communication Activities

Audio Tape
for *What's Cooking?: Chicken Sunday*

Amazing Grace

Amazing grace!
How sweet the sound
That saved a wretch like me!
I once was lost,
But now am found,
Was blind,
But now I see.

'Twas grace that taught
My heart to fear.
And grace my fears relieved;
How precious did
that grace appear
The hour
I first believed!

by John Newton (1725–1807)

Informal Assessment

Circulate among the groups and encourage students to tell what they picture in their minds as they listen to the music.

Listening and Speaking

Listening to Gospel Music

Invite students to listen to gospel music, such as the songs on Mahalia Jackson's *Gospels, Spirituals & Hymns*. Ask students if the singer's voice sounds like slow thunder and sweet rain. Have students hum the melody and clap out the rhythm. What do they picture in their minds as they listen? Suggest that students sing a hymn, such as "Amazing Grace."

Resources
Gospels, Spirituals & Hymns
by Mahalia Jackson (Columbia/Legacy)

Live…We Come Rejoicing
by the Brooklyn Tabernacle Choir (Warner/Alliance)

Speaking Russian

Multicultural Link Play a recent recording in the Russian language. Have students compare the language to English and other languages they speak. Then teach students the following Russian phrases.

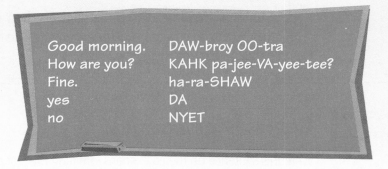

Good morning.	DAW-broy OO-tra
How are you?	KAHK pa-jee-VA-yee-tee?
Fine.	ha-ra-SHAW
yes	DA
no	NYET

Listening to Klezmer Music

Multicultural Link Invite students to listen to Jewish music called Klezmer. Have them close their eyes. When the music ends ask students how the music makes them feel. Do they feel happy? Sad? Students may want to compare gospel music with Klezmer.

Resources
Master of Klezmer Music: Russian Sher by Harry Kandel (Global Village)

Viewing

Comparing Patricia Polacco's Artwork

Provide students with other books by Patricia Polacco, such as *The Keeping Quilt.* Have them compare the illustrations with those in *Chicken Sunday,* noting similarities and differences in art styles. (Students may notice the illustration in *The Keeping Quilt* of a grown-up Stewart Washington at Polacco's wedding.) Have students also compare pictures of Patricia Polacco as a child in both books with the photograph of her as an adult on page 92.

Watching a Video

Tape a TV gospel music show and play it for the class. Have students describe the choir robes, the staging, and the number of singers in each group. After viewing the tape, some students may wish to form a group and sing a gospel song for the class.

Looking at Hats

Suggest that the next time students are walking around town they look for hats in stores and on people. Challenge them to spot many different hats. When they are back in class, have them describe the different kinds of hats worn.

- Which hats seemed the most popular style on passers-by?

- In which kind of weather do most people wear hats?

- What kinds of hats do *you* have?

Instruct and Integrate

Cross-Curricular Activities

Book List

Science

Chickens Aren't the Only Ones
by Ruth Heller

Egg
by Pascale De Bourgoing

Materials

- hard-boiled eggs
- crayons
- paper cups
- food coloring (blue, green, yellow)
- vinegar
- spoons
- egg carton

Art

Making *Pysanky* Eggs

Invite students to use the directions for making a variation of *pysanky* eggs. Students first use crayons to create different patterns and symbols on hard-boiled eggs.

1 Pour food coloring in several cups. Add a teaspoon of vinegar.

2 Carefully put a decorated egg in the coloring for a couple of minutes.

3 Remove the egg with a spoon and dry on the carton.

Challenge Suggest that students locate Ukraine on a map and discuss its proximity to Russia. Then have them research the story of the Ukrainian egg decorating art called *pysanky*.

Science

Experimenting with Eggs

Challenge Ask students under what conditions raw eggs break. Mention that people who have experimented by dropping raw eggs from different heights have discovered that not every egg broke. Have students work in groups to set up an experiment to test the theory. They could

- drop the same number of eggs from various heights

- think of ways of protecting the eggs so they would not break

- record their results by putting the data in a table

Choices for Math

Hat Prices

Suggest that students look through store advertisements for hat prices. Ask them to determine how much they would have to charge for every decorated egg in a dozen in order to buy a hat of their choice. Have them report their findings to the class. Challenge them to design a hat using different materials. What would they need to know in order to price the hat if it was for sale? Why?

Shaping Up Eggs

Have students use only geometric shapes to decorate either a hard-boiled egg or egg-shaped paper. Some students may wish to practice on the egg-shaped paper before applying their designs to the boiled egg. Encourage students to use as many different shapes as possible, such as a triangle, trapezoid, circle, oval, rectangle, rhombus, etc. Have them discuss which shapes consist of straight lines and which consist of arcs.

Portfolio Opportunity

Save students' drawings of egg designs for discussions in math on geometric shapes.

Activating Prior Knowledge

Ask students if they have eaten or drunk any of the following in the past day: *soft drinks, ice cream, popcorn,* and *hot dogs.* Have them share how frequently they enjoy these foods and in what situations they usually consume them.

Then challenge students to try to measure how much of each of these foods they eat in a year. Suggest that they first calculate on a daily or weekly basis using measurements such as:

can of soda	12 ounces	.237 liters
bowl of ice cream	8 ounces (half-pint)	.355 liters
bag of popcorn	1.75 ounces (vending machine-size)	50 grams

Tell them to save their guesses in order to compare them to the facts in the article.

Building Background

Have students preview the article. Discuss how the information is presented. Point out that the information in the article is laid out in such a way that a reader can skim it easily. They do not need to read in a sequential pattern, from the first paragraph to the last.

Purpose Setting Have students read to find out what the funniest fact about food is.

Fun Food Facts

Average Americans guzzle 40 gallons of soft drinks a year. That's enough to fill your bathtub and have 10 gallons left over to fill the kitchen sink.

Average Americans eat nearly 2,000 pounds of food a year — that's as much as the weight of a small two-door car.

Each year, enough ice cream is produced in the United States to fill the Grand Canyon. The average American eats 15 gallons of ice cream per year — that would fill a washing machine.

122

Students Acquiring English

Point out that *guzzle* means "to drink" and that a *soft drink* is usually carbonated. Ask students to name some soft drinks. They might also share their favorite kinds of ice cream and what they like to add to hot dogs, when they eat them.

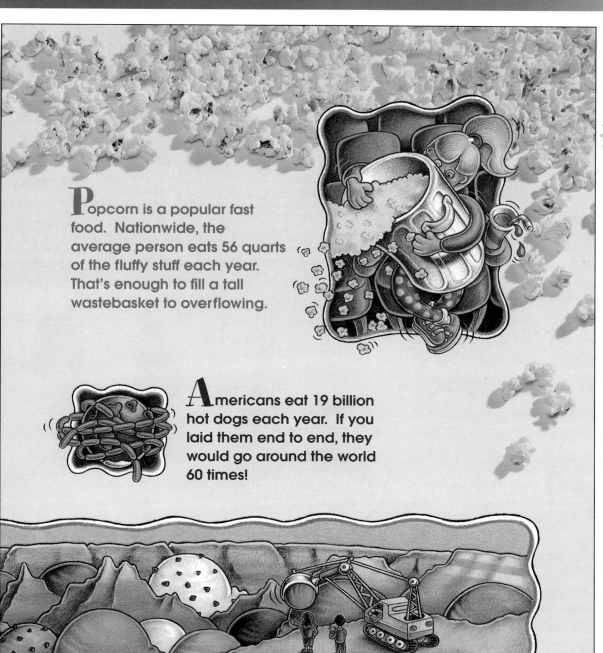

Popcorn is a popular fast food. Nationwide, the average person eats 56 quarts of the fluffy stuff each year. That's enough to fill a tall wastebasket to overflowing.

Americans eat 19 billion hot dogs each year. If you laid them end to end, they would go around the world 60 times!

123

Math Link

Explore with students the customary units used in the United States to measure weight (ounce, pound, ton) and liquids (cup, pint, quart, gallon). For example, have them fill a gallon container with water; then put the water into quart containers. How many quart containers are needed? Continue to explore other equivalencies. Some students acquiring English may want to share metric units.

Writing Stories

Use these facts to inspire students to write funny stories. For example, they might write about:

- a person who followed a trail of hot dogs around the world
- a family vacation to a Grand Canyon filled with ice cream
- a contest in which Americans go on a diet and try to eat only 1,000 pounds of food a year

Health Link

Cooperative Learning

Ask students to save the Nutrition Facts on a food package the next time they have a snack. Then have them work in small groups to compare and contrast the information for various foods.

Discussion

- Which food fact did you think was the funniest? Why?
- Do you think you consume more or less of each of these foods than the average American?

Theme Assessment Wrap-Up

Time: About 1 hour

Evaluates:

1 **Theme Concept:** Food is an important aspect of a culture's identity.

2 **Skills:** Problem Solving/Decision Making, Following Directions

This is a brief, informal performance assessment activity. For a more extended reading-writing performance assessment, see the Integrated Theme Test.

Literacy Activity Book, p. 52

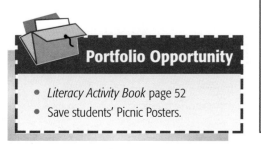

Planning a Picnic

Work in groups to plan a picnic. Each person in the group should plan to take one or two kinds of food. Fill out the chart to help you plan your project.

Where will your picnic be? _____

What food will you take? _____

List the good and bad things about the food that you'll bring.

+ (pros)	— (cons)

Make a poster of your picnic plan. With your group, follow these steps. Make sure to read all of the directions before you start.

1. Give your poster a title. Write it at the top.
2. On separate sheets of paper, draw pictures of the food you plan to take.
3. Cut out and paste your pictures on the poster. Under each drawing, write the reasons you think your food is a good choice for a picnic.
4. Present your poster to the class.

Portfolio Opportunity

- *Literacy Activity Book* page 52
- Save students' Picnic Posters.

PERFORMANCE ASSESSMENT

Planning a Picnic

LAB, p. 52

Materials
- tag board
- drawing paper
- crayons
- pencils

Introducing

Invite students to work in groups to make a poster that presents their plan for a picnic. Have them use *Literacy Activity Book* page 52 to plan their project, following steps like these:

2 Groups follow directions on *Literacy Activity Book* page 52 to make picnic poster.

1 Groups choose the food they'll bring.

3 Present the poster to the class.

Evaluating

Students should explain what considerations led to their decisions about what food to bring. They should address how they met the criteria on the *Literacy Activity Book* page 52 Checklist. Evaluate using the scoring rubric.

Scoring Rubric

Criterion	1	2	3	4
Makes realistic attempt to plan a picnic	Does not plan picnic	Some elements are consistent with a picnic	Most elements are consistent with a picnic	All elements are consistent with picnic
Makes decisions	Does not make practical decisions about food	Some decisions about food are practical	Most decisions are practical	Picnic plan is creative and practical
Follows directions	Does not follow directions	Follows some directions	Follows most directions	Follows all directions

Choices for Assessment

Informal Assessment

Review the Informal Assessment Checklist and observation notes to determine:

- Which selections did students enjoy most?
- How well did students apply comprehension skills to the theme?
- In what areas do students need more practice or support?

Formal Assessment

Select formal tests that meet your needs:

- Integrated Theme Test for What's Cooking?
- Theme Skills Test for What's Cooking?
- Benchmark Progress Test

See the *Teacher's Assessment Handbook* for guidelines on administering and scoring tests.

Portfolio Assessment

Helping Students Make Selections for the Portfolio

- Make a list of reasons for choosing an item for a portfolio, such as one's best work, a favorite, or a piece that emphasizes a certain skill or type of work. Then model the process, thinking aloud about the reasons for making a selection.
- In the beginning, have students talk about their choices and reasons. Later, students could complete entry slips, explaining their choices.

Evaluating Oral Language

- During class discussion or small group work, focus on one or two students. Note your observations on the Oral Language Checklist.
- Provide structured opportunities to help students self-evaluate their oral language abilities.
- Role-playing or dramatizing a story will give students acquiring English opportunities for practice and evaluation.

Managing Assessment

Evaluating Writing

Question: How can I evaluate students' writing?

Answer: Try these tips for evaluating writing processes, informal writing, and formal writing:

- Use the Writing Process Checklist. Discuss the process with students, as needed.
- Use first drafts and journal writing to evaluate writing fluency.
- For more formal writing assessment, use the rubrics in the *Teacher's Assessment Handbook* for criteria for different types of writing.
- When evaluating writing, identify one area of concern and concentrate on this area. Periodically collect representative samples to use in checking for growth.
- As students learn usage and mechanics skills, have them keep a list of the skills. Ask them to become responsible for using these skills by referring to their checklists when they are writing for an audience.

See also the *Teacher's Assessment Handbook.*

MINILESSON ASSESSMENT

Spelling Review

Review with students the Spelling Words and, if appropriate, the Challenge Words from the spelling lessons on pages 37J, 58I, 84I, 91E, and 121J. Have volunteers summarize each spelling principle and explain how the words in each lesson illustrate the principle.

Pretest/Test

1. Please set the <u>table</u> for <u>dinner</u>.
2. Did you <u>want</u> a <u>slice</u> of bread?
3. Will we eat <u>here</u> or <u>there</u>?
4. Let's eat lunch with the <u>new</u> <u>girl</u>.
5. That <u>yellow</u> <u>apple</u> looks good.
6. Let's <u>invite</u> <u>our</u> classmates to a party.
7. Buy grape <u>jam</u> at the <u>market</u>.
8. I <u>never</u> <u>hear</u> the lunch bell.
9. Do you see those boys? I think <u>they're</u> our <u>age</u>.
10. Do you live in a <u>large</u> <u>city</u>?

Challenge Words

11. The <u>princess</u> <u>wouldn't</u> eat.
12. I <u>wonder</u> who dug this <u>hole</u>?
13. He tried to <u>ignore</u> the <u>whole</u> class.
14. It is a long <u>distance</u> to the <u>village</u>.
15. Please wait <u>while</u> I get <u>another</u> book.

See

5-Day Planner

Spelling Plan p. 121J

Challenge

Challenge Words Practice Have students use the Challenge Words to write a summary of a story idea.

Literacy Activity Book

Spelling Practice: pp. 139–140
Take-Home Word Lists: pp. 173–174

Celebrating the Theme

Choices for Celebrating

Food Fest

Cooperative Learning Hold a food fest in which you enjoy both the dishes described in this theme and any recipes students might like to share from their homes. Assemble students into small teams and assign responsibility for various tasks, such as collecting ingredients, measuring, mixing, cooking, serving, and clean-up. Also consider inviting students from other classrooms to come and enjoy what's cooking in your classroom.

1. Make a large chart of different recipes so that students can follow them easily.

2. Encourage students to research different recipes for the same dish and prepare the one they find easiest or most desirable.

Home Connection You may wish to have parents and other family members visit in order to help in the preparation of the food and to share how they first learned to cook it.

Materials
- measuring cups
- trays
- disposable dishware
- hot plate
- pots and pans
- silverware
- chopsticks
- napkins
- cutting board
- vegetable peeler

Sukiyaki

Ingredients:
1 lb. sirloin (sliced thinly)
1 bunch scallions
3 medium onions, cut in rings
2 pounds spinach
half-lb. mushrooms
1 celery cabbage
Soy sauce
Sugar

1. Put small amount of vegetables in hot skillet. Add the meat last.
2. Sprinkle sugar over the mixture. Add soy sauce.
3. Serve with rice.

Chili

Ingredients:
1 small onion
half-lb. ground beef
4 cups of canned tomatoes
2 teaspoons of salt
2 tablespoons chili powder
6 tablespoons of flour

1. Brown onion. Add ground beef and cook until done.
2. Mix chili powder, flour, and salt. Add to meat and onion mixture.
3. Add tomatoes and cook until mixture thickens. Serves 12.

Make a World Map

Have students work together to make a large world map in which they label where the various foods they read about in this theme originated. For example, they would label Korea for the kimbap from *Halmoni and the Picnic* and Italy for the panettone in *Tony's Bread.*

Students Acquiring English
Encourage students to add foods from their native countries to the map and to share with their classmates how these foods are prepared.

Master Exhibit

Create a master exhibit featuring the best student work from this theme. Encourage students to be creative in how it is arranged. Then invite other classes and family members to enjoy the exhibit.

Self-Assessment

Have students meet in small groups to compare and discuss their Selection Connection charts (*Literacy Activity Book,* p. 2). Ask groups to share answers to questions such as the following:

- Why is food a good way of bringing people together?
- Why was this theme called *What's Cooking?*
- Who was your favorite character in the stories in this theme?

Glossary

Some of the words in this book may have pronunciations or meanings you do not know. This glossary can help you by telling you how to pronounce those words and by telling you the meanings for the words as they are used in this book.

You can find out how to pronounce any glossary word by using the special spelling after the word and the key that runs across the bottom of the glossary pages.

The full pronunciation key on the next page shows how to pronounce each consonant and vowel in a special spelling. The pronunciation key at the bottom of the glossary pages is a shortened form of the full key.

324

Full Pronunciation Key

Consonant Sounds

b	**bib**, ca**bb**age	kw	**ch**oir, **qu**ick	t	**t**igh**t**, stopp**ed**
ch	**ch**ur**ch**, sti**tch**	l	**l**id, need**l**e, ta**ll**	th	ba**th**, **th**in
d	**d**ee**d**, maile**d**, pu**dd**le	m	a**m**, **m**an, du**mb**	*th*	ba**th**e, **th**is
		n	**n**o, sudde**n**	v	ca**v**e, **v**al**v**e, **v**ine
f	**f**ast, **f**i**f**e, o**ff**, **ph**rase, rou**gh**	ng	thi**ng**, i**nk**	w	**w**ith, **w**olf
		p	**p**o**p**, ha**pp**y	y	**y**es, **y**olk, on**i**on
g	**g**a**g**, **g**et, fin**g**er	r	**r**oa**r**, **rh**yme	z	**r**o**s**e, **s**i**z**e, **x**ylophone, **z**ebra
h	**h**at, **wh**o	s	mi**ss**, **s**au**c**e, **sc**ene, **s**ee	zh	gara**g**e, plea**s**ure, vi**s**ion
hw	**wh**ich, **wh**ere				
j	**j**udge, **g**em	sh	di**sh**, **sh**ip, **s**ugar, ti**ss**ue		
k	**c**at, **k**i**ck**, s**ch**ool				

Vowel Sounds

ă	r**a**t, l**au**gh	ŏ	h**o**rrible, p**o**t	ŭ	c**u**t, fl**oo**d, r**ou**gh, s**o**me
ā	**a**pe, **ai**d, p**ay**	ō	g**o**, r**ow**, t**oe**, th**ough**	û	c**i**rcle, f**u**r, h**ea**rd, t**e**rm, t**u**rn, **u**rge, w**o**rd
â	**ai**r, c**a**re, w**ea**r				
ä	f**a**ther, k**oa**la, y**a**rd	ô	**a**ll, c**au**ght, f**o**r, p**aw**		
ĕ	p**e**t, pl**ea**sure, **a**ny	oi	b**oy**, n**oi**se, **oi**l	yōō	c**u**re
ē	b**e**, b**ee**, **ea**sy, p**ia**no	ou	c**ow**, **ou**t	yōō	**a**buse, **u**se
ĭ	**i**f, p**i**t, b**u**sy	ōō	f**u**ll, t**oo**k, w**o**lf	ə	**a**bout, sil**e**nt, penc**i**l, lem**o**n, circ**u**s
ī	b**y**, p**ie**, h**igh**	ōō	b**oo**t, fr**ui**t, fl**ew**		
î	d**ea**r, d**ee**r, f**ie**rce, m**e**re				

Stress marks

Primary Stress ´: bi•ol•o•gy [bī **ŏl´** ə jē]
Secondary Stress ´: bi•o•log•i•cal [bī˝ ə **lŏj´** i kəl]

325

A

ad•o•ra•tion (ăd´ ə **rā´** shən) *noun* Great love: *The bride and groom gave each other rings to show their* **adoration** *for each other.*

a•lert (ə **lûrt´**) *noun* A warning: *The siren on an ambulance is an* **alert** *to people driving cars or crossing the street.*

> **ALERT**
> *Alert comes from the Italian all'erta, meaning "on the watch."*

a•pol•o•gize (ə **pŏl´** ə jīz´) *verb* To say that one is sorry: *Nicole* **apologized** *to Malcolm for having lost his library book.*

ar•gu•ment (**är´** gyə mənt) *noun* A disagreement: *The two boys had an* **argument** *about what to watch on TV.*

as•sure (ə **shōōr´**) *verb* To make certain: *The teacher* **assured** *me that if I studied, I would do well on the test.*

C

car (kär) *noun* **1.** An automobile: *Mom drives her* **car** *to work, but Dad takes a train.* **2.** A section of a train: *A freight train has many* **cars** *for carrying goods.*

freight cars

> **CAR**
> In ancient times, the Celts (who lived in Europe) had a kind of wagon called a *karros*. It was used to move armies from place to place. The ancient Romans changed the word *karros* to *carrus*.

cau•tious•ly (**kô´** shəs lē) *adverb* In a careful way, without taking chances: *Children who walk to school should cross streets* **cautiously**.

clat•ter (**klăt´** ər) *verb* To make a loud, rattling sound: *The baby sat on the kitchen floor and* **clattered** *the pots and pans.*

326

coax (kōks) *verb* To try to persuade: *Gloria* **coaxed** *the cat to come down from the tree by offering it a bowl of milk.*

court (kôrt) *verb* To try to win the love of someone: *The young man sent red roses to the woman he wished to* **court**.

creak (krēk) *verb* To squeak: *Olga tried to tiptoe quietly down the stairs, but then one of the old floorboards* **creaked**.

D

dam•age (**dăm´** ĭj) *noun* Harm: *Our new puppy did some* **damage** *to Dad's slipper when she chewed on it.*

damage

de•cent (**dē´** sənt) *adjective* Proper: *It's not* **decent** *to borrow something from a friend and then not return it.*

de•fi•ant (dĭ **fī´** ənt) *adjective* Showing a refusal to obey: *If you stamp your feet and shout "NO!" when told to do something, you are being* **defiant**.

dig•ni•fied (**dĭg´** nə fīd´) *adjective* Acting in a proper or serious way: *The mayor is a* **dignifed** *woman, whom people of our town respect and look up to.*

dis•turb (dĭ **stûrb´**) *verb* To break in on or bother: *Do not* **disturb** *your sister while she is doing her homework.*

E

em•bank•ment (ĕm **băngk´** mənt) *noun* A small hill of dirt or rocks: *The* **embankment** *along the river keeps the water from flooding our fields during a storm.*

embankment

327

em•bar•rassed (ĕm bărˊ əst) *adjective* Feeling ill at ease: *Eli felt nervous or **embarrassed** when he saw that everyone else had brought a present to the party.*

en•gi•neer (ĕnˊ jə **nir**ˊ) *noun* A person who runs the locomotive on a train: *When the **engineer** saw a deer on the tracks, he blew the whistle to scare the animal off.*

engineer

ENGINEER
This word was formed by adding the ending -er, meaning "one who," to the word engine. Engine comes from an Old French word meaning "skill."

 G

glare (glâr) *verb* To look at someone in an angry way: *Mr. Brooks **glared** at Nan when he saw her taking a shortcut through his yard.*

glow•er (glouˊ ər) *verb* To stare at in an angry or threatening way: *Mr. Brooks **glowered** at the kids who batted a baseball through his window.*

 H

hail (hāl) *noun* Small pieces of frozen rain. Hail usually falls during a thunderstorm.

hail

 I

in•dig•nant (ĭn **dĭg**ˊ nənt) *adjective* Showing anger: *Jordan gave me an **indignant** look when I told him to sit down and be quiet.*

in•fec•tion (ĭn **fĕk**ˊ shən) *noun* A disease that can be passed from one person or animal to another: *The doctor gave Vanessa medicine to take for her throat **infection**.*

à rat / à pay / à care / à father / è pet / ē be / ĭ pit / ī pie / î fierce / ŏ pot / ō go / ô paw, for / oi oil / ŏŏ took

328

---

in•sist (ĭn **sĭst**ˊ) *verb* To demand: *Grandpa **insisted** that Ari stop reading and go to sleep.*

 L

lo•cal (lōˊ kəl) *adjective* Making lots of stops: *The **local** train takes longer than the express because it makes more stops.*

LOCAL
Local comes from a Latin word meaning "place."

 M

mend (mĕnd) *verb* To heal or get better: *Mara's broken arm is **mending**, but it must remain in a cast for two more weeks.*

mend

MEND
Mend is a shortened form of the word amend, which means "to change."

mod•est•ly (mŏdˊ ist lē) *adverb* In a humble way: *Lynn bragged about winning the girls' race, but José accepted his first-place prize **modestly**.*

 N

no•ble•man (nōˊ bəl mən) *noun* A man of high rank, often with a title: *The king gave the **nobleman** land, money, and the title of duke.*

nobleman

NOBLEMAN
Long ago, when people used the word nobleman, it meant "well-known man."

 O

op•er•ate (ŏpˊ ə rātˊ) *verb* To do surgery, as a doctor does: *Dr. Brady **operated** on Bobby to take out his tonsils.*

ŏŏ boot / ou out / ŭ cut / û fur / hw which / th thin / th this / zh vision / ə about, silent, pencil, lemon, circus

329

 P

pan•ic (pănˊ ĭk) *verb* To suddenly feel great fear: *When a wave washed Suki off her float, she started to **panic**.*

PANIC
The word panic comes from the name Pan. Pan was a god worshipped by the ancient Greeks. Pan caused fear in herds of cattle as well as in crowds of people.

pa•tient (pāˊ shənt) *noun* One being treated by a doctor or dentist: *Dr. Ramirez gave flu shots to many of her **patients**.*

patient

PATIENT
Patient comes from a Latin word meaning "suffering."

plod (plŏd) *verb* To walk with great effort: *The snow was deep now, and people were **plodding** through it to get home.*

PLOD
Plod is a sound word. It imitates the sound someone makes as he or she walks with heavy footsteps.

pro•pos•al (prə pōˊ zəl) *noun* A plan or an offer: *Dad said, "I'll make you a **proposal**. If you clean your room, I'll take you to the movies."*

pro•test (prōˊ tĕstˊ) *verb* To complain: *Julio wanted to keep on swimming, so he **protested** when I said, "It's time to go home."*

 R

re•lieved (rĭ **lēvd**ˊ) *adjective* Less worried: *I felt so **relieved** to see Rex that I didn't punish him for running off.*

re•luc•tant•ly (rĭ **lŭk**ˊ tənt lē) *adverb* In a way that shows unwillingness: *Fran turned the TV off **reluctantly** because she didn't want to go to bed.*

à rat / à pay / à care / à father / è pet / ē be / ĭ pit / ī pie / î fierce / ŏ pot / ō go / ô paw, for / oi oil / ŏŏ took

330

---

rum•ble (rŭmˊ bəl) *noun* A deep, rolling sound, like distant thunder: *As we neared the amusement park, we could hear the **rumble** of the old roller coaster.*

 S

sched•ule (skĕjˊ ŏŏl) *or* (skĕjˊ əl) *noun* A list of the times when trains, buses, or planes arrive and depart: *Mike checked the **schedule** to see what time our train would arrive.*

schedule

SCHEDULE
Schedule comes from the Latin word for "sheet of papyrus." Papyrus was what ancient Romans (and Egyptians) used for paper.

scoff (skŏf) *or* (skôf) *verb* To mock or laugh at: *Ted was surprised when Anna got a home run; he had **scoffed** at the idea of having a girl on the team.*

scowl (skoul) *verb* To frown angrily: *Jennifer **scowled** when she couldn't find her skates.*

scowl

snick•er (snĭkˊ ər) *verb* To laugh in a mean way: *Tony **snickered** when his dog jumped up and grabbed the hamburger I was about to eat.*

sol•emn (sŏlˊ əm) *adjective* Very serious: *To be on the team, you have to make a **solemn** promise to obey all the rules.*

spoil (spoil) *verb* **1.** To hurt someone's character by always giving in or by praising too much: *That little boy cries whenever he can't have what he wants; I think his family has **spoiled** him.* **2.** To ruin: *The rip **spoiled** Sam's new jacket.*

ŏŏ boot / ou out / ŭ cut / û fur / hw which / th thin / th this / zh vision / ə about, silent, pencil, lemon, circus

331

---

sput•ter (spŭt′ ər) *verb* To speak in a confused way; to stammer: *When we shouted "Happy birthday!" Helen was so surprised that she **sputtered** words no one could understand.*

strained (strānd) *adjective* Tense and uncomfortable: *Ken and I had had a fight, so our next phone conversation was **strained.***

stride (strīd) *verb* To walk forward: *Gina **strode** up to the front of the classroom to give her report.*

sur•ger•y (sûr′ jə rē) *noun* Operating on someone to remove or repair diseased body parts: *The doctor will need to perform **surgery** on Grandpa to repair his heart.*

surgery

T

tem•per•a•ture (tĕm′ pər ə chər) *noun* Hotness of one's body, as measured by a thermometer: *If your **temperature** is much above 98.6°F, you have a fever and may be sick.*

tor•na•do (tôr nā′ dō) *noun* A violent kind of storm, in which winds spin around in a funnel-shaped cloud.

tornado

TORNADO
Tornado comes from the Spanish word *tronada,* which is a form of the verb *tronar,* meaning "to thunder."

ă rat / ā pay / â care / ä father / ĕ pet / ē be / ĭ pit / ī pie / î fierce / ŏ pot / ō go / ô paw, for / oi oil / o͝o took
332

tri•um•phant•ly (trī ŭm′ fənt lē) *adverb* In a way that shows happiness at having won or been successful: *After winning the football game, the team ran **triumphantly** from the field.*

TRIUMPHANTLY
This word comes from the Latin word *triumphus.* In ancient Rome, it referred to a parade honoring a general for victory over an enemy.

trudge (trŭj) *verb* To walk very slowly and with effort: *The children had to **trudge** through the deep snow to get to the bus stop.*

W

whine (wīn) *verb* To make a crying sound: *Whenever our dog wanted to go out, she sat at the front door and **whined.***

whoop (ho͞op) *or* (hwo͞op) *or* (wo͞op) *verb* To cry out loudly: *When Scott got a home run, his team **whooped** with joy.*

wrecked (rĕkt) *adjective* Ruined: *I cried as I looked at my **wrecked** bike; I shouldn't have left it in the driveway.*

Y

yield (yēld) *verb* To give in: *The horse wanted to run, but Betsy held the reins tightly and wouldn't **yield.***

o͞o boot / ou out / ŭ cut / û fur / hw which / th thin / *th* this / zh vision / ə about, silent, pencil, lemon, circus
333

ACKNOWLEDGMENTS

For each of the selections listed below, grateful acknowledgment is made for permission to excerpt and/or reprint original or copyrighted material, as follows:

Selections

Brave Irene, written and illustrated by William Steig. Copyright © 1986 by William Steig. Reprinted by permission of Farrar, Straus & Giroux, Inc.
"A Calendar for Kids," from *The Second Kids' World Almanac of Records and Facts*, by Margo McLoone-Basta and Alice Siegel. Copyright © 1987 by Margo McLoone-Basta and Alice Siegel. Reprinted by permission of Funk & Wagnalls Corporation.
"Celebration," by Alonzo Lopez, from *Whispering Wind*, by Terry Allen. Copyright © 1972 by the Institute of American Indian Arts. Reprinted by permission of Doubleday, a division of Bantam Doubleday Dell Publishing Group, Inc. Illustration by Tomie dePaola, from *Tomie dePaola's Book of Poems.* Copyright © 1988 by Tomie dePaola. Reprinted by permission of G. P. Putnam's Sons.
Chicken Sunday, written and illustrated by Patricia Polacco. Copyright © 1992 by Patricia Polacco. Reprinted by permission of Philomel Books.
"Fun Food Facts," copyright © 1994 by Meredith Corporation. Reprinted by permission of *Crayola Kids™* magazine. All rights reserved. Crayola® and Crayola Kids™ are trademarks of Binney & Smith Properties, Inc.
"Get the Facts on Fast Foods," from September 1993 *Current Health 1* magazine. Reprinted by permission. Copyright © 1993 Weekly Reader Corporation.
"The Great Hair Argument," from *Ramona and Her Mother*, by Beverly Cleary. Copyright © 1979 by Beverly Cleary. Reprinted by permission of Morrow Junior Books, a division of William Morrow & Company, Inc.
"The Greatest Storms on Earth," from December 1992 *Kids Discover* magazine. Copyright © 1992 by Kids Discover Magazine. Reprinted by permission.
Halmoni and the Picnic, by Sook Nyul Choi, illustrated by Karen Milone Dugan. Text copyright © 1993 by Sook Nyul Choi. Illustrations copyright © 1993 by Karen Milone Dugan. Reprinted by permission of Houghton Mifflin Company. All rights reserved.
"How snowmaker was taught a lesson," from *How we saw the world*, by C. J. Taylor. Copyright © 1993 by C. J. Taylor. Reprinted by permission of Tundra Books.
Mac & Marie & the Train Toss Surprise, by Elizabeth Fitzgerald Howard, illustrations by Gail Gordon Carter. Text copyright © 1993 by Elizabeth Fitzgerald Howard. Illustrations copyright © 1993 by Gail Gordon Carter. Reprinted by permission of Simon & Schuster Books for Young Readers, Simon & Schuster Children's Publishing Division.
"Pronunciation Key," from the *American Heritage Children's Dictionary.* Copyright © 1994 by Houghton Mifflin Company. Reprinted by permission. All rights reserved.
"Ribsy and the Roast," from *Henry and Beezus*, by Beverly Cleary. Copyright © 1952 by Beverly Cleary. Reprinted by permission of Morrow Junior Books, a division of William Morrow & Company, Inc.
"Sandwiches from Around the World," by Ann Hinga Klein. Copyright © 1994 by the Meredith Corporation. Reprinted by permission of *Crayola Kids™* magazine. All rights reserved. Crayola® and Crayola Kids™ are trademarks of Binney & Smith Properties, Inc.
Say Woof! written and illustrated by Gail Gibbons. Copyright © 1992 by Gail Gibbons. Reprinted by permission of the author.
Storm in the Night, by Mary Stolz, illustrated by Pat Cummings. Text copyright © 1988 by Mary Stolz. Illustrations copyright © 1988 by Pat Cummings. Reprinted by permission of HarperCollins Publishers.
"This has been a good day!" from *As You Like It, Charlie Brown*, by Charles M. Schulz. Copyright © 1963, 64 by United Feature Syndicate, Inc. Reprinted by permission.
Tony's Bread, written and illustrated by Tomie dePaola. Copyright © 1989 by Tomie dePaola. Reprinted by permission of G. P. Putnam's Sons.
Tornado Alert, by Franklyn M. Branley. Copyright © 1988 by Franklyn M. Branley. Reprinted by permission of HarperCollins Publishers.
"Wind and Weather," from *175 Science Experiments to Amuse and Amaze Your Friends*, by Brenda Walpole, illustrated by Kuo Kang Chen and Peter Bull. Copyright © 1988 by Grisewood & Dempsey Ltd. Reprinted by permission of Random House, Inc.

Poetry

"I'd Never Eat a Beet," from *The New Kid on the Block*, by Jack Prelutsky. Copyright © 1984 by Jack Prelutsky. Reprinted by permission of Greenwillow books, a division of William Morrow & Company.
"Snowflakes," from *Half Past Four*, by Suk-Joong Yoon. Copyright © 1978 by Suk-Joong Yoon. Reprinted by permission of F. T. Yoon Company.

334

"Spaghetti! Spaghetti!" from *Rainy Rainy Saturday*, by Jack Prelutsky. Copyright © 1980 by Jack Prelutsky. Reprinted by permission of Greenwillow Books, a division of William Morrow & Company. Art from *Never Take a Pig to Lunch and Other Poems About the Fun of Eating*, by Nadine Bernard Westcott. Copyright © 1994 by Nadine Bernard Westcott. Reprinted by permission of Orchard Books.
"Sunflakes," from *Country Pie*, by Frank Asch. Copyright © 1979 by Frank Asch. Reprinted by permission of Greenwillow Books, a division of William Morrow & Company, Inc.
"That Kind Of Day," from *Under the Sunday Tree*, by Eloise Greenfield, paintings by Amos Ferguson. Text copyright © 1988 by Eloise Greenfield. Paintings copyright © 1988 by Amos Ferguson. Reprinted by permission of HarperCollins Publishers.
"Who Has Seen the Wind?" by Christina Rossetti, traditional domain.

Additional Acknowledgments

Special thanks to the following teachers whose students' compositions are included in this level:

Leticia Albright, E. A. Jones Elementary School, Missouri City, Texas; Alice Holstein, Dana Hall School, Newton, Massachusetts; Ron Gunter, Taylors Elementary School, Taylors, South Carolina; Theresa Callicott, North Jackson Elementary School, Jackson, Mississippi; Betsy Turner, Clays Mill Elementary School, Lexington, Kentucky; Jane Merritt, Mountainside Elementary School, Fort Carson, Colorado

CREDITS

Illustration **18–35** Tomie dePaola; **43–57** Karen M. Dugan; **62–81** Alan Tiegreen; **93–120** Patricia Polacco; **122–123** Greg Valley; **130–148** George Guzzi; **195–218** William Steig; **220, 222** C. J. Taylor; **232–253** Alan Tiegreen; **265–286** Gail Gordon Carter; **295–320** Gail Gibbons; **322** Tomie dePaola; **323** Charles M. Schulz

Photography **36** Suki Coughlin (1994) **42** Courtesy of Sook Nyu Choi/Houghton Mifflin Co. (tl) Courtesy of Karen Dugan (br) **82** Courtesy of Beverly Cleary (t); Courtesy of Alan Tiegreen (b) **82-83** Gary Cralle/The Image Bank (background) **83** Lee Hunt **91** Courtesy of Christina Vela **92-93** © 1994 Lawrence Migdale 1994 **125** ©Jeffrey Brown/Liason International **126-7** J. Amos/H. Armstrong Roberts **128-9** ©Naoki Okamoto/The Stock Market **130** Courtesy of Franklyn M. Branley (tl); Courtesy of George Guzzi **135** J.H. Golden/Photo Researchers (br) **142-143** Frank Rossotto/The Stock Market **150-1** ©Jeff Heger 1985/FPG International **152** ©Frank Rossotto/The Stock Market; ©Viviane Moos/The Stock Market **156** Courtesy of Mary Stolz; Courtesy of Pat Cummings **156-157** © 93 Wolf Maehl/ Zefa/The Stock Market **187** ©Chip Porter/©Tony Stone Images/Chicago Inc **189** Courtesy of Annie Holstein **190** Merrilee Thomas (cover); Kent Wood/Photo Researchers (m) **191** The Granger Collection (bl); Sigrid Heilig/Photo Researchers (br); Howard Bluestein/Photo Researchers (t) **192** D. Olsen/Weatherstock; Hasler & Pierce, NASA /GSFC/Science Photo Library **193** Library of Congress (tr); Brian Brake/Photo Researchers (br); Lawrence Migdale/Photo Researchers (tl); NOAA/ National Geophysical Data Center (bl) **194-5** ©Richard Pasley/Liason International **194** ©Rob Nelson/ Courtesy of William Steig (bl) **224-225** © 1995 Museum of Modern Art (m) **254** William Morrow & Co./ Courtesy of Beverly Cleary (tl); Courtesy of Alan Tiegreen (b) **257** Courtesy of Andy Costa **258** Obremski/The Image Bank (br) **259** The Bettmann Archive (tl); Guido Rossi/The Image Bank (m); David Jeffrey/The Image Bank (bm); UPI/Bettmann (bl) **260** The Bettmann Archive (br); Benn Mitchell/The Image Bank (tr); G.V. Faint/The Image Bank (ml); Ron Rovtar/FPG International (bm) **261** Jeff Hunter/The Image Bank (tl); The Bettmann Archive (mr); Kevin Forest/The Image Bank (bl); Mel Digiacomo/The Image Bank (bm) **262** Michel Tcherevkoff/The Image Bank (m); Co Rentmeester/The Image Bank (bl); Micheal Quackenbush/The Image Bank (bm) **263** The Bettmann Archive (ml); The Stock Market (br); Phillip Kretchmar/The Image Bank (tl); Richard Hutchings/Photo Researchers (tm) **264** Courtesy of Elizabeth Fitzgerald Howard; Courtesy of Gail Gordon Carter **264-5** ©James Randklev/Tony Stone Images/Chicago Inc **286** Courtesy of Elizabeth Fitzgerald Howard (m) **290** Courtesy of Jamie Coleman (br) **291** Rohan/ Tony Stone Images/Chicago Inc; Courtesy of Matthew Uckotter (tr) **292** Max Gibbs/Animals Animals; Courtesy of Beverly Hernandez (tl) **293** W. Anthony/West Stock; Courtesy of Joe Sturdivant (tr) **294** Courtesy of Gail Gibbons (tm) **326** John Vachon/The Image Bank (r) **327** Steve Dunwell/The Image Bank (l); The Image Bank (r) **328** Edward Bower/The Image Bank (l); Phil Degginger/Animals Animals (r) **329** Stock Boston (l); Robert Frerck/Tony Stone Images (r) **330** Chris Jones/The Stock Market (l) **332** The Image Bank (l); Eric Meola/The Image Bank (r)

335

Glossary 123F

Teacher's Handbook

TABLE OF CONTENTS

Study Skills

Globes

INTERACTIVE LEARNING

Teach/Model

Display a globe and have students share what they know about globes. Explain that a globe is a spherical model of the earth. Tell students that a globe shows the locations of the earth's features.

As you display the classroom globe, use the Think Aloud to model how to use it. Point to specific places as you identify them.

Think Aloud

I can use this globe to find places. I can point to the North Pole, which is at the top of the globe, or to the South Pole, which is at the bottom of the globe. I know that the large land areas are continents. Inside the continents are countries in different colors. I can find China, a country where many people use chopsticks. I can also find Italy, a country famous for its spaghetti.

Oceans are blue. I can point to the Pacific Ocean and to the Atlantic Ocean. I can tell that the Atlantic Ocean is smaller than the Pacific Ocean.

I know that the United States lies between the Pacific Ocean and the Atlantic Ocean. I look for the words *United States*. I can even find the state I live in. I can see how far my state is from China. Reading a globe teaches me a lot about places in the world.

Practice/Apply

Have students take turns demonstrating how to use a globe. When they are done, ask questions like these.

- Where is Great Britain, the country where the sandwich got its name?

- Many people in the United States enjoy Mexican food. Where is Mexico located in relation to the United States?

- German cooking and French cooking are different. Are Germany and France located far apart?

Have students summarize what they have learned about reading a globe by answering these questions.

- What is a globe?

- What information can you find by looking at a globe?

- How is a globe different from a map?

SKILL FINDER — Minilesson, p. 39

Library: Fiction Books

INTERACTIVE LEARNING

Teach/Model

If possible, take the class to a library. Ask students if they know the difference between fiction and nonfiction. If necessary, tell them that books with made-up characters and stories are fiction. Books that are factual, telling about real people, places, things, and events, are nonfiction.

Display Transparency H–8. Tell students they will learn how to find books in the fiction section of the library.

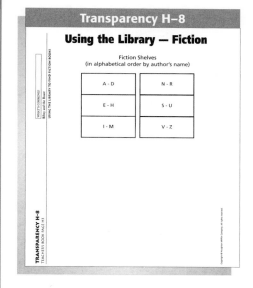

Transparency H–8

Using the Library — Fiction

Fiction Shelves
(in alphabetical order by author's name)

A - D	N - R
E - H	S - U
I - M	V - Z

Think Aloud

To find a fiction book in the library, I know I must go to the fiction section. Fiction books appear in alphabetical order by the last name of the author. I want to find a book by William Steig. Steig begins with *S*, so I look for the shelves that include the letter *S*. The shelves marked **S–U** contain the letter *S*. William Steig's books will be on these shelves. If the first letter of two last names is the same, I would look at the second letter. Elizabeth Shub's books come before books by William Steig because *h* comes before *t*. I can find any fiction book in the library if I know the author's name.

Practice/Apply

Have students take turns demonstrating how to locate a fiction book. When they are done, ask questions like these.

- On what shelves would you find books by Beverly Cleary?

- Would Jane Yolen's books come before or after Chris Van Allsburg's? (If necessary, point out that Van Allsburg is one last name.)

- On what shelves would you find the Narnia books by C. S. Lewis?

Have students summarize what they have learned about using the library by answering these questions.

- What have you learned today?

- What is a fiction book?

- How are fiction books arranged in the library?

SKILL FINDER Minilesson, p. 79

Reading Charts

Reading Charts

Sales of Bagels at Laura's Bagels

Time Sold	Types of Bagels			Hourly Total
	Plain	Sesame	Onion	
8:00 - 9:00 A.M.	14	8	9	31
9:00 -10:00 A.M.	9	11	0	20
10:00 -11:00 A.M.	13	9	12	34
12:00 - 1:00 P.M.	12	15	10	37
Total Kinds of Bagels Sold	48	43	31	

INTERACTIVE LEARNING

Teach/Model

Discuss with students how they can use a chart to share information. Point out that a chart allows information to be read quickly and easily. Display Transparency H–9. Note that the chart tells about the sales at a restaurant, Laura's Bagels.

Think Aloud

The first things I read on a chart are the title and labels. The title tells me that the chart shows the sales of bagels at Laura's Bagels. The labels on the top tell what kinds of bagels are sold: plain, sesame, and onion. The label at the left tells when the bagels were sold. The first row of numbers tells how many bagels were sold between 8:00 and 9:00 A.M. The first number on the left is under the label "Plain." That means that Laura sold 14 plain bagels between 8:00 and 9:00 A.M. The number 31 on the far right is under the label "Hourly Total." That means that Laura sold a total of 31 bagels between 8:00 and 9:00 A.M.

Reading down the first column of numbers, I can compare how many plain bagels Laura sold at different times. The bottom row of numbers tells the total number of each kind of bagel Laura sold. This chart can give me a lot of information if I know how to read it.

Practice/Apply

Have students take turns demonstrating how to read the chart. Ask questions like these:

- How many onion bagels were sold between noon and 1:00 P.M.?

- How many sesame bagels were sold altogether?

- Which kind of bagel had the most sales?

- At what time were the most bagels sold?

- Which kind of bagel did not sell at all at a certain time?

Have students summarize what they have learned about reading a chart by answering these questions.

- What is a chart?

- What do you read first when looking at a chart?

- Why is a chart a good way to organize information?

SKILL FINDER ▸ Minilesson, p. 87

Teach/Model

Explain to students that taking notes as they read will help them remember important information. Stress the following points:

- Use a separate sheet of paper or index card for each topic.

- Write a main heading (a key word or phrase) for each topic.

- Below the heading, write important details about the topic. Number these details in order of importance.

Read aloud a paragraph from an encyclopedia and model how you would take notes.

Think Aloud

My topic to research is "What Pigs Eat." I can find this topic in the P book of the encyclopedia. I have a sheet of paper for notes. I will write the topic, "What Pigs Eat," at the top of the sheet. Next I will read the article about pigs in the encyclopedia. When I come to information about what pigs eat, I will write the important details in order. (Some encyclopedias have the information under the topic "Hogs.") For example, farmers feed pigs grains such as corn, wheat, rye, and oats. My first detail would read:

    1. Corn, wheat, rye, and oats.

I will write other numbered details telling other foods that pigs eat. When I am done, I will have the information written in a form I can use.

Practice/Apply

Have groups of students research animal topics. When students have completed their notes, ask questions like these:

- What information does the heading on your note paper give?

- What does each detail have to do with the topic?

- If you researched another topic, where would that information go?

Have students summarize what they have learned about reading a chart by answering these questions.

- How do you take notes?

- What is the importance of taking notes?

- Taking notes might be helpful in what other activities?

SKILL FINDER — Minilesson, Level 3.1, Theme 1

Library: Nonfiction Books

Transparency H–10

Using the Library — Nonfiction

Nonfiction Shelves
(by call number)

000 - 299	600 - 799
300 - 399	800 - 899
400 - 599	900 - 999

I N T E R A C T I V E   L E A R N I N G

Teach/Model
Take the class to the school or local library. Review the fact that the library has two main kinds of books: fiction and nonfiction. Ask a volunteer to tell the difference between the two. Students should recall that storybooks and books with made-up characters are fiction, while books that contain facts about real people, things, and events are nonfiction. Display Transparency H–10, which shows a sample library floor plan. Tell students they will learn how to find books in the nonfiction section of the library.

Think Aloud

I can find nonfiction books by subject in their own section of the library. Each subject has a special number, named a call number. To find the call number of a nonfiction book, I look in the card catalog or on the library computer. These sources list every book in the library. Once I know the call number, I look for the shelf that has that number. I know that the nonfiction shelves start with the lowest call numbers. A book on grasshoppers, call number 595.7, comes before a book on snakes, call number 597.9. Finding nonfiction books is easy when I know the call-number system.

Practice/Apply
Have groups of students work together to find books on the following topics: kangaroos, jazz, the Civil War, electricity, football. If you can't get to a library you might affix call numbers to the spines of nonfiction books with removable tape. Then have students work together to describe where they can find each library book. Have a volunteer point to that section on the transparency.

Ask students to summarize what they have learned about using the library by answering these questions.

- What is a nonfiction book?

- How are nonfiction books arranged in a library?

- Is it important to know an author's name to find a nonfiction book?

SKILL FINDER Minilesson, Level 3.2, Theme 6

INFORMAL ASSESSMENT CHECKLIST

Student Names

Record observations of student progress for those areas important to you.

− = **Beginning Understanding**
✔ = **Developing Understanding**
✔+ = **Proficient**

Tony's Bread									
Reading									
Responding									
Comprehension: Following Directions									
Writing Skills: Writing a Play									
Word Skills: Multiple-Meaning Words									
Spelling: First Sound in *city* and *just*									
Grammar: Helping Verbs									
Listening and Speaking									

Halmoni and the Picnic									
Reading									
Responding									
Comprehension: Predicting Outcomes									
Writing: Writing an Invitation									
Word Skills: Using Context									
Spelling: Words Ending with *-er* or *-le*									
Grammar: Irregular Verbs									
Listening and Speaking									

Henry and Beezus									
Reading									
Responding									
Comprehension: Sequence									
Writing Skills: Avoiding Stringy Sentences									

INFORMAL ASSESSMENT CHECKLIST

Record observations of student progress for those areas important to you.

− = **Beginning Understanding**
✔ = **Developing Understanding**
✔+ = **Proficient**

	Student Names							
Henry and Beezus *(continued)*								
Word Skills: Prefixes *un-* and *re-*								
Spelling: The VCCV Pattern								
Grammar: Punctuating Dialogue								
Listening and Speaking								
Reading-Writing Workshop								
Spelling: Words Often Misspelled								
Chicken Sunday								
Reading								
Responding								
Comprehension: Problem Solving/ Decision Making								
Writing Skills: Avoiding Stringy Sentences								
Word Skills: Homophones								
Spelling: Homophones								
Grammar: Commas in a Series								
Listening and Speaking								
Performance Assessment								
Spelling Review								
General Observation								
Independent Reading								
Independent Writing								
Work Habits								
Self-Assessment								

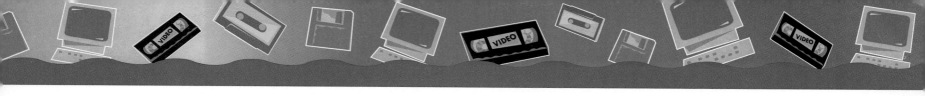

Audio-Visual Resources

Adventure Productions
3404 Terry Lake Road
Ft. Collins, CO 80524
970-493-8776

AIMS Media
9710 DeSoto Avenue
Chatsworth, CA
91311-4409
800-367-2467

Alfred Higgins Productions
6350 Laurel Canyon
Blvd.
N. Hollywood, CA
91606
800-766-5353

Audio Bookshelf
174 Prescott Hill Road
Northport, ME 04849
800-234-1713

Audio Editions
Box 6930
Auburn, CA 95604-6930
800-231-4261

Audio Partners, Inc.
Box 6930
Auburn, CA 95604-6930
800-231-4261

Bantam Doubleday Dell Audio
1540 Broadway
New York, NY 10036
212-782-9489

Bullfrog Films
Box 149
Oley, PA 19547
800-543-3764

Clearvue/EAV
6465 Avondale Ave.
Chicago, IL 60631
800-253-2788

Coronet/MTI
2349 Chaffee Drive
St. Louis, MO 63146
800-777-8100

Dial Books for Young Readers
375 Hudson St.
New York, NY 10014
800-526-0275

Direct Cinema Ltd.
P.O. Box 10003
Santa Monica, CA 90410
800-525-0000

Disney Educational Production
105 Terry Drive,
Suite 120
Newtown, PA 18940
800-295-5010

Encounter Video
14825 NW Ash St.
Portland, OR 97231
800-677-7607

Filmic Archives
The Cinema Center
Botsford, CT 06404
800-366-1920

Films for Humanities and Science
P.O. Box 2053
Princeton, NJ 08543
609-275-1400

Finley-Holiday Film Corp.
12607 E. Philadelphia St.
Whittier, CA 90601
562-945-3325

Fulcrum Publishing
350 Indiana St.
Golden, CO 80401
303-277-1623

HarperAudio
10 East 53rd Street
New York, NY 10022
212-207-6901

Houghton Mifflin/Clarion
181 Ballardvale St.
Wilmington, MA 01887
800-225-3362

Kidvidz
618 Centre St.
Newton, MA 02158
617-965-3345

Kimbo Educational
Box 477
Long Branch, NJ 07740
800-631-2187

Let's Create
50 Cherry Hill Rd.
Parsippany, NJ 07054
973-299-0633

Listening Library
One Park Avenue
Old Greenwich, CT
06870
800-243-4504

Live Oak Media
P.O. Box 652
Pine Plains, NY 12567
518-398-1010

McGraw-Hill
220 East Danieldale Rd.
Desoto, TX 75115
800-843-8855

Media Basics
Lighthouse Square
705 Boston Post Road
Guilford, CT 06437
800-542-2505

MGM/UA Home Video
2500 Broadway St.
Santa Monica, CA
90404-3061
310-449-3000

Milestone Film and Video
275 W. 96th St.
Suite 28C
New York, NY 10025
212-865-7449

Miramar
200 Second Ave.
Seattle, WA 98119
800-245-6472

National Geographic
1145 17th Street NW
Washington, DC 20036
800-368-2728

The Nature Company
P.O. Box 188
Florence, KY 41022
800-227-1114

PBS Video
1320 Braddock Place
Alexandria, VA
22314-1698
800-424-7963

Philomel Books
200 Madison Ave.
New York, NY 10016
212-951-8400

Premiere Home Video
755 N. Highland
Hollywood, CA 90038
213-934-8903

Puffin Books
375 Hudson St.
New York, NY 10014
212-366-2000

Rabbit Ears Books/Simon and Schuster
1230 Avenue of the
Americas
New York, NY 10020
800-223-2336

Rainbow Educational Media
4540 Preslyn Drive
Raleigh, NC 27616
800-331-4047

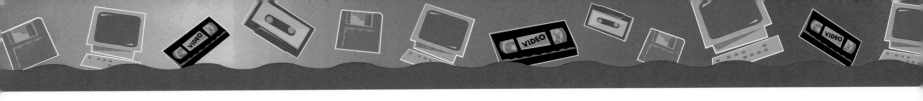

Audio-Visual Resources *(continued)*

Random House Media
400 Hahn Road
Westminster, MD 21157
800-733-3000

Recorded Books
270 Skipjack Road
Prince Frederick, MD
20678
800-638-1304

SelectVideo
5475 Peoria St., Unit 4C
Denver, CO 80239
800-742-1455

Silo/Alcazar
Box 429
Waterbury, VT 05676
802-844-5178

Spoken Arts
8 Lawn Ave.
New Rochelle, NY
10801
914-633-4516

SVE and Churchill Media
6677 N. Northwest
Highway
Chicago, IL 60631
800-334-7830

Time-Life Education
P.O. Box 85026
Richmond, VA
23285-5026
800-449-2010

Video Project
200 Estates Drive
Ben Lomond, CA 95005
800-475-2638

Warner Home Video
4000 Warner Blvd.
Burbank, CA 91522
818-954-6000

Weston Woods
12 Oakwood Ave.
Norwalk, CT 06850
800-243-5020

Wilderness Video
P.O.Box 3150
Ashland, OR 97520
541-488-9363

BOOKS AVAILABLE IN SPANISH
Spanish editions of English titles referred to in the Bibliography are available from the following publishers or distributors.

Bilingual Educational Services, Inc.
2514 South Grand Ave.
Los Angeles, CA
90007-9979
800-448-6032

Charlesbridge
85 Main Street
Watertown, MA 02172
617-926-0329

Children's Book Press
246 First St., Suite 101
San Francisco, CA 94105
415-995-2200

Econo-Clad Books
P.O. Box 1777
Topeka, KS 66601
785-233-4252

Farrar, Straus & Giroux
19 Union Square West
New York, NY 10003
212-741-6900

Grolier Publishing Co.
P.O. Box 1796
Danbury, CT 06816
800-621-1115

Harcourt Brace
6277 Sea Harbor Drive
Orlando, FL 32887
800-225-5425

HarperCollins
10 E. 53rd Street
New York, NY 10022
717-941-1500

Holiday House
425 Madison Ave.
New York, NY 10017
212-688-0085

Kane Press
48 W. 25th St.
New York, NY 10010
800-528-8273

Alfred A. Knopf
201 E. 50th St.
New York, NY 10022
800-726-0600

Lectorum
111 Eighth Ave.
New York, NY 10011
800-345-5946

Santillana
2105 NW 86th Ave.
Miami, FL 33122
800-245-8584

Simon and Schuster
1230 Avenue of the
Americas
New York, NY 10020
800-223-2336

Viking
357 Hudson Street
New York, NY 10014
212-366-2000

Index

Boldface page references indicate formal strategy and skill instruction.

Expanding literacy. *See* Literacy, expanding.

Expository text, 38–40, 122–123

Fluency, 21, 30, 37M, 50, 76, 104

Focus Skills, 37L, 41D, 58K, 121L

G

Generalizations, making, 84J

Genre. *See* Literary genres.

Glossary in Student Anthology, 123D–123F

Grammar and usage
 parts of sentence
  predicates, 37L
 parts of speech
  adjectives, 121B
  nouns
   abbreviations, 33
   singular and plural, 32
  verbs
   helping, **37K–37L.** *See also* Reading-Writing Workshop.
   irregular verbs, **58J–58K.** *See also* Reading-Writing Workshop.
   past tense, 58J–58K
 punctuation
  commas, 84J, 84K, 91E, 121K
  end marks, 84J, 84K
  quotation marks, **84J,** 84K. *See also* Reading-Writing Workshop.
 revising, 37L, 58K, 84K, 91E, 121L
 spelling connection, 91E

Graphic information, interpreting
 charts, 58A, **87,** 88, **H3**
 globes, **39,** 58O, **H2**
 maps, 19, 37P, 39, 107, 121N
 nutrition labels, 37P
 schedules, 55

Graphic organizers
 bulletin boards, 16G, 61
 charts, 33, 37P, 39, 41D, 53, 55, 58B, 58H, 58P, 65, 67, 84P, 87, 88, 91A, 91E, 99, 117, 121C, 123C
 cluster diagrams, 62

diagrams, 77, 88
graphs, 84O, 91E
lists, 21, 37D, 37N, 37P, 67, 71, 84E, 84H, 84O, 91A, 121H, 121I
maps, 37P, 39, 91E, 123C
research logs, 91B
semantic charts, 41C
semantic webs, 61C
steps, 31
storyboards, 41C
story maps, 80
tables, 37P, 58O, 121P
time lines, 33
Venn diagrams, 47
webs, 41C
word maps, 121F
word walls, 61C
word webs, 38, 41C, 58E, 61C, 112

Guided reading. *See* Reading modes, guided reading.

H

Home Connection, 16G, 16H, 37, 40, 55, 58, 58A, 62, 81, 84, 84M, 89, 90, 100, 121

Home-Community Connections, 37N, 55, 58E, 84N, 84P, 119, 121, 121N, 121P, 123, 123C

Home-school communication. *See* Home Connection.

Homework. *See* Home Connection.

I

Idioms, 89

Illustrate original writing, 37F, 84N, 91E

Illustrators of selections in Anthology
 dePaola, Tomie, 18, 36
 Dugan, Karen M., 43
 Polacco, Patricia, 92
 Tiegreen, Alan, 83

Independent reading
 suggestions for, 15A, 16A, 16B, 16E, 16F, 16H, 17B, 18, 35, 37H, 37I, 37O, 41B, 42, 58G, 58H, 58N, 61A, 61B, 84G, 84H, 84N, 91H, 92, 115, 121B, 121H, 121I, 121N, 121O

Independent reading option. *See* Reading modes, independent reading.

Independent writing
 suggestions for, 16F, 16H, 37, 37E, 58, 58E, 84, 84E, 121F

Individual needs, meeting
 challenge, 16E, 19, 37B, 37J, 37M, 37P, 41C, 53, 58H, 58I, 58O, 59, 71, 78, 84H, 84N, 84O, 98, 121J, 121P
 extra support, 16E, 20, 39, 41D, 47, 52, 61C, 66, 70, 75, 81, 94, 106
 guided reading, 18, 28, 34, 44, 46, 52, 56, 62, 68, 74, 80, 94, 100, 106, 120
 reteaching, 37D, 37L, 58C, 58G, 58K, 84C, 84G, 84K, 121D, 121H, 121L
 Students Acquiring English, 16E, 18, 22, 26, 27, 31, 32, 33, 37, 37A, 37B, 38, 41C, 48, 50, 56, 58, 59, 60, 61C, 62, 63, 65, 67, 68, 70, 71, 73, 74, 75, 76, 77, 80, 84, 85, 86, 89, 95, 99, 100, 102, 105, 107, 108, 111, 112, 114, 116, 120, 121, 122, 123C
 support in advance, 41C, 61C

Inferences, making
 about characters' actions and feelings, 50, 62, 64
 by drawing conclusions, 27, 34, 91A, 91B, 121C
 from illustrations, 44
 by predicting, 44, 50, 62, 64, 106

Inflected forms, 32

Information skills, 19, 37I, 37N, 37P, 38, **39,** 58D, 58O, 60, 67, **79,** 84G, 84O, 87, 107, H2, H3, H4

Interactive Learning
 building background, **17C, 41C, 61C, 91I**
 comprehension, **37C, 58B, 84B, 121C**
 grammar, **37K-37L, 58J-58K, 84J-84K, 121K-121L**
 prior knowledge, **17C, 41C, 61C, 91I**
 selection vocabulary, **17D, 41D, 61D, 91J**
 theme, launching the, **16G-16H**

58P, 60, 61C, 62, 69, 84P
photos, 84P
section headings, 84P
text, 38, 69, 122
title, 58P

Prewriting. *See* Reading-Writing Workshop, steps of.

Prior knowledge, 37I, 38, 41C, 58P, 60, 61C, 84P, 122. *See also* Background building.

Problem solving, 19, **49,** 58O, **99, 121C–121D,** 122, 123, 123A. *See also* Theme 2.

Process writing. *See* Reading-Writing Workshop, steps of.

Proofreading. *See* Reading-Writing Workshop, steps of.

Publications, student-produced, 16H, 91E

Punctuation. *See* Mechanics, language.

Purpose setting for reading, 18, 22, 28, 44, 46, 52, 60, 62, 68, 74, 84P, 94, 99, 106, 122

Q

Questions, generating, 37B, 39, 40, 44, 54, 91A–91B, 94, 100

R

Reader's Theater, 37E, 37M, 84A

Reading across the curriculum
art, 16G, 16H, 37F, 37N, 38, 58E, 58M, 84M, 89, 96, 104, 106, 121B, 121I, 121O
health, 16H, 30, 37O, 37P, 58N, 59, 61, 67, 79, 84N, 87, 89, 97, 105, 123
language arts, 20, 22, 23, 26, 27, 28, 34, 35, 44, 48, 50, 52, 54, 56, 58L, 69, 78, 80, 95, 108, 121M
math, 19, 30, 31, 84N, 84O, 88, 98, 112, 121P, 122–123
media literacy, 64, 85

multicultural, 24, 37M, 44, 50, 51, 52, 54, 58E, 58L, 58M, 61, 65, 95, 97, 99, 109, 110, 121, 121M
music, 37F, 84L, 116, 121M
science, 31, 37P, 71, 72, 84O, 88, 89, 121P
social studies, 19, 25, 29, 34, 37P, 39, 41, 41P, 44, 54, 55, 61D, 75, 85, 100, 107, 115, 121O

Reading fluency. *See* Fluency.

Reading modes
cooperative reading, 22, 46, 58P, 60, 68, 81, 104, 121A, 121G
guided reading, 18, 22, 28, 34, 44, 46, 52, 56, 62, 68, 74, 80, 84, 94, 100, 106, 120, 121A
independent reading, 16H, 22, 37F, 46, 58E, 60, 68, 74, 100, 121F
oral reading, 21, 30, 37A, 37F, 37M, 50, 53, 58, 60, 73, 76, 84, 84H, 84L, 91A, 91C, 104
teacher read aloud, 16B, 58P, 60, 121I
See also Vocabulary, during reading; Vocabulary, selection.

Reading strategies. *See* Strategies, reading.

Reading-Writing Workshop (process writing)
connecting to literature, 90
evaluating, 91F
introductions and conclusions, **91C**
introducing the student model, 90, 91
reflecting/self-assessment, 91F
spelling, words often misspelled, **91E**
steps of
drafting, **91C**
prewriting, **91A–91B,** 91D
proofreading, 91, **91E**
publishing, 91E, **91F**
revising, **91C–91D**
strategies
drafting, 91C
research, 91B
revising, 91D
subjects
writing a research report, 90–91F

supporting details, **91B**
writing a topic sentence, **91A**

Reference and study skills. *See* Study skills.

Rereading
comprehension, 58, 69, 121A, 121B
cooperatively, 37M, 58C, 81, 121A, 121G
extra support, 81
for fluency, 21, 30, 37A, 37M, 50
independently, 30, 69, 76, 77, 84L, 91C, 104
informal assessment, 30, 50, 58, 84, 104
noting details, 91C
orally, 37A, 50, 84, 84L

Research activities, 58N, 58O, 84L, 84M, 84N, 84O, 90–91F, 121O, 123C

Responding to literature, options for
art, 37A, 37B, 58A, 84A, 121B
discussion, 37A, 58A, 84A, 91, 121A
drama, 37A, 37B, 58A, 84A, 121, 121B
writing, 37, 37B, 58, 58A, 84, 84A, 121, 121B

Reteaching, 37D, 37L, 58C, 58G, 84C, 84G, 121H, 121L. *See also* Individual needs, reteaching.

Revising. *See* Reading-Writing Workshop, steps of.

Rhyme, 37F, 59, 61

S

Science activities. *See* Cross-curricular activities.

Scoring Rubric, 91F, 123A

Selecting books. *See* Independent reading.

Selections in Anthology
autobiography
Chicken Sunday by Patricia Polacco, 91A–121A
fiction
Halmoni and the Picnic by Sook Nyul Choi, 41A–58

oral presentation, 91F
Reader's Theater, 37E, 37M,
    84A
storytelling, 21, 37F
summary, 102
guidelines
    for Reader's Theater, 37M
purpose
    analyzing/evaluating literature,
        21, 27, 46, 55
    contributing information, 18, 20,
        28, 41C, 50, 58D, 58M, 69,
        70, 71, 79, 84H, 84M, 84P,
        85, 87, 88, 99, 111, 119,
        121H, 121O
    enjoyment, 21, 58L
    giving opinions, 60, 84D, 85,
        123
    quizzes, 40
    role-playing, 41C, 56, 65, 112,
        121A, 121D
    singing, 121M, 121N.
    See also Creative dramatics;
        Fluency, speaking; Modeling,
        student writing; Oral, reading.

Speech, parts of
    adjectives, 121B
    nouns
        singular and plural, 32
    See also Grammar and usage;
        Language and usage.

Spelling
    assessment, 37I, 58I, 84I, 84J, 121J
    integrating grammar and spelling,
        91E
    integrating spelling and reading
        ending in *er* or *le*, **58I**
        first sound in *city* and *just*, **37J**,
        37L
        homophones, **121G**, 121H,
        121J, 121L
        phonograms, **121H**
        r-controlled vowels, **58G**
        words often misspelled, **91E**
    spelling review, **123B**
    revising, 58K, 91E
    rules, 32
    VCCV pattern, **84I**, 84K.
    See also additional spelling lists
        with pratice on pages 149–158
        of the level 3.2 *Literacy Activity
        Book*; Decoding skills.

Spelling, personal word lists for, 37J,
    84I, 91E, 121J, 123B

Story elements/story structure
    character, 21, 22, 37E, 37F, 41C, **55**
    ending, 21, 34
    events, 26, **33**, 34, 37F, 41C, 58C,
        77, 80, 112, **117**
    setting, 21, 37E, 37F, 53, 106
    solution, 37F, 53
    titles, 58N.
    See also Graphic organizers, story
        map; Literary devices.

Storytelling, 21, 37A, 37F

Strategic reading. *See* Strategies,
    reading; Vocabulary, during
    reading.

Strategies, reading
    Evaluate, 94, 114
    Monitor, 18, 26
    Predict/Infer, 44, 50, 62, 64
    Self-question, 54, 94, 102, 112
    Summarize, 94, 102, 112
    Think About Words, 18, 20, 28, 48,
        62, 70, 104

Structural analysis, 84F. *See also*
    Vocabulary, selection; Vocabulary,
    extending.

Student self-assessment. *See*
    Assessment: Self-assessment; Self-
    assessment.

**Students Acquiring English, activities
especially helpful for**
    background, building, 61C, 67, 68,
        112, 114
    expressions/idioms, 22, 27, 31, 37,
        60, 65, 67, 73, 74, 75, 85, 89, 95,
        100, 102, 108, 111, 116, 120
    mentoring, 37L
    picture clues, 41C, 48, 62, 76, 105
    previewing, 38
    sharing, 56, 71, 73, 97, 99, 102,
        112, 121, 123C
    vocabulary, 32, 33, 37B, 38, 58A,
        77, 80, 86, 105
    word meanings, 18, 26, 48, 50, 59,
        63, 67, 89, 97, 99, 107, 122
    written English, 58, 58O, 84.
    See also idioms.

Study skills
    graphic sources
        charts, creating, 33

charts, reading, 87, **H3**
globes, 39, 58O, **H2**
maps, using, 19, 39, 58O, 107,
    121O
information skills
    locating information quickly, 39
    organizing/recording, 33, 37P
    taking notes, **H4**
    using the library, **79, H5**
    writing a research report,
        90–91F
reference sources
    globe, **39, H2**
    maps, using, 23, 39, 107, 121O
study strategies
    directions, following, **31, 69**
    K-W-L strategy, 91A, 91D
See also Research activities.

Study strategies. *See* Skills, major;
    Strategies, reading; Study skills.

Summarizing,
    oral summaries, 37M, 80, 102, 112

Symbols, 18, 58M

T

Teacher-guided reading. *See* Reading
    modes.

Teaching across the curriculum. *See*
    Content areas, reading in the;
    Cross-curricular activities.

Teaching and management
    grouping students flexibly, 41C,
        61C
    managing assessment, 16F, 123B
    managing instruction, 16C-16D,
        41B, 61B, 90
    managing program materials, 16C-
        16D, 41B, 61B, 90, 123B
    special needs of students, meeting.
        See Individual needs, meeting.

Technology resources
    audiotapes, 16B, 17B, 37M, 41B,
        61B, 76, 91H, 121M
    Channel R.E.A.D., 16B, 16E, 61B,
        84C
    Filmstrips, 16B
    Great Start CD-ROM, 16E, 17B,
        41B, 41C, 61B, 61C, 91H
    Internet: Education Place, 16B,
        16E, 16G

37L, 61, 84E, 84K, 95, 111, 114, 121, 121F, 123

independent. *See* Independent writing.

modes of organization
    classificatory, 16H, 37M, 58O, 84N
    descriptive, 16H, 58, 58E, 61C, 84E
    expressive, 23, 37B, 37E, 37J, 37L, 37F, 61, 95, 111, 114, 121, 121H, 123
    functional, 61C, 94
    informative, 58D, 58E, 58O
    narrative, 16H, 84E, 84K
    persuasive, 37A, 37B, 37F, 37J

types
    about learning, 58A
    advertising, 37J
    booklets, 16H
    cookbook, 16H

description, 16H, 58, 58K
dialogue, 37F, 84E, 84K
funny stories, 123
handbooks, 58O, 84N
invitations, 37A
Italian phrase book, 37M
journal. *See* Journal.
letter, 37L, 84A
memory, 16H, 121L
menu, 61, 121L
pictionary, 58A
personal narrative, 84E, 84K
poems, 16H, 61, 121H
poetic language, **95**
predictions, 61C
questions, 39, 40
quick writing, 58P, 61C
rhyme, 61
sequel, 37B
similes, 95
steps of an activity, 31

thought balloons, 84K, 114
tips for pets, 84I

Writing as a process. *See* Reading-Writing Workshop (process writing).

Writing conferences, 91D

Writing skills,
    avoiding stringy sentences, **84D**
    introductions and conclusions, **91C**
    invitation writing, **58D**
    poetry writing, 121E
    supporting details, **91B**
    topic sentences, **91A,** 91C, 91D
    word processor, using, 91D, 91E
    See also Language and usage; Reading-Writing Workshop.